La Cucina Siciliana della Casa

Sicilian Home Cooking

La Cucina Siciliana della Casa

Sicilian Home Cooking

Family Recipes
from Gangivecchio

Wanda and Giovanna Tornabene

with Michele Evans

Photographs by Michele Evans

Alfred A. Knopf   New York   2001

THIS IS A BORZOI BOOK PUBLISHED BY ALFRED A. KNOPF

www.aaknopf.com

Knopf, Borzoi Books, and the colophon are registered
trademarks of Random House, Inc.

ISBN: 0-375-40399-X
LCCN: 2001012345

Manufactured in the United States of America
First Edition

Ai nostri antenati, che ci hanno donato Gangivecchio per
la serena felicitá della gente che qui ha vissuto, e per tutti
coloro, che, anche per un solo giorno ci vivranno.

(To our ancestors, who left us Gangivecchio, for the happy
peace of the people who have lived here, and for all those
who, even for one day, will live here.)

Contenuto (Contents)

Ringraziamenti—Fra Noi

(Acknowledgments—Between Us)

As we complete our second cookbook, our thoughts are filled with many happy memories of another amazing adventure. We think of the countless hours spent *fra noi* (between us), mother and daughter, recounting stories of our lives, discussing food and testing and writing recipes, while running our restaurant at Gangivecchio. But a cookbook, like any production, is the result of an enormous collaboration. So, between the two, we want to acknowledge all the players in this work. We cannot forget the enthusiasm of many family members and friends who were eager to share their recipes with us. These recipes, added to ours, are the backbone of this book.

We think first of Paolo, our son and brother, our sparkling competitor in the kitchen, but always so generous with his own ideas, especially pasta sauces, and really, help of every kind.

If we have wonderful fish and seafood recipes, we owe many of them to Mariuccia Schiavone and Sofia LoCoco. From their own tables the taste of the Mediterranean Sea will be transported to tables in America.

The secret of the "real" *amatriciana* pasta sauce was revealed to us by Tiziana Carapezza, born in Amatrice, where this great dish originated.

A friend of forty years, Kery Mollica, hand wrote and sent her best soup and focaccia recipes to us.

A warm thanks to Angela De Santis for her couscous lesson and delicious recipes.

From the deep well of our memories we thank Granny Giovanna and Granny Elena. They are ever with us in the form of their recipes filling page after page of an old exercise book, so very precious to us.

If the recipes are the backbone of this book, absolutely vital was the collaboration again with Michele Evans, our multitalented, inexhaustible co-author. And through her eyes, she has captured our food and the world of Gangivecchio in photographs throughout this book. She is our English-speaking alter ego. In Michele, we have found a daughter and a sister for life.

We must thank Tully Plesser, Michele's husband, who, along with her, has

always made their home our home. Tully and Michele also created an American family for us of friends like Margot Bachman and Ken and Binky Auletta. These dear people have also opened their homes to us many times.

But neither of our books would ever have been written without Peter Gethers, our brilliant editor. It was he who discovered us hidden in this remote part of the world. He arrived with Norton, his handsome little cat, and his lovely companion, Janis Donnaud. The three of them gave us the tremendous gift of trust and friendship.

We thank Esther Newberg, Michele's literary agent, for recommending her to Peter Gethers as the perfect co-author for us. Esther was absolutely right.

Peter's assistant editor, Shauna Toh, who recently visited Gangivecchio, has done excellent work editing our manuscript, especially the recipes.

At Knopf, we are grateful to the talented men and women whose splendid individual work was so vital to the creation of this book: Amy Stackhouse and Kevin Bourke for copyediting; Anthea Lingeman for the interior design; Susan Carroll for the design of the cover; and Tracy Cabanis and Avery Fluck for production.

Special thanks to Christopher Hirsheimer, who took the cover photograph of us in our home kitchen at Gangivecchio.

Here at Gangivecchio, we must mention our important collaborators. First, Peppe Bevacqua, with us for over thirty years in the kitchen, restaurant, and garden; and also our dependable and loyal workers, Mario Cavoli and Giovanni Salerno.

Our gratitude to Renata Pucci for her English translation of the poem, "Momenti 1965."

In our quiet times at home, as we wrote we had the tender, loving glances and comforting company of our beloved little dogs, Silla and Ciccio, and cats, Perlina and Billy.

We must thank Alfonso Cucchiara and Alfio Noto, Director and President of our bank, and they know why!

Finally, we want to thank Gangivecchio, because we are honored to live in such a beautiful and peaceful place. We end our acknowledgments in the spiritual company of all those who collaborated on this book, and, in many, many ways contributed to our lives. Grazie.

December 15, 2000
Gangivecchio, Sicily

Storia Cronologica di Gangivecchio e La Famiglia Tornabene

(Chronological History of Gangivecchio and the Tornabene Family)

1299	The King of Aragon, Frederick II, during battles with his brother in Sicily, James, destroys the village of Engium (Gangi's name after Roman domination), located in the Madonie Mountains in north-central Sicily. The only surviving building is the chapel of the Church of St. Mary of the Annunciation.
1363	Benedictine monks obtain permission to build a priory around the Church of St. Mary of the Annunciation, which becomes known as Gangivecchio (Old Gangi). Count Ventimiglia, master of the Madonie, donates approximately sixteen hundred acres of adjacent land to the order.
1366	The priory is completed, and the monks begin their activities: teaching their students reading, writing, miniature drawing, and new farming methods.
1413	The priory is elevated to the high rank of abbey.
1577	A Sicilian artist, Pietro Billio, completes painting frescoes on the vaulted ceilings of the abbey's refectory dining room.

Gangivecchio's imperial coat of arms

1653   After a black plague, the surviving monks leave l'Abbazia de Gangivecchio, moving to Castelbuono, thirty kilometers from Gangivecchio. Only one member of the order remains as guardian and revenue collector. After his death, the abbey is completely abandoned and crumbles to ruin.

1770   Francesco Bongiorno, a wealthy local squire from Gangi, obtains a perpetual lease from the church and begins restoration of the dilapidated former abbey, converting it into a summer residence.

1786	The Bongiorno family buys Gangivecchio from the church. They restore the building, adding neoclassical structures.
1788	King Ferdinand IV designates the estate a barony. A two-headed eagle becomes Gangivecchio's imperial coat of arms in honor of the Bourbon king's Austrian wife, Maria Carolina.
1828	With the death of Francesco Bongiorno's only surviving heir, the property is given as a gift to the archbishop of Palermo.
1856	After years of tedious negotiations, the church sells Gangivecchio to Vincenzo Tornabene. He begins restoration of the abbey, transforming the land into a working farm.
1885	Vincenzo Tornabene meets and marries Giulia Colombari, twenty-six years his junior, from Bologna.
1886	Giulia gives birth to a son, Mariano.
1911	Mariano marries a young woman from Palermo, Giovanna Randazzo.
1912	The son of Mariano and Giovanna is born. His name is Vincenzo.
1948	Vincenzo marries Wanda di Paola, a young woman from Palermo. Their children are Giovanna (1950) and Paolo (1952).
1978	During a financial crisis, Wanda opens a restaurant in the west wing of the abbey to save Gangivecchio and the remaining 140-acre property. The restaurant succeeds.
1984	Vincenzo Tornabene dies suddenly on August 20.
1992	An American editor and writer, Peter Gethers, arrives at Gangivecchio for lunch. After a second visit, he invites Wanda and Giovanna to write a cookbook. Paolo converts stables and in November they become the nine-room *albergo* called Tenuta Gangivecchio.

1994	Paolo Tornabene marries Palermo-born Betty Loiacono at Gangivecchio.
1996	Our cookbook, *La Cucina Siciliana di Gangivecchio,* written with American food writer Michele Evans, is published by Alfred A. Knopf.
1997	*La Cucina Siciliana di Gangivecchio* wins the 1997 James Beard Foundation Award for the best Italian cookbook of the year.
1998	Wanda, Giovanna, and Michele begin collaborating on a second cookbook for Alfred A. Knopf.
1999	La Casa di Annunziata, a one-bedroom stone cottage on the grounds of Gangivecchio, is refurbished and becomes an addition to Paolo's *albergo,* Tenuta Gangivecchio.
2000	Gangivecchio, 637 years old, enters the new millennium with a satellite dish for television transmission perched on its antique roof; inside the abbey, the household is connected to the Internet.
2001	Our second cookbook, *Sicilian Home Cooking,* is published by Alfred A. Knopf.

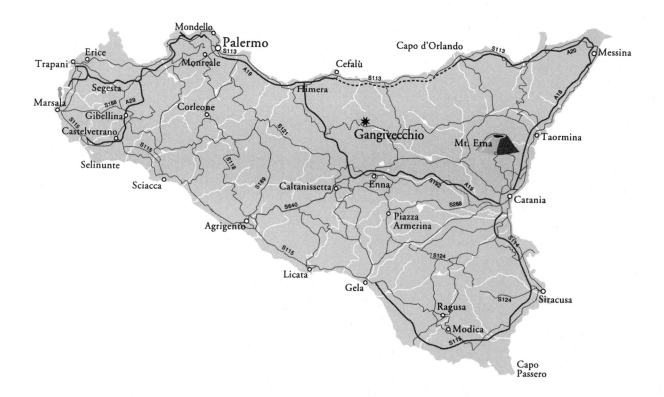

Trapani
Erice
Mondello
Palermo
Monreale
Marsala
Segesta
Gibellina
Castelvetrano
Corleone
Selinunte
Sciacca
S188
A29
S115
S113
A19
Himera
Cefalù
Capo d'Orlando
S113
S113
A20
Messina
A18
Gangivecchio
Mt. Etna
Taormina
S121
S118
S189
Caltanissetta
Enna
S192
A19
Catania
S640
Piazza
Armerina
S288
Agrigento
S115
Licata
Gela
S124
S124
Ragusa
Modica
Siracusa
S114
S115
Capo
Passero

Introduzioni

(Introductions)

L'Appetito nel Terzo Millennio e La Cucina Siciliana della Casa

(Appetites in the Third Millennium
and Sicilian Home Cooking)

When our editor, Peter Gethers, proposed that we write another cookbook, Giovanna and I were, of course, thrilled. Our first book, *La Cucina Siciliana di Gangivecchio,* remains, in my mind, a glorious fantasy, even though I see and touch it, as my talisman, every day. The fantasy continued when we traveled across America, promoting our book, appearing on television for cooking demonstrations, giving radio and newspaper interviews, and, eventually, even winning a big culinary award. Giovanna will tell you in her introduction how dramatically the publication of that book affected our lives.

Although we included more than two hundred of our treasured classic Sicilian recipes in our first book, we had to leave out many other recipes due to lack of space. *La Cucina* contained personal stories of our past experiences and information about specific foods indigenous to Sicily, as well as a detailed history of the abbey and the Tornabene family. You can examine Gangivecchio's historical chronology, dating from 1299, on pages xi–xiii. (A full account of our history, along with more delicious recipes, is included in *La Cucina Siciliana di Gangivecchio.*)

In this new book, there are more personal and gastronomical stories as well as revelations about some of Sicily's great foods, like cardoons, nuts, and blood oranges. But once again the real focus is on our recipes, the food we know and love best: our own robust Sicilian home cooking. The dishes we eat at home are primarily hearty soups, the freshest vegetables, and simple, tasty egg dishes. And pasta, topped with a variety of fragrant sauces, has always reigned as queen in our home. But we also include delicious antipasti, risottos, main courses of meat and fish and seafood, and more recipes in my favorite food category, Sicilian desserts.

Giovanna insisted that we devote a chapter to *cuscus* (couscous), the unique, aromatic Arabian dish she so admires. *Cuscus* is served throughout the western part

of Sicily, in the Trapani region—from there, the Tunisian coast is only ninety miles away. A Tunisian friend, Angela De Santis, who has lived in Sicily most of her adult life, spent a day at Gangivecchio teaching us the authentic method for making *cuscus*. When she was done, twelve of us devoured the delicious result of her lesson.

Giovanna is also responsible for the chapter on pizza and *focacce*—wonderful Sicilian versions of these savory flatbreads. After cooking a multicourse luncheon feast for a hundred people in the abbey's restaurant on a Sunday, nothing is more satisfying to me than eating a simple, scrumptious pizza that Giovanna prepares for me that night at home. She knows my favorite toppings: tomatoes, mozzarella cheese, and chopped anchovies with an explosion of fresh basil.

To better appreciate our lives and our cooking (often, the two cannot be separated), some background of our culinary heritage might be helpful.

Our home, Gangivecchio, is an old Benedictine abbey, built in 1363. After three centuries it became privately owned property. It was occupied first by the Bongiornos, then, in 1856, by the Tornabene family. Giovanna, my daughter, Paolo, my son, and I are the last Tornabenes (at least, so far—I still hold out hope, but my children tell me that I would be the oldest granny in the world).

In 1978, during a financial crisis, I opened a restaurant in the west wing of the abbey, trying to scrape up enough income to save Gangivecchio and the rest of our 140-acre property. The success of the restaurant made that possible. In 1992, Paolo built and opened a small nine-room inn, which we call Tenuta Gangivecchio, with his own restaurant. He too has become a formidable presence in front of the stove. We were blessed that his *albergo* and restaurant were prosperous too.

To be honest, when I first came here, more than fifty years ago, the culinary art was not bubbling in my veins. Born and raised in Palermo, I knew little of the remote Sicilian countryside, and apart from a healthy appetite, absolutely nothing about cooking. My secret aspiration was to become an actress. I am what people call a cook by fate—a very happy fate, I must add. You see, I happened to fall in love with a man—the only child of a wonderful cook—who lived in an immense, ancient place, surrounded by all the genuine foods of the earth. It was only natural for me to awaken from my childish dream and surrender to such a wondrous fate.

I was also most fortunate to be welcomed into Gangivecchio's kitchen and taught how to cook by my generous, patient mother-in-law, Giovanna (my daughter's namesake), who was a highly skilled cook. She gave confidence to a willing student, convincing me that I showed promise.

Giovanna and Enzo, my husband, are no longer with us, but they remain with

me always. Looking at their faces in picture frames, I hear their voices, their suggestions, and receive their endless *amore ogni giorno* (love each day).

Since the opening of the restaurant, Giovanna has been at my side. She is my guardian angel, my assistant and pupil (and she cooks very well, nowadays). She is the amazing English translator and chief administrator of our restaurant at Gangivecchio. Without her there would be no cookbooks.

Many changes are happening in Sicily and Gangivecchio. For some time I have witnessed the world I know vanishing around me. Anna Mazzola, our superb cheese maker, retired. Many dear old friends have died. Hundreds of people have left the countryside and moved to cities for better opportunities. Few youth of today are interested in dedicating their lives to the cultivation of the earth. Instead, if they stay, they open a big business, like a gelato factory, such as the one near us in Gangi. Our best staff member, Peppe, though he is nearing seventy, is still busy with me in the kitchen. He recently decided to revive our home garden, with his beloved peppers and tomatoes, and is now fighting with Mario, another worker, about who is more skilled in this area. We once had an enormous, flourishing home garden, but with Peppe in the kitchen we didn't have anyone to do the garden work. For too many years, the only garden at Gangivecchio was the small one

Peppe shows off the day's giant ferla mushroom harvest.

behind Paolo's inn. It still supplies him with fresh vegetables and herbs—tomatoes, eggplants, peppers, green beans, zucchini and their bright orange blossoms, arugula, lettuces, basil, sage, oregano, thyme, and mint. Paolo is quite proud of his garden, but he is happy Peppe has replanted a sizable garden for me. I suspect Paolo pays visits to my garden when his own vegetables are finished.

Of course, it is very reassuring that we will always have great bushes of rosemary, and meters and meters of bay laurel hedges that are covered with thousands of fragrant leaves. (Giovanna makes an incredibly good bay laurel leaf liqueur; see page 224.) Our fruit trees continue to provide us with luscious cherries, figs, and pears, and our nut trees give us all the pine nuts, hazelnuts, and almonds that we could ever possibly use. We even have pure water from a natural spring. We are quite blessed to have this wealth of natural resources.

But in the midst of our bountiful, idyllic country home environment, other astonishing changes are sneaking into our lives.

At Gangivecchio, on an early-December day in 1999, a young man arrived from the telephone company, lugging the tools of his trade. He was there to install an additional phone line in the walls of our fourteenth-century home, this one providing an additional Internet connection. As he drilled and hammered, I sat in a nearby room at my old walnut table, my old pen held in my seventy-two-year-old hand, a plain pad of paper in front of me. I wasn't composing a food shopping and errand list for the day, as is my morning habit, but was beginning my introduction for this book. The top page of the pad remained blank, because at that particular moment I could concentrate on nothing but an enveloping and threatening feeling of becoming obsolete. Fortunately, this thought stayed in my mind only briefly. I then decided it was not a question of becoming obsolete, but of my two crazy children's desire to be so up-to-date.

I am unable to share my children's enthusiasm for technology. I view this sorcery as some unauthorized, invisible surgeon snipping away at my orderly, sensible, and perfectly contented life. Yes, yes, I know e-mails and faxes are invaluable

for people wanting to make reservations for dinner at our abbey and for rooms at my son's *albergo,* and these diabolical machines have enabled Giovanna and Michele, our coauthor, to communicate almost instantly for work on our books. But as the phone man continued to work, I didn't care about any of that. I reminisced about the hand-written recipes in the old black exercise book that had been lovingly assembled and patiently written by my mother-in-law, Giovanna, and her mother-in-law, Giulia. My own recipes fill that book's last pages. These frail sheets of paper seemed to me a mystical communication. Unlike the words typed on a computer, these precious pages showed the importance of faithfully preserving our past, at least in terms of our cuisine.

Startling me from my thoughts, the telephone man announced that he would soon complete his work. Then he commented, "That delicious aroma smells just like my grandmother's tomato sauce." A big pot of fresh *salsa di pomodoro* was indeed simmering on the stove in the kitchen and this starving man gobbled up two big plates of spaghetti before he left. He said the sauce was even better than his granny's—but he wouldn't tell her that. Then he rushed off to install more Internet lines.

It wasn't long before the phone rang. It was Paolo, who announced, "Mamma, sixteen unexpected guests are coming for lunch. Can you give me two liters of your tomato sauce?"

"Ah, so I am not obsolete," I told him. "Are you not fortunate that I am still alive?"

"Mamma, what are you talking about? Are you ill? *Allora,* Mamma, at least don't die until after the New Year's celebration. You must make your wonderful desserts for that dinner. Forty people are coming! Mamma? Do you have the *salsa di pomodoro?*"

I repeat this short conversation because it lightened my dark mood, and also because it proved two things to me: first, the uninvited technical world is here to stay, but second, the telephone man, my son, his many guests, and everyone else in the world will still be hungry in the third millennium.

With a new peace of mind, I returned to fulfilling our goal: to write a book dedicated to the flavors and perfumes of authentic Sicilian home cooking. These are the dishes that have evolved throughout our history, an extraordinary combination of the foods introduced by our conquerors, from the Greeks, Romans, and Arabs to the French and Spanish. We Sicilians add our preferences and touches, naturally. A few recipes in this book are from the harvest of the gardens of my modern son's and daughter's minds.

My attitude has changed entirely from the time we began our first book, when I was so reluctant to part with any of our secret family recipes. As I come to the end of this introduction, I can now say what perhaps should have been the opening sentence: "*Questa volta ho iniziato un nuovo libro con il proposito di dividere il suo contenuto con altri e mi sorprende di farlo con immenso piacere.* [I begin this new book with the purpose of sharing its contents with others, and I'm surprised I'm doing this with so much pleasure.]"

I have been a very lucky woman, because somehow I have been able to transfer my genuine love of cooking and my passionate love and dedication to Gangivecchio on to my children. After all, they have shared in all Gangivecchio's hardships and glories, and it has been their home since birth. Someday it will be theirs to protect.

My children are my greatest gifts, my future. They are my critics, but also my strength and enthusiasm. I believe that human beings, like plants and trees, can only thrive with good roots, loving care, and nourishment. And like most strong plants and trees, they can survive the storms.

To know and be close to your family, nothing is more important than dining together at home, as often as possible, on delicious home cooking.

It gives me great pleasure to imagine people sitting at tables in their American homes with their families and friends, conversing and laughing, while dining on the Sicilian dishes from within these pages. *Salute!*

—Wanda Tornabene

Incontri Incantevoli
e Vita con Mia Madre

(Enchanting Encounters and
Life with My Mother)

*H*istorians have said that we Sicilians *sopravviviamo brillantemente* (are brilliant at surviving), that when faced with adversity, we thrive. We say, "*Non abbiamo altra scelta che arrangiarci.* [We have no choice but to be resourceful.]" At least, that has always been my mother's philosophy.

Mamma saved us from losing Gangivecchio by opening the restaurant back in 1978. Almost twenty years later, when our first cookbook, *La Cucina Siciliana di Gangivecchio,* was published, in December of 1996, we were once again in economic trouble—both personally and nationally. There have been more leaders of government in Italy than pasta shapes. We wonder if someone will ever take over who finally can get the country's finances right. Anyway, taxes were then and are still exorbitant, like the cost of telephones, electricity, and petrol for cars. In 1996, people were still coming to our restaurant, but our bookkeeping figures revealed a marked decline in guests. Paying more attention to their lire, Sicilians were going out less and eating at home much, much more.

So it was with this worry on our minds, and mixed feelings of *agrodolce* (sweet and sour, like some of our favorite Sicilian dishes), that Mamma and I left for New York to begin an exciting new adventure—something called a "national book

tour." We'd been warned that it would be very tiring, but to Mamma and me, it turned out to be a fascinating holiday.

When we arrived in New York, as always, we had to pass through the dreaded customs inspection—dreaded because hidden deep inside our suitcases, we always bring fresh foods with us for cooking demonstrations—fresh cheeses, Gangivecchio's fresh rosemary and bay leaves, *pasta frolla* (prepared cake dough), lard, and many other prohibited foods. A stern-faced examiner called us forward and asked Mamma (with me as interpreter), "Why are you visiting America? Business or pleasure? You marked both on your form."

"Because it is both business and pleasure," Mamma replied, smiling at the man. "We are here to promote the Sicilian cookbook we have written." Mamma proceeded to produce a copy of our book from the briefcase she had bought for the sole purpose of holding our printed treasure. (She carries the book everywhere she goes, even to the butcher.)

Mamma told me to show the man that it was us pictured on the book's cover. After congratulating us, he told us that his mother was half Italian, as her father was from Naples. He made a big check on our form, and we were free to go. Mamma's diversional tactic had worked. Relieved that the danger was over, we were thrilled to be in America again.

We traveled like a sirocco across America, flying in and out of each city in two or three days. In New York, Los Angeles, San Francisco, Chicago, and Boston, we talked to radio hosts about the recipes in our book and about our lives. Newspaper columnists interviewed us and took our pictures. We cooked our dishes on television after makeup artists and hairdressers made us look like movie stars. We met enchanting, welcoming people everywhere. Alice Waters, in her restaurant, Chez Panisse, in Berkeley, California, and Nancy Silverton and Mark Peel at their restaurant Campanile, in Los Angeles, held special dinners for their clients featuring menus from our cookbook. Mamma and I were amazed and touched by their generosity.

We returned to New York at the end of the terrific journey to celebrate with Michele, Peter, and Amy Scheibe, our Knopf publishing family, and other old and new friends. Then the party came to an end, and it was back to reality again: two Sicilian women trying to *sopravviviamo brillantemente*.

But our new reality turned out to be a surprise. Not only did Americans buy our book, they began coming to Sicily, traveling the long distance to the Madonie Mountains to stay at Tenuta Gangivecchio and to meet and dine with us. Some stayed for a day, some up to a week.

Wanda, Michele, and Giovanna at the 1997 James Beard Awards, with Alice Waters (far left)

On May 5th, 1997, we returned to New York to attend the James Beard Foundation awards dinner in the huge ballroom at the Marriott Marquis on Broadway in Manhattan. Incredibly, our book had been nominated for the best Italian book of the year award. Of course, Michele joined us from St. Thomas. Honestly, none of us expected to win. But we very much wanted to experience this important ceremony. More than a thousand distinguished food writers, chefs, restaurateurs, publishers, and editors were to attend.

When it was time for our category, we held hands. The presenter began slowly announcing the winner syllable by syllable:

"La Cucina Siciliana di . . ."

Before he could finish the title, we jumped up, screaming with glee. On the stage, long purple ribbons with large medallions were placed over our heads. Mamma threw kisses to the audience, repeating over and over again *"Grazie! Grazie! Grazie!"* I was in such shock I don't even remember what Michele or I said.

What happened in the coming months was nothing less than a miracle, like winning the award had been. There was an American invasion. More and more Americans were faxing for reservations. When Mamma opened the restaurant, in 1978, she saved our home the first time; nearly twenty years later, our cookbook and the award were saving Gangivecchio again.

Paolo's nine-room inn soon was booked for months in advance. Mamma decided to refurbish a stone cottage on the property so we would have more space for guests. Tour groups from America and Europe began booking the entire *albergo* and the cottage for several weeks at a time in both the spring and the fall. And they booked on a yearly basis! It was fantastic to be balancing the books again.

But success can also be a battle. It took quite some time, plus extra help, and hard work, to settle in to this hectic new schedule. Not only were we running our restaurant in the abbey, we were helping Paolo cook two meals a day in his *albergo*. For the pleasure of the large groups, we organized old-fashioned *schittichiate* (picnics) on a nearby mountaintop. And we also gave cooking classes!

I worried that writing another book in the midst of all this extra work would be difficult, but Mamma insisted: "*Certo* [of course] we can do this. I have enough space in my briefcase for another book."

Life with my mother reminds me of how Sicilians respond to a red traffic light: it's merely a suggestion. "Run through the red lights of life" is her philosophy: "*Vai! Vai!* [Go ahead! go ahead!]" is what she likes to instruct me to do while I'm driving. When we appeared on TV, the directors in America told Mamma, "When the red light on the camera goes on, that's the signal. It means *Now!* Then you're on!" My mother liked the sound of that. Today when we approach a red stoplight in Palermo, she yells, "Now! Now!"

Living and working with someone with such a strong personality, being at her beck and call twenty-four hours a day—especially if that someone is your mother—can be exasperating. Fortunately, our common goal and mutual commitment have been the glue of our relationship. It helps that we are also each other's best friend. And it helps even more that we somehow manage to find humor in the worst possible crises. And time has taught me, my brother Paolo, and Peppe and our other workers how to survive and still admire and love the perilous boss of our lives: that incredible person named Wanda.

At least the kitchen is no longer our personal battleground. My sauces are almost perfect, my eggs and puddings turn out well. From my mother's cooking instructions over the years I have also learned many useful lessons of life: never surrender to a difficult mayonnaise *or* the tax collector.

Now that the success of our *albergo* and restaurants makes it possible for beloved Gangivecchio to remain securely in our future (we hope and pray, at least, since one can never predict life), we can mentally and physically adjust to our new work rhythm. We can also take even more pride and pleasure in this ancient place that was my father's splendid gift to us.

This book, like our first, is an invitation to all those wanting to enter Gangivecchio's Sicilian kitchen and dining rooms. Be sure to bring along your appetites, because we invite you to taste the genuine flavors of our island's traditional dishes. You can listen to our stories and breathe in some of the scents of the Sicilian countryside. The protagonists of this book are the recipes, and there are more than 175 of them. We hope you will enjoy our dishes at your own table, remembering that they come from two Sicilian women with a passion for home.

—Giovanna Tornabene

Antipasti
(Appetizers)

Polpettine Agrodolce di Gangivecchio
(*Gangivecchio's Sweet-and-Sour Meatballs*)

Fuiulate di Lucia (*Lucia's Fritters*)

Frittata di Spaghetti con Capperi e Olive Nere
(*Spaghetti Omelette with Capers and Black Olives*)

Bigne' Piccanti (*Spicy Beignets*)

La Bruschetta (*Grilled Bread with a Topping*)

Bruschetta con Pesce Spada e Menta
(*Bruschetta with Swordfish and Mint*)

Bruschetta alla Casalinga
(*Home-Style Bruschetta*)

La Bruschetta di Peppe (*Peppe's Bruschetta*)

Peperoni di Siracusa (*Syracuse-Style Peppers*)

Melanzane di Concetta (*Concetta's Eggplant*)

Melanzane di Campagna
(*Country-Style Eggplant*)

La Cucina Allegra (*The Happy Kitchen*)

Panini Caldi di Melanzane
(*Hot Eggplant Sandwiches*)

I Carciofi alla Maniera di Gangi
(*Gangi-Style Artichokes*)

Caponata (*Sweet-and-Sour Eggplant Stew*)

Carciofi "Lasciatemi Sola"
(*Artichokes "Leave Me Alone"*)

Tortino di Carciofi con Sarde e Ricotta
(*Artichoke Tart with Sardines and Ricotta*)

Fonduta di Verdure (*Vegetable Fondue*)

Fagioli Vellutina con la Menta
(*Beans with Mint*)

Le Olive della Zia Elvira (*Aunt Elvira's Olives*)

Le Olive dell' Attore (*The Actor's Olives*)

Pecorino Fresco con Miele e Pistacchi
(*Fresh Pecorino with Honey and Pistachios*)

Caciocavallo con Mandarini
(*Mandarins with Caciocavallo*)

Torta di Gorgonzola e Pere
(*Gorgonzola and Pear Tart*)

Torta con Lattuga (*Lettuce Tart*)

La Torta di San Giuseppe (*Saint Joseph's Tart*)

Torta di Ricotta e Nocciole
(*Ricotta and Hazelnut Tart*)

Sformato di Peperoni e Cipolle
(*Pepper and Onion Soufflé*)

Melone con Aceto Balsamico e Menta
(*Melon with Balsamic Vinegar and Mint*)

Mezze Lune di Ricotta (*Half Moons with Ricotta*)

Uno Strudel Mediterraneo
(*A Mediterranean Strudel*)

Pizza Calabrese (*Calabrian Pizza*)

Panini di Modica di Nina
(*Nina's Little Sandwiches, Modica Style*)

Il Pane del Re (*The King's Bread*)

In addition to the recipes in this chapter, many of the dishes in the *verdure* (vegetable) section (beginning on page 171) are excellent candidates for antipasti.

Il Prologo

(The Prologue)

*Come un innamora-
mento, un pasto comin-
cia con un flirt, che
chiamiamo antipasti.*

(Like a love affair, a
meal begins with a
flirtation, which we
call antipasti.)

In Italian, antipasti literally means "before the meal." Appropriately enough, antipasti are small portions of foods that are served as a tantalizing overture to the fundamental courses in a menu. In Old Sicilian, they're called *vucativi,* from the Latin *vocare,* meaning to call—in this case, what we are calling is the appetite. In our Sicilian dialect, we also say *isca i viviri,* which is difficult to translate but roughly means something like bait to be drunk or like an almost-liquid bait so light it can be swallowed like water.

Antipasti are the most felicitous part of a menu—not too serious, yet extremely seductive. Mamma loves preparing classic antipasti dishes as well as inventing new ones, perhaps because in the past no such course existed in Sicilian homes, particularly in the countryside where we live. In Sicily, until the last several decades, antipasti were served only at special celebrations or large functions like weddings and official receptions. Many Sicilians were too poor and too busy to prepare antipasti.

Restaurants really invented antipasti, which were and are often still temptingly displayed on a long table containing as many as two dozen or more dishes. These dishes ranged from stuffed vegetables to marinated seafood, usually served at room temperature. I believe that this enormous offering was developed by clever restaurant owners as a sensible way of satisfying their hungry, demanding customers while the pasta and other dishes were being cooked to order in the kitchen. As much as my mother enjoys a delicious, big antipasti table, she also believes it defeats the purpose of a balanced menu. There is so much food that these temptations can become an entire meal, especially if diners return for second helpings, like my mother always does. (When I read Mamma what I'd just written, she protested and corrected me. She explained that she *never* has second helpings; she

returns with her plate to the antipasti table for the sole purpose of tasting each dish presented . . . *fare ricerca* [to do research].)

At our restaurant at Gangivecchio, we typically serve three or four of an assortment of our *antipasti rustici*. A small amount of each antipasto is arranged on individual plates for every diner. In the summer there might be *bruschetta* (grilled bread) spread with either a simple puree of tuna or a spicy tomato sauce with tiny dice of swordfish (page 22), along with a few specially seasoned olives, salami or mortadella, and thin slices of melon with mint and balsamic vinegar (page 40). The season dictates the selection, of course. In fall or winter, we serve fried pecorino with pistachios, drizzled with honey (page 34), *polpettine agrodolce* (little sweet-and-sour meatballs) (page 19), crisp fritters (page 19), or a slice of Paolo's sumptuous gorgonzola and pear tart (page 36).

Polpettine Agrodolce di Gangivecchio

(Gangivecchio's Sweet-and-Sour Meatballs)

SERVES 6

In a bowl combine the veal, egg, bread crumbs, parsley, and pecorino and season with salt and pepper. Shape lightly into 1-inch balls (about 36).

Heat 2 tablespoons of the oil in a frying pan. Cook the veal balls over medium heat until brown all over and just cooked through, about 12 minutes. Transfer to a plate lined with paper towels to drain.

Add the remaining 2 tablespoons of oil to the pan and stir in the onions. Season with salt and cook over medium-low heat until the onions are limp, about 15 minutes, stirring often. Don't let the onions brown.

Stir in the vinegar, sugar, and water.

Return the meatballs to the pan and gently turn to coat them lightly in the sauce. Cover and cook over medium-low heat for 5 minutes, shaking the pan frequently. Transfer to a serving dish and cool. Serve at room temperature.

1 pound ground veal
1 large egg
1 cup fresh bread crumbs
2 tablespoons freshly chopped Italian parsley
2½ tablespoons freshly grated pecorino cheese
Salt and freshly ground pepper
4 tablespoons olive oil
2 medium onions, thinly sliced
3 tablespoons red wine vinegar
1½ tablespoons sugar
2 tablespoons water

Fuiulate di Lucia

(Lucia's Fritters)

SERVES 4

In a bowl combine the pecorino, eggs, bread crumbs, garlic, and mint and season with salt and pepper.

Heat ½ inch of oil in a large frying pan. Drop mixture into the pan by tablespoons, forming individual fritters. Fry in batches over medium heat until golden on each side. Drain, season lightly with salt, and serve at once.

1 cup freshly grated pecorino cheese
5 large eggs
1 cup dried bread crumbs
2 garlic cloves, minced
10 mint leaves, chopped
Salt and freshly ground pepper
Olive oil

Frittata di Spaghetti con Capperi e Olive Nere

(Spaghetti Omelette with Capers and Black Olives)

SERVES 6

¾ pound cooked spaghetti, coarsely chopped

4 large eggs

¼ cup pitted and chopped black olives

1 small onion, chopped

1 tablespoon capers, rinsed and patted dry

1 tablespoon freshly chopped Italian parsley

¼ cup freshly grated Parmesan cheese

6 tablespoons olive oil

Put the chopped spaghetti into a large bowl. In another bowl beat the eggs with the olives, onion, capers, parsley, and cheese. Pour mixture over the spaghetti and combine well.

Heat 3 tablespoons of the oil in a 10-inch nonstick frying pan with curved sides. Pour the spaghetti mixture into the pan and flatten top evenly. Cook over medium heat until the bottom is golden brown.

Carefully invert the frittata onto a flat lid or plate. Slide back into the pan, browned side up. Add remaining 3 tablespoons of oil to the side of the pan. Cook until other side is golden brown.

Cut into wedges and serve immediately.

Bigne' Piccanti (Spicy Beignets)

SERVES 6

1 cup water

⅓ cup unsalted butter

Pinch salt

1 cup all-purpose flour

5 large eggs

¼ cup diced boiled ham

¼ cup freshly grated Parmesan cheese

Pour water into a medium saucepan and add the butter and salt. Bring to a boil, then remove from the heat. Add the flour all at once and stir immediately with a wooden spoon. Return pan to medium heat and stir until the mixture pulls away from the side of the pan and forms a ball. Let cool for 5 minutes.

Stir in each egg 1 at a time until it is incorporated into the mixture. Add the ham, cheese, parsley, and hot pepper flakes and combine well.

Roll the mixture into little balls the size of walnuts.

In a skillet, heat the lard, vegetable shortening, or sunflower oil. (The depth of the liquid fat or oil should be about 1½ inches.) Fry the balls in batches until puffy and golden brown all over. Drain on paper towels and serve hot.

2 tablespoons freshly chopped Italian parsley
Pinch hot pepper flakes
Lard, vegetable shortening, or sunflower oil, for deep-frying

La Bruschetta (Grilled Bread with a Topping)

The word *bruschetta* comes from the verb *abbruscare,* which in Italian means "to burn without flames." In the fall in the Sicilian countryside, it is common to see clouds of smoke slowly drifting off at an angle, rising from large patches of land: the *contadini* burning the land to sterilize it. We say that they *"abbruscano la terra."*

Bruschetta is a slice of good Italian bread put on a grill over a fire and toasted until it is crispy and light brown on both sides. If you don't have a grill, the bread can be toasted under a broiler.

The classic bruschetta is a slice of bread rubbed with a pungent slice of garlic and grilled. The topping is simply a brush stroke of extra virgin olive oil and a sprinkle of salt and freshly ground pepper. If Mamma is napping and I'm alone in the late afternoon, and hungry, I prepare myself a *merenda* (snack) of two or three of these classic bruschetta. I might have a glass of chilled white wine. And I also might listen to Bach—he is nourishment, too.

Beyond the classic bruschetta, there are countless other toppings. One of the most admired is a fragrant mixture of chopped tomatoes, fresh basil, olive oil, vinegar or lemon juice, and salt and pepper. Sometimes people add a little diced mozzarella to this combination. We give a few examples of our favorite toppings here, but the choice is really up to the cook's own fantasy.

Bruschetta con Pesce Spada e Menta

(Bruschetta with Swordfish and Mint)

Olive oil
1 pound swordfish, diced
8 mint leaves, finely chopped
2 garlic cloves
¼ cup diced tomatoes
Salt and freshly ground pepper
1 slice of white sandwich bread,
    crusts removed, and torn apart
    into small pieces
2 tablespoons milk
Twelve ¾-inch-thick slices Italian
bread, toasted

SERVES 6

In a large frying pan, put enough olive oil to just cover the bottom of the pan. Add the swordfish and cook over high heat, stirring, until white and just cooked. Add the mint, garlic, and tomatoes. Season to taste with salt and pepper. Cook over medium heat for 10 minutes, stirring occasionally.

Meanwhile, soak the pieces of bread in the milk.

Remove the garlic from the pan and discard. Add the soaked bread. Season mixture with salt and pepper and crush lightly with a fork.

Put the mixture into a serving bowl. Place the bowl on a platter and surround with the toasted bread. Serve immediately.

Bruschetta alla Casalinga

(Home-Style Bruschetta)

Our home-style bruschetta is toasted in the oven in one long row of overlapping slices topped with mozzarella, then separated at serving time. Mamma did this to serve bruschetta in a different manner for a change. It's one of her fantasies.

8 thin slices mozzarella cheese
    (fresh, if possible)
Eight ½-inch-thick slices lightly
    toasted Italian country-style
    bread

SERVES 4

Preheat the oven to 375 degrees.

Put a slice of mozzarella on top of each slice of bread. In a shallow rectangular baking dish, arrange the mozzarella-topped slices of bread in a single row, each slice overlapping the next by about ½ inch. Put into the oven and cook until the cheese has melted.

Meanwhile, in a small frying pan, melt the butter with the anchovies, mashing them with a fork.

Carefully transfer the cheese-topped bruschetta with two spatulas, using one at each end, to a serving dish. Spoon the hot anchovy butter sauce over the top. Serve hot.

6 tablespoons unsalted butter
2 anchovies

La Bruschetta di Peppe

(Peppe's Bruschetta)

Peppe thought up this very simple but delicious stuffed *bruschetta* after a long day of labor in our home garden. We think he was so thirsty that day that he invented just a little something to swallow with the enormous amount of wine he drank.

SERVES 4

Preheat the oven to 375 degrees.

Mash the anchovies with the parsley and garlic in a bowl. Add the olive oil and pepper to taste. Mix to a creamy consistency, adding a little more oil if necessary.

Spread the mixture in equal amounts over 8 slices of bread. Top each with the remaining slices of bread. Gently press down the top of each. Place the bruschetta on a large baking sheet. Bake for 10 minutes or until the bread is just toasted. Serve immediately with cold white wine.

12 anchovies, chopped
⅓ cup freshly chopped Italian parsley
1 garlic clove, minced
3 tablespoons extra virgin olive oil
Freshly ground pepper
16 thin slices Italian bread

Peperoni di Siracusa

(Syracuse-Style Peppers)

3 large yellow bell peppers
3 large red bell peppers
⅓ cup olive oil
Salt
10 fresh mint leaves, chopped
1 large garlic clove, crushed
2 tablespoons toasted bread
    crumbs
⅓ cup blanched almonds, toasted
    and coarsely chopped
Red wine vinegar

SERVES 4 TO 6

Remove the cores and seeds from the peppers and cut them into ¼-inch-thick strips.

In a large frying pan, heat the oil over medium-high heat. Add the peppers and season to taste with salt. Cook until softened and slightly browned, stirring often.

Stir in the mint, garlic, bread crumbs, and almonds. Sprinkle lightly with vinegar. Combine well and cook for 5 minutes over low heat. Taste for seasoning.

Transfer peppers to a shallow serving dish and cool completely. Cover and refrigerate for at least 2 hours. Mix before serving cold.

Melanzane di Concetta

(Concetta's Eggplant)

Concetta, a former maid of friends of ours, was famous for this dish. During a memorable lunch about twenty years ago, she gave Mamma the recipe. Mamma remembers that lunch well because so many dishes were served. She always refers to it as "The Fatal Invitation."

SERVES 6

1 cup plus 3 tablespoons olive oil
8 small eggplants
1 large onion, thinly sliced
1½ cups fresh tomato sauce (Salsa
    di Pomodoro, page 95)
2 tablespoons raisins
Red wine vinegar
10 fresh mint leaves, chopped
6 slices (about 8 ounces) caciocavallo or soft pecorino cheese

Heat ½ cup of the olive oil in a large skillet. Cut eggplants into thin slices. Fry half of the slices until golden on each side. Drain them on paper towels. Add another ½ cup of oil to the pan. Fry the remaining eggplant slices. Drain on paper towels.

In a clean large frying pan, heat 3 tablespoons of oil and sauté the onion until soft, about 15 minutes.

Preheat the oven to 350 degrees.

Arrange the eggplant slices on the bottom of a shallow 9-by-13-inch baking pan. Spoon the Salsa di Pomodoro evenly over the eggplant.

Combine the onion and raisins. Spoon them over the top of the eggplant mixture. Sprinkle lightly with vinegar and mint. Bake for 10 minutes. Remove from the oven, and cover with the cheese slices. Return the pan to the oven and bake until the cheese has melted, about 15 minutes. Remove from the oven and cool. Serve at room temperature.

Melanzane di Campagna

(Country-Style Eggplant)

SERVES 6

Cut eggplants into ⅓-inch-thick slices, lengthwise. Cook the slices over a grill until golden on both sides. Transfer to a large serving dish.

In a medium frying pan, cook the garlic in the oil for 1 minute over medium heat. Add the vinegar and sugar and cook for 2 minutes.

Spoon this mixture over the eggplant slices. Sprinkle the top with the oregano, mint, and hot pepper flakes.

2 medium-sized eggplants
3 garlic cloves, chopped
½ cup olive oil
2 tablespoons red wine vinegar
1 tablespoon sugar
1 teaspoon dried oregano
1 tablespoon freshly chopped mint
Pinch hot pepper flakes

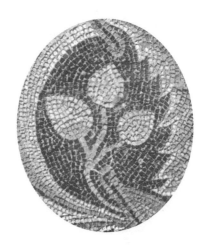

La Cucina Allegra (The Happy Kitchen)

In Palermo, the Via Ruggero Settimo runs from Politeama Square to Massimo Square. Known as "The Lounge of Palermo," this street is no more than five hundred meters in length, and is home to some of the city's most luxurious and expensive shops. The Via Ruggero Settimo is also where Palermo's wealthy inhabitants like to walk in the late afternoon to window-shop and look at all the other people. During this walk (*passeggiata,* in Italian) you can learn *tutto di tutti* (everything about everyone). We call this circle of meandering strollers "*la Palermo bene.*"

Via Ruggero Settimo was a trendy place in Palermo in the early 1960s, before the unrest of 1968 temporarily altered this custom (read more about this on page 84). After that, the street became the symbol of *i nuovi ricchi* (the new rich). Only in the 1980s did it return to its former status and relaxed atmosphere. This came as a big relief to everyone, because nothing is missed more during a serious revolution than good, juicy gossip.

Back in the 1960s, there was a tiny place where you could buy wonderful snacks to enjoy during your walk. It was called La Cucina Allegra (The Happy Kitchen), and it was one of my favorite stops going to and from school. La Cucina Allegra was located just off the Ruggero Settimo, inside a doorway leading to the courtyard of an aristocratic hall of a nineteenth-century *palazzo.* There was always a queue. I didn't care, because I knew that from behind the beaded curtain (there to help keep out the flies), freshly made *panzerotti con besciamella, arancini,* tiny *timballi di pasta, crocche di patate,* puff pastry bowls filled with ragù and green peas, and other delicious savories were waiting for me.

Despite the name of the place, the owners and cooks were eternally sad. Busily working behind the white marble countertop, dressed all in black, the workers seemed more like undertakers than happy cooks, as if in an unresolved conflict between their personalities, clothes, the name of the shop, and the incredibly good food.

During one of Michele's recent visits, I wanted to show her La Cucina Allegra, mostly to see if it still existed. After thirty-five years I felt strong emotions as we turned into the entranceway to the courtyard and saw a beaded curtain in front of the door. The location was the same, but the shop had been modernized. The present owners had

renamed it I Cuochini (The Little Cooks). After a ten-minute wait, we each bought little brown bags filled with some of the same steaming specialties I remembered and walked out onto the sunlit street to eat them. The food was as wonderful as before. But deep in my heart, I missed the original place, the name, the gloomy "happy cooks," and the other ingredients that time has taken away.

Panini Caldi di Melanzane

(Hot Eggplant Sandwiches)

SERVES 6

Cut the eggplants into ½-inch-thick slices. Dust each side with flour.

Put the eggs in a shallow dish and beat lightly. Coat both sides of the eggplant slices with the egg.

Heat about ¼ inch of olive oil in a large frying pan. Fry the eggplant slices until golden brown on each side, cooking them in batches. Add more oil as needed. Drain the fried eggplant slices on paper towels.

Preheat the oven to 350 degrees.

Place half of the fried eggplant slices on a large baking sheet. Cover them with the mozzarella. Sprinkle lightly with oregano and salt. Cover each with 1 of the remaining eggplant slices. Secure each sandwich with a toothpick and bake for 15 minutes. Discard toothpicks and serve hot.

2 medium-sized eggplants
All-purpose flour
3 large eggs
Olive oil
8 ounces mozzarella cheese, cut into tiny cubes
Oregano
Salt

I Carciofi alla Maniera di Gangi

(Gangi-Style Artichokes)

6 large artichokes
1 lemon, halved and seeded
2½ cups Caponata (recipe below)
6 thin slices caciocavallo or pecorino cheese

SERVES 6

Trim the artichokes: Squeeze the juice of the lemon into a large bowl filled halfway with cool water, and add the lemon halves. Trim and peel each artichoke's stem, leaving about 1 inch of stem attached. Cut about 1 inch off the tough tops—this varies with the size of the artichokes. Pull off the outer leaves, trim the sharp ends off the remaining leaves, and remove the fuzzy choke center. As each artichoke is cleaned, drop it into the lemon water. When you are ready to use the artichokes, drain and pat them dry.

Steam the artichokes in lightly salted water until tender, about 30 minutes. Drain them well in a colander.

Gently spread the top opening in each artichoke apart with your fingers. Spoon equal amounts of the Caponata into the center of each. Top each with a slice of the cheese. Serve immediately.

Caponata (Sweet-and-Sour Eggplant Stew)

Although only 2½ cups of caponata are required in the recipe for I Carciofi alla Maniera di Gangi, this recipe makes about 1½ quarts. When you take the time to prepare caponata, you might as well make a little extra (it's so good!), especially since it improves with flavor as it marinates. It keeps well for three or four days in the refrigerator. Caponata is a delicious appetizer eaten plain or on grilled bread as a bruschetta topping. It's also a savory condiment that can accompany chicken, meat, or fish dishes.

MAKES ABOUT 1½ QUARTS

Olive oil
3 large eggplants, cut into 1-inch cubes
1 large onion, coarsely chopped

Heat ½ inch of olive oil in a large frying pan and fry the eggplant in batches until golden brown on all sides. Add extra oil to the pan, as needed. Drain the fried eggplant on paper towels.

In a large, heavy-bottomed saucepan or pot, heat another ½

cup olive oil and sauté the onion for 5 minutes, stirring often. Add the remaining ingredients and the drained eggplant. Combine gently but thoroughly and simmer over low heat for 30 minutes, stirring occasionally. Taste for seasoning. The caponata should have a pleasant, sweet-and-sour flavor. Transfer the caponata to a large bowl and let cool. Serve at room temperature or cover, refrigerate overnight, and serve cold.

3 cups fresh tomato sauce (Salsa di Pomodoro, page 95)
¾ cup pitted and chopped green olives (Sicilian, if possible)
½ cup capers, drained and rinsed
1 cup thinly sliced celery hearts, including 2 tablespoons chopped leaves
5 anchovy fillets, finely chopped
About ½ cup red wine vinegar
About 1 tablespoon sugar
Salt and freshly ground pepper

Carciofi "Lasciatemi Sola" (Artichokes "Leave Me Alone")

The strange name of this dish comes from my first, unsuccessful preparation of it. I spent all morning in the kitchen trying to make it. It turned out an awful mess—and everyone was kind enough to repeat over and over: "the worst dish I've ever tasted," "too salty," "too soggy," etc. Finally I cried, "*Basta! Lasciatemi sola con il mio dolore!* [Enough! Leave me alone with my pain!]" Of course my mother remade the dish and it was perfect. But since then, whoever makes it, my family calls the dish Carciofi "Lasciatemi Sola."

SERVES 4

Trim the artichokes: Squeeze the juice of the lemon into a large bowl filled halfway with cool water, and add the lemon halves. Trim and peel each artichoke's stem, leaving about 1 inch of stem attached. Cut about 1 inch off the tough tops—this varies with the size of the artichokes. Pull off the outer leaves, trim the sharp ends off the remaining leaves, and remove the fuzzy choke center. As each artichoke is cleaned, drop it into the lemon water. When you are ready to use the artichokes, drain and pat them dry.

Cut the prepared artichokes into thin slices. Arrange half of the sliced artichokes in the bottom of a saucepan. In a medium bowl, combine the bread crumbs, Parmesan cheese, onion, garlic, pars-

8 large artichokes
1 lemon, halved and seeded
½ cup toasted bread crumbs
½ cup freshly grated Parmesan cheese
1 medium onion, chopped
1 garlic clove, thinly sliced
1 tablespoon freshly chopped Italian parsley
Salt and freshly ground pepper
Olive oil

ley, and salt and pepper to taste. Sprinkle half of the mixture on the artichokes and drizzle generously with olive oil. Make 1 more layer in the same manner. Cover and cook over medium heat for 30 minutes or until artichokes are tender.

Tortino di Carciofi con Sarde e Ricotta

(Artichoke Tart with Sardines and Ricotta)

This dish is a specialty from the small mountain town of Petralia, thirty minutes from Gangivecchio. Originally the dish was made with sardines preserved in salt, since that was the only way we could keep fish for any length of time in the mountains.

The sardines in the center of the tart are the noble filling between two layers of a delicious ricotta and artichoke mixture. In Petralia, the tart is so beloved that it is served as a main course. But we think it makes a wonderful antipasti dish.

SERVES 6

4 large artichokes
1 lemon, halved and seeded
1¼ pounds ricotta cheese (fresh, if possible)
Salt and freshly ground pepper
⅓ cup freshly chopped Italian parsley
⅓ cup olive oil
1 small onion, finely chopped
⅓ cup dry white wine
½ cup water
2½ pounds whole fresh sardines, or thawed frozen sardines, scaled, cleaned, boned, finned, and deheaded. (After cleaning, only 1 pound of fillets remain.

Trim the artichokes: Squeeze the juice of the lemon into a large bowl filled halfway with cool water, and add the lemon halves. Cut off each artichoke's stem end and about 1 inch off the tough tops—this varies with the size of the artichokes. Trim the sharp ends off the leaves and remove the fuzzy choke center. Cut the artichokes into thin slices and put them into the lemon water.

Put the ricotta into a medium bowl and mash it with a fork. Season well with salt and pepper and add the parsley. Mix well and set aside.

In a large frying pan, cook the olive oil and the onion over medium heat for 3 minutes, stirring often. In the meantime, drain the artichokes and pat them dry.

Add the artichokes to the onion and sauté for 5 minutes, stirring a few times. Add the wine and water. Cover and cook on low heat for 20 minutes. Remove from heat and let cool.

Preheat the oven to 375 degrees.

Add the artichokes to the ricotta mixture and combine well.

Grease an 8-inch round baking pan with olive oil. Coat the pan on the bottom and the side with bread crumbs. Knock out extra crumbs.

With half the ricotta and artichoke mixture, make a smooth, even layer in the pan. Cover with the sardine fillets. Top with the remaining half of the mixture. Bake for 30 minutes or until the top is golden brown. Serve hot.

Ask your fishmonger to prepare them for you—order 1 pound filleted sardines.)
Dried bread crumbs for dusting pan

Fonduta di Verdure (Vegetable Fondue)

SERVES 4

Cover each vegetable with lightly salted boiling water separately in saucepans and cook until just tender. Drain and allow to cool.

In a nonstick saucepan, melt the cheeses over low heat, stirring often.

Sprinkle in the flour, stir, and add the wine. Cook until sauce is smooth and creamy, stirring frequently. Stir in the kirsch, nutmeg, and salt and pepper to taste.

Lightly grease a 4½-by-9-inch loaf pan. Pour a thin layer of the sauce into the bottom. Add layers of each vegetable, 1 at a time. Spoon the remaining sauce over the top and sprinkle with the Parmesan cheese. Put under the broiler for 5 minutes or until golden on top. Let cool for 10 minutes, and then cut into slices. Serve hot.

4 medium carrots, peeled and cut into 1-inch lengths
4 celery stalks, cut into 1-inch lengths
1 small cauliflower head, broken into small florets
1 pound broccoli, stalks peeled, trimmed, and cut into slices, and heads broken into small florets

FOR THE SAUCE:

8 ounces Gruyère cheese, cut into small cubes
4 ounces Emmentaler cheese, cut into small cubes
2 tablespoons all-purpose flour
⅔ cup dry white wine
1 tablespoon kirsch
Pinch freshly grated nutmeg
Salt and freshly ground pepper
2 tablespoons freshly grated Parmesan cheese

Fagioli Vellutina con la Menta (Beans with Mint)

SERVES 8

1 pound barlotti (cranberry)
   beans
½ cup chopped celery hearts
3 garlic cloves, minced
3 tablespoons extra virgin olive oil
½ cup white wine vinegar
Salt and freshly ground pepper
About ½ cup freshly chopped
   mint leaves

Rinse the beans thoroughly and soak them 8 hours or overnight. Drain them well.

Put the beans into a large saucepan and cover with 2 inches of cool water. Add the celery and garlic. Bring to a boil, then reduce heat to a simmer and cook until tender, about 2 hours. (Some American beans need less cooking time, so after 1 hour, taste the beans for doneness every 10 minutes.)

Drain the cooked beans well and place them in a large serving bowl. Dress lightly with the oil, vinegar, salt and pepper to taste, and mint. Toss gently to combine well. Allow to rest at room temperature for 30 minutes before serving. Toss and taste again before serving.

Variation: If you have any leftover beans, puree them with a tablespoon or 2 of olive oil for 10 to 15 seconds in a food processor or until mixture is a slightly rough paste. Taste for seasoning. This puree makes a fantastic spread for bruschetta.

Le Olive della Zia Elvira (Aunt Elvira's Olives)

My *zia* (aunt) Elvira, the originator of this olive recipe, was one of the most fascinating characters of my childhood. She was one of the three sisters of my mother's mother, Elena. All the other sisters married, but Elvira never did. She lived with one of her sisters, Enrica, until she was seventy. Then she moved to Elena's house, which is where I first met this strange woman.

At the time, my grandmother lived in an apartment in a seventeenth-century building in the historic center of Palermo, ai Quatro Canti di Citta', the famous four corners. It was a large apartment, with many rooms on two floors. Elvira spent a lot of time in her locked room on the second floor.

She was quite tall and striking, with long blond hair gathered in a chignon at the nape of her neck. Her blue eyes always sparkled. She wore odd, old, mismatched clothes and spoke in a deep voice. She told great stories with theatrical gestures. When she cooked—and she was an outstanding cook—she liked to sing songs from the First World War. I thought she was fantastic company. If she were alive today, I'm sure she would have made a fortune in show business.

After she died, at eighty, we finally discovered what had kept her so occupied behind her closed door. In her room, we found an amazing collection, neatly stored little things in boxes under her bed, in the closet, and in her dresser: thousands of bus ticket stubs, used matches, broken buttons, old shoestrings, and hair from combs and brushes rolled up and tied in tiny little rings.

My granny immediately threw everything away. But for several weeks she swore that she heard the sounds of drawers opening and closing in Elvira's room at night, as if someone was looking for something. No one ever wanted to sleep in that room again.

SERVES 6

Preheat the oven to 350 degrees. Spread the bread crumbs in a baking sheet and put them into the oven. Stir after 5 minutes. Remove the bread crumbs when they are golden (after 3 to 5 minutes). Spread out on a plate to cool. Set aside.

Put the olives into a shallow dish or bowl. Stir in the remaining ingredients. Sprinkle the bread crumbs over the top and combine well. Serve immediately.

Note: If you want to prepare this dish in advance, don't add the bread crumbs. Refrigerate the olive mixture in a covered container; it will keep for 3 or 4 days. To serve, bring the olives back to room temperature and just before serving, toss with the bread crumbs.

½ cup fresh bread crumbs
2 cups pitted green olives
    (Sicilian, if possible)
1 celery stalk, diced
½ cup capers, rinsed and drained
¼ teaspoon fennel seeds
2 tablespoons white wine vinegar
¼ cup olive oil

Le Olive dell' Attore (The Actor's Olives)

When I was a child, an actor appearing in a show in the area came to see the abbey. We invited him to stay for lunch. The next day we received a glass jar containing his special olives. A note with them read "I hope you will appreciate this modest creation." It was signed "The Actor."

SERVES 6

2½ cups pitted black olives (Gaeta, if possible)

Zest of 1 orange, cut into very thin strips

Zest of 1 lemon, cut into very thin strips

Juice of 1 lemon

3 garlic cloves, peeled and left whole

1 teaspoon fennel seeds

1 cup extra virgin olive oil

Put the olives into a bowl and combine with the remaining ingredients. Transfer to a glass jar with a tight-fitting lid. Seal and let rest at room temperature for at least 12 hours or up to 3 days. Remove and discard the garlic cloves. Spoon olives into a bowl with a slotted spoon. Toss again before serving. You can serve the olives with toothpicks, but you'll still need to offer guests napkins.

Pecorino Fresco con Miele e Pistacchi

(Fresh Pecorino with Honey and Pistachios)

You might be surprised to see a microwave oven used as a cooking method in our cookbook, but this is Paolo's recipe, and he often uses a microwave to melt or heat food in his restaurant at Tenuta Gangivecchio. "Mamma," he tells me, "everybody's got them. They're very useful and fast, like cars." Anyway, I've always preferred walking to driving or riding in a car. And I've never touched this piece of mischief, and don't intend to. But if you are brave enough, try this recipe—I admit it is delicious.

SERVES 4

4 tablespoons sunflower oil

Four 3½-ounce, ½-inch-thick slices fresh pecorino cheese

In a small nonstick frying pan, heat 1 tablespoon of the oil. When the oil is hot but not smoking, fry a slice of cheese for 2 minutes on each side. Transfer the slice to an individual, small microwave-

able dish. Repeat with remaining oil and cheese slices. Spoon 1 tablespoon of honey over the top of each slice and microwave for 30 seconds. Sprinkle each with a teaspoon of pistachios and serve immediately.

¼ cup honey
4 rounded teaspoons chopped
   pistachios

Caciocavallo con Mandarini

(Mandarins with Caciocavallo)

This recipe, like so many others, was born of desperation. On a cold winter day, a sophisticated group of four arrived at Gangivecchio for lunch, without reservations. We hadn't expected any guests on that particular day, but it was impossible to send them away in the freezing weather with nothing to eat. So we welcomed them inside and sat them at a table by the hearth, where Peppe quickly lit a fire. In a quivering voice, one of the ladies asked Mamma to make her "*Qualcosa di indimenticabile* [something unforgettable]." "You will have it," Mamma promised.

As always, we had pasta and quick sauces that Mamma could prepare. Unfortunately, we had little other food in the pantry except for staples such as dried herbs, eggs and cheese, and a big basket of mandarins. Mamma scurried to the kitchen and told me to bring her the bottle of rum we kept locked in an armoire's secret compartment. (It is not a good idea to leave any opened bottle of liquor where Peppe can find it.) But why did Mamma want rum now? I couldn't imagine.

Here is the recipe for Mamma's delectable invention. I can also tell you that more than two tablespoons of rum disappeared from the bottle that day, and that Peppe's siesta was longer than usual.

SERVES 4

Preheat the oven to 400 degrees.

In a frying pan, heat the butter and add the tangerines. Cook over low heat for 5 minutes, turning once halfway through. Sprinkle with the sugar and rum. Remove from the heat.

In 4 small, shallow, ovenproof dishes, place 1 slice of the cheese and equal amounts of the tangerine slices and juice from the pan.

¼ cup unsalted butter
4 mandarins or tangerines,
   peeled, seeded, membranes
   removed, thinly sliced
   crosswise
4 teaspoons sugar

2 tablespoons white rum
Four ⅓-inch-thick slices of cacio-
    cavallo or soft pecorino cheese
Dried oregano
Salt and freshly ground pepper

Bake for 5 minutes or until the cheese is just melted. Sprinkle the top of each dish with oregano, salt, and pepper to taste and serve immediately.

Torta di Gorgonzola e Pere
(Gorgonzola and Pear Tart)

½ pound gorgonzola cheese, at
    room temperature
⅓ cup heavy cream
1 sheet (½ pound) frozen puff
    pastry, thawed at room tem-
    perature for 30 minutes
4 pears, peeled, cored, seeded,
    and cut into thin slices

SERVES 6

Preheat the oven to 400 degrees.

Coarsely chop the cheese and heat it in a small saucepan with the heavy cream over very low heat, stirring often. When the mixture is smooth, remove from the heat. Let cool for 10 minutes.

Meanwhile, roll out the puff pastry on a lightly floured surface. Cut it into a 9-inch circle and fit into a 9-inch round tart or baking pan. Prick the surface of the pastry in a dozen or so places with a fork. Spoon half of the cheese mixture over the surface of the puff pastry. Arrange layers of the pear slices in 2 overlapping circles on top of it. Spoon the remaining cheese mixture evenly over the top of the pears.

Bake for 30 minutes or until the top is golden.

Let rest for 15 minutes. Cut in wedges and serve.

Torta con Lattuga (Lettuce Tart)

Bring 2 quarts of water to a boil. Add the lettuce and boil for 2 minutes. Drain well, pat dry, and set aside.

Grease and flour an 8-inch cake pan. Fit the Pasta Frolla Piccante into the pan, pressing it halfway up the side.

Preheat the oven to 350 degrees.

Heat the butter in a large frying pan. Add the lettuce, sprinkle lightly with salt, and sauté for 10 minutes over low heat, stirring occasionally. Remove lettuce from heat and cool for 15 minutes.

To make the béchamel sauce, melt the butter in a saucepan. Stir in the flour and cook over low heat, constantly stirring, for about 2 minutes. Slowly pour in the milk, whisking constantly, and turn the heat to high. Whisk until the sauce has thickened. Season to taste with salt.

Spoon the lettuce evenly over the Pasta Frolla. Spoon the Salsa di Pomodoro over it and top with the béchamel sauce. Sprinkle lightly with Parmesan cheese. Bake for 45 minutes.

Remove from the oven and let cool. Serve at room temperature.

2 small heads romaine lettuce hearts, coarsely chopped
Pasta Frolla Piccante (recipe follows)
2 tablespoons unsalted butter
Salt
½ cup fresh tomato sauce (Salsa di Pomodoro, page 95)
Freshly grated Parmesan cheese

SALSA BESCIAMELLA
(BÉCHAMEL SAUCE)

3 tablespoons unsalted butter
3 tablespoons all-purpose flour
1¼ cups milk
Salt

Pasta Frolla Piccante
(Pastry Dough for Vegetable Tarts)

Put the flour, salt, sugar, and baking powder into a large bowl. Combine. Add the eggs and vanilla, and mix together with a pastry blender or the blades of 2 ordinary kitchen knives. Little by little, incorporate the butter. Coat your hands with a little flour and knead the dough only enough so that it sticks together; take care not to overwork it or it will toughen. Shape the dough into a ball.

Pasta Frolla Piccante can also be made in a food processor: Put the flour, salt, sugar, baking powder, and butter into the bowl of the processor and blend until coarse-crumb consistency. With the machine running, add the eggs and vanilla through the feed tube. Process just a few seconds, until the dough is combined.

With a little flour on your hands, form the dough into a ball, then cover with plastic wrap and refrigerate overnight, if possible, but at least for 1 hour. The dough also freezes well for future use.

2 cups all-purpose flour
1 teaspoon salt
½ cup plus 2 tablespoons sugar
1 tablespoon baking powder
3 large eggs, at room temperature
½ teaspoon vanilla extract
½ cup plus 3 tablespoons unsalted butter, melted then cooled to room temperature

La Torta di San Giuseppe (Saint Joseph's Tart)

SERVES 6

2 cups all-purpose flour

1½ tablespoons unsalted butter,
   at room temperature

2 large egg yolks

¼ cup tepid water

Pinch salt

½ cup olive oil

1 large onion, chopped

3 large artichoke hearts, cooked
   and sliced

2 cups cooked green peas

2 cups fresh spinach, chopped

⅔ cup celery, chopped

⅔ cup fennel, chopped

¼ cup finely chopped feathery
   green fennel tops

1 tablespoon freshly chopped basil

1 tablespoon freshly chopped
   mint

2 tablespoons raisins

2 tablespoons pine nuts

Salt and freshly ground pepper

1 large egg, lightly beaten

Combine the flour with the butter, egg yolks, water, and salt until the dough is smooth. Shape into a ball and let rest in a bowl covered with a dish towel.

Heat the olive oil in a large saucepan. Add the onion and sauté for 5 minutes over medium heat, stirring often. Stir in the remaining vegetables, basil, and mint. Combine thoroughly. Add the raisins and pine nuts, blending well. Season to taste with salt and pepper and set aside.

Preheat the oven to 400 degrees.

Lightly butter and flour an 8-inch round cake pan.

Divide the dough into 2 parts, 1 slightly larger than the other. Roll out the larger piece of dough into a 10-inch circle. Fit it into the pan, letting the extra dough hang over the edges.

Spoon the vegetable mixture onto the dough and pat down evenly. Roll out the second piece of dough to a 9-inch circle. Gently place it on top of the vegetables. Seal the tart by pressing together the edges of the upper and lower pieces of dough evenly, with your fingers. Cut off and discard any excess dough. With a fork, prick the top layer of dough in 8 places, spaced a few inches apart.

Brush the top of the dough with the beaten egg.

Bake for 40 minutes or until the top crust is golden brown. Serve hot.

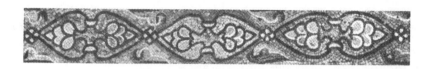

Torta di Ricotta e Nocciole (Ricotta and Hazelnut Tart)

SERVES 6

Lightly butter and flour an 8-inch round baking pan.

Roll out the Pasta Frolla and fit into the pan. Set aside.

Preheat the oven to 350 degrees.

In a large frying pan, heat the butter and water. When the butter has melted, add the potatoes, leek, lettuce, and salt and pepper to taste. Simmer for 5 minutes. Add the wine and cook 5 minutes longer. Let rest.

In a bowl, combine ricotta, egg, Parmesan cheese, and cream.

Using a slotted spoon, place the vegetables on the dough in the pan. Cover the vegetables with the ricotta-cream mixture. Spread evenly. Sprinkle the hazelnuts evenly over the top. Bake for 30 minutes. Let the tart cool. Serve at room temperature.

Pasta Frolla Piccante (page 37)
2 tablespoons unsalted butter
1 tablespoon water
2 medium potatoes, boiled and cubed
1 leek, white part only, chopped
1 large head romaine lettuce, center leaves only (about 8), chopped
Salt and freshly ground pepper
¼ cup dry white wine
¾ cup ricotta cheese
1 large egg
¼ cup freshly grated Parmesan cheese
1 cup heavy cream
¾ cup toasted and chopped hazelnuts

Sformato di Peperoni e Cipolle
(Pepper and Onion Soufflé)

SERVES 6

Preheat the oven broiler. Roast the peppers and onions 5 to 6 inches under the heat source on the rack until the skin is blackened all over. You will need to turn each vegetable several times with tongs. Remove the peppers and onions from the oven and place in a brown paper bag. Close the top securely and let rest about 15 minutes.

Preheat the oven to 350 degrees.

Remove the vegetables from the bag. When cool enough to handle, remove the stem ends, cores, and seeds from the peppers. Remove the skins with a small, sharp knife. Cut the peppers into thin strips.

3 large yellow bell peppers
2 large onions
4 large eggs
¼ cup freshly grated pecorino cheese
½ teaspoon dried oregano
Salt
Olive oil
¼ cup toasted bread crumbs, or as needed

Peel the onions and cut them in half lengthwise. Slice them into thin slivers.

In a large bowl, beat the eggs with the cheese, oregano, and salt to taste. Add the vegetables and combine well.

Lightly grease a 10-inch round baking pan with olive oil and coat it lightly with toasted bread crumbs.

Spoon the vegetable mixture into the pan and pat down the top evenly with the back of a spoon. Cover the top lightly and evenly with more toasted bread crumbs. Bake for about 15 minutes, until the eggs are set. Serve hot or at room temperature.

Melone con Aceto Balsamico e Menta

(Melon with Balsamic Vinegar and Mint)

In the summer we often serve this simple, wonderfully refreshing antipasto. The cantaloupe should be ripe and sweet, and a good-quality balsamic vinegar is important. Sometimes Paolo adds two or three thin slices of prosciutto to each dish. The prosciutto complements the melon nicely. Along with some bread, this dish makes a delicious lunch or light dinner.

2 tablespoons extra virgin olive oil
2½ tablespoons good-quality
  balsamic vinegar
12 mint leaves, finely chopped
1 medium-sized ripe cantaloupe
8–12 thin slices prosciutto
  (optional)

SERVES 4

Combine the oil, balsamic vinegar, and mint in a small bowl. Let rest for 10 minutes.

Quarter the cantaloupe. Scoop out the seeds and peel each quarter. Cut into thin slices and arrange in a fan shape on each of 4 plates. Spoon equal amounts of the oil, vinegar, and mint mixture over the cantaloupe slices. If desired, garnish each serving with 2 or 3 slices of prosciutto. Serve at once.

Mezze Lune di Ricotta (Half Moons with Ricotta)

SERVES 6

Place the pizza dough on a lightly floured work surface and let rest.

In a bowl, combine the ricotta, mozzarella, salami, egg yolk, Parmesan, butter, parsley, and pepper to taste.

Divide the dough into 12 equal pieces. Roll each piece into a circle about 4 inches in diameter. Spoon equal amounts of the filling into the center of each. Fold half of each dough circle over the filling and press the edges together, forming a semicircle. Make sure you have sealed the sides securely.

Grease a baking sheet lightly with olive oil. Place the half moons on it about 3 inches apart. Brush the tops with lightly beaten egg white. Let them rise for 1 hour.

Preheat the oven to 400 degrees. Bake the half moons for 20 minutes or until they are golden brown. Serve hot.

½ recipe for pizza dough (Paste Base per la Pizza, page 79)
¾ cup ricotta cheese
¾ cup diced mozzarella cheese
½ cup diced salami
1 large egg, separated
¼ cup freshly grated Parmesan cheese
¼ cup melted unsalted butter
⅓ cup freshly chopped Italian parsley
Freshly ground pepper
Olive oil

Uno Strudel Mediterraneo (A Mediterranean Strudel)

Years ago, I knew a wonderful young woman who became a nun. As a nun, her personality dramatically changed. She lost her sense of humor, became very solemn and strict, and was thoroughly disagreeable company. Then, after ten years, to everyone's surprise, she gave up her holy garments. She immediately started smoking, playing poker, going to the hairdresser, and collecting all kinds of bizarre hats. She also began eating like a wolf and entertaining. Her elaborate dinners were food and wine extravaganzas. What delicious meals we ate at her joyful gatherings! When I asked her if she felt uncomfortable living such an excessive, jolly life after so many years of prayer and humble living, she answered, "Not in the least. It was the Lord who wished this life for me." Here is one of her recipes.

SERVES 4

1¼ cups all-purpose flour

1 teaspoon baking powder

2 tablespoons olive oil

3–4 tablespoons lightly salted
   water

¾ cup diced mozzarella cheese

¾ cup diced tomatoes

1 tablespoon capers

2 anchovies, chopped

2 tablespoons pitted and chopped
   green olives (Sicilian, if
   possible)

1 teaspoon dried oregano

Salt and freshly ground pepper

1 large egg yolk

2 tablespoons milk

In a bowl, combine the flour with the baking powder. Mix in the oil and water. When dough is soft and smooth, put it into a clean bowl and cover with a dish towel. Let rest for 45 minutes.

Combine the mozzarella, tomatoes, capers, anchovies, olives, and oregano in a bowl. Season with salt and pepper.

Preheat the oven to 350 degrees.

Divide the dough into 2 parts, 1 slightly larger than the other. On a lightly floured work surface, roll the smaller piece of dough into a thin rectangle about 8 inches long and 4½ inches wide. Roll the other piece of dough into a thin rectangle about 9 inches long and 5 inches wide. Grease a baking sheet lightly with oil. Place the smaller piece of dough on it. Gently move the ends of the rectangle toward each other to form a C shape. Spoon the filling evenly over the top, keeping about ¾ inch from the edge of the pastry. Place the other piece of dough over the top of the filling. Seal the edges of the dough by pressing them with your fingers.

In a small bowl, combine the egg yolk with the milk and brush it over the dough. Bake for 30 minutes. Turn off the oven and let the strudel rest there for 15 minutes. Remove and cool to room temperature. Transfer to a serving dish, slice, and serve.

Pizza Calabrese (Calabrian Pizza)

After Betty, my former sister-in-law, left Gangivecchio, one of the main things I missed was her mother's marvelous recipes from Calabria. But, as an old Italian proverb says, "God sees and acts"—eventually, my brother met another young woman from Calabria whom he liked. Her name was Rose, and she was a guest at his inn. During the brief time she was at Gangivecchio, she gave me only a few recipes, but they were very tasty, especially this one. There is no question that I got the best part of Paolo and Rose's unrequited romance: a new antipasto!

Serves 4

Put the yeast and water in a bowl and set aside for 5 minutes or until frothy. Put the flour in a bowl and make a well in the center. Combine the yeast, olive oil, and salt in the well. Draw the flour into the wet ingredients and knead the mixture into a dough on a lightly floured work surface. Let the dough rest in a clean bowl, covered with a dish towel, for 2 hours.

Preheat the oven to 350 degrees.

Divide the dough in half. Flatten each piece with your hands into an 8-inch circle and place 1 of them on a lightly greased baking sheet. Spread the ricotta over the dough, leaving 1 inch of the dough uncovered around the outer edge. Sprinkle the top with the pancetta and arrange the egg slices over it. Sprinkle with the parsley and hot pepper flakes and drizzle lightly with olive oil. Cover the pizza with the second circle of dough and seal the edges of the dough by pressing them together. Brush the top with the beaten egg yolk. Bake for 40 minutes or until golden. Serve hot.

2 teaspoons active dry yeast
½ cup warm water
1¼ cups all-purpose flour
1½ tablespoons olive oil
Pinch salt
¾ cup ricotta cheese
⅓ cup cubed pancetta
2 large hard-boiled eggs, thinly sliced
1½ tablespoons freshly chopped Italian parsley
Pinch hot pepper flakes
1 large egg yolk, lightly beaten

Panini di Modica di Nina

(Nina's Little Sandwiches, Modica Style)

Modica is a beautiful baroque town in southeastern Sicily, famous for its pastries. It also has some excellent antipasti. Our friend Nina, who had the good fortune to marry a man from Modica, shared this recipe with us.

Serves 8

Combine yeast and water and set aside for 5 minutes or until frothy. Put the flour into a bowl and make a well in the center. Mix the yeast, olive oil, and salt in the well. Combine wet and dry ingredients. Shape dough into a ball and let rise in a bowl, covered with a dish towel, for 2 hours.

To prepare the filling, combine the ricotta, egg yolk, parsley,

1 package active dry yeast
½ cup warm water
1¾ cups all-purpose flour
1 tablespoon olive oil
Pinch salt
1½ cups ricotta cheese

1 large egg yolk

⅓ cup freshly chopped Italian parsley

Pinch hot pepper flakes

¼ cup milk

1 garlic clove, minced

2 tablespoons capers, minced

⅓ cup diced salami

⅓ cup chopped boiled ham

1 medium tomato, cubed and blotted between paper towels

hot pepper, milk, and salt to taste. Stir in the remaining ingredients.

Roll the dough out on a lightly floured work surface until it is about ⅛ inch thick. Using a 4-inch round cookie cutter, cut out 16 circles. (To get 16, you will have to gather the scraps and re-roll the dough.)

Lightly grease a baking sheet. Arrange 8 of the circles of dough on the sheet, 4 inches apart. Spoon a rounded tablespoon of the ricotta mixture on top of each circle of dough and flatten slightly, being careful not to come closer than ½ inch from the edge of the dough. Top each with 1 of the 8 remaining circles of dough. Press the edges of the top and bottom pieces of dough securely together. Let the *panini* rise for 30 minutes.

Preheat the oven to 350 degrees. Bake for 30 minutes. Serve immediately.

Il Pane del Re (The King's Bread)

This savory stuffed bread is a local specialty of our area. It is unusual because it contains meat—in this case, chicken. In the past, the *contadini* rarely ate meat, since they couldn't afford it. Hence, the name "The King's Bread." Even today it's usually only served for special celebrations.

SERVES 6

1 medium onion, chopped

½ cup olive oil

2½ pounds equal portions of chicken legs and thighs

Salt and freshly ground pepper

½ cup dry white wine

2 hard-boiled eggs, coarsely chopped

¼ cup chopped Italian parsley

Juice of 1 lemon

In a large frying pan, sauté the onion in olive oil for 5 minutes over medium heat. Season the chicken well with salt and pepper. Add the chicken and wine to the pan and cook over medium heat until very tender, about 40 minutes, turning halfway through.

Take the chicken from the pan and let rest on a cutting board until cool enough to handle. Discard the skin. Remove the meat from the bones and coarsely chop it. Transfer the chicken to a bowl and add the cooking juices and onion from the pan, the eggs, parsley, lemon juice, almonds, pine nuts, and capers. Combine well. Taste for seasoning.

Preheat the oven to 300 degrees.

Cut the top half off the loaf of bread and remove most of the soft part inside each half. Drizzle the top and bottom of the inside of the bread halves lightly with olive oil. Spoon the chicken mixture into the bottom half of the bread. Cover with the top half of the bread and press down lightly.

Transfer the stuffed bread to a baking sheet and bake for 10 minutes or until the filling is just heated.

Cut the bread in half. Cut each half into 3 equal-sized wedges and serve hot.

2 tablespoons blanched, toasted, and chopped almonds
2 tablespoons pine nuts
1 tablespoon capers
One 8-inch-round loaf crusty Italian bread

Minestre

(Soups)

Fagioli e Festoncini di Nonna Elena
  (Granny Elena's Bean and Pasta Soup)

Palline di Patate in Brodo *(Potato Balls in Broth)*

Dadi *(Bouillon Cubes)*

Minestra di Funghi e Patate
  (Mushroom and Potato Soup)

Minestrone Rustico Siciliano *(Sicilian Rustic Soup)*

Minestra di Broccoletti *(Broccoli Soup)*

Minestra di Cime di Rapa *(Broccoli Rabe Soup)*

Minestra di Ditali con Lattuga *(Ditali and Lettuce Soup)*

Zuppa di Pesce di Maria *(Maria's Fish Soup)*

Zuppa d'Inverno di Carne di Wanda
  (Wanda's Winter Meat Soup)

I Tenerumi *(Cucuza Tendrils and Leaves)*

Minestra di Tenerumi *(Tenerumi Soup)*

Una Luce in Cucina

(A Light in the Kitchen)

All'alba di molti grigi e scuri mattini d'inverno, quando vedevo una luce filtrare da sotto la porta della cucina, sapevo che qualcuno stava cucinando una minestra, per prendersi cura di me.

(At dawn, on many gray and dark winter mornings, when I saw a light coming from under the kitchen door, I knew someone was cooking soup, caring about me.)

—Wanda Tornabene

Winters in Palermo, where I grew up, never seemed terribly cold to me. It was in 1949, when I arrived at Gangivecchio, high in the Madonie Mountains, that I discovered the meaning of a cold winter. Here, sometimes the snow would fall silently throughout the night, burying everything under a thick blanket of icy white. My mother-in-law, Giovanna, trying to comfort me, cheerfully told me that snow was one of nature's most beautiful elements to experience, and always a joyous occasion too, because it was the signal that it was time for soup.

I can still smell her hot, rich chicken broth simmering in the kitchen. I can also hear the arguments that followed about whether to choose beans or lentils to go into the broth. Giovanna always made the final decision, despite our wishes. She preferred beans.

Gangivecchio has been my home now for more than fifty years. I wonder how many bowls of soup have been consumed within these ancient walls. This reflection takes me on a childhood reverie as I smell the aroma of another bean soup cooking.

At the beginning of winter, when rain started falling over Palermo, my brothers and sister and I waited for the words we knew my mother would soon speak: "Children, remind me to put the beans in the water tonight." Promptly we would reply, in unison, in old Sicilian, "*Chiovi, chiovi, pasta coi fasoli* [Rain, rain, pasta with beans]," a well-known lullaby. Now when I ask my own children to remind me about soaking the beans, they do not answer with that old refrain, but with, "Please, Mamma, why not potatoes with mushrooms or rice balls in broth, or something different?" Each time they complain, I become angry. It is I who decide, and I prefer beans now, too. Perhaps it is an affliction of old age to prefer the food from a happy past. While in this dark mood, I swear that one day I will

tell them that when I am no longer with them in this life, they will remember, as I do, the sweet feeling of the "light in the kitchen." I'll say, "At dawn, on gray and dark winter mornings, remember when you saw a light coming from under the kitchen door and knew someone was cooking soup, caring about you. It didn't matter *what* kind of soup. It was a sign of love to warm the body and soul." Of course, I will never say that. Instead, I take a deep breath and get on with the business of offering what is demanded in my household today: variety. I will create new soups and resurrect delicious old ones—anything to please my beloved children in the third millennium.

For Sicilians, soup is normally hearty fare, whatever the season. In our household, it takes the place of our cherished "due spaghetti."

The prince ladled out the *minestra* himself, a pleasant chore, symbol of his proud duties as paterfamilias.

—From *The Leopard,* by Giuseppe Tomasi di Lampedusa

Fagioli e Festoncini di Nonna Elena

Fagioli e Festoncini di Nonna Elena

(Granny Elena's Bean and Pasta Soup)

Mamma often made this wonderful bean and pasta soup—and in enormous quantities. My brothers, sister, and I competed over how many bowls of it we could devour. Afterward, my brothers rushed off to whichever sport they were playing that day. My sister and I also disappeared, perhaps collecting our skates as we went. Whatever the activity, we had energy to burn for hours, which is probably exactly the effect Mamma had in mind.

SERVES 6

Rinse the beans thoroughly. Soak them overnight in a bowl covered with 3 inches of cool water.

Transfer the beans and soaking water to a large pot. Add the onion, potato, baking soda, and celery. Bring to a boil, reduce the heat, and cook over medium heat until the beans are tender. (After 1 hour of cooking taste beans every 10 minutes, as some beans cook faster than others.)

When the beans are tender, remove the onion, potato, and pieces of celery. Pass them through a food mill and save the puree.

Add the tomatoes and liquid, sugar, oil, and vegetable puree to the beans. Season to taste with salt and pepper. Bring the mixture to a boil and cook for 5 minutes, stirring often. Stir in the pasta, adding a little more water if needed, and cook until the pasta is done. Stir in the hot pepper flakes.

Transfer the soup to a tureen or soup bowl. Top with the chopped parsley. Sprinkle with a little olive oil, and, if you like, Parmesan cheese. Serve immediately.

1 pound dried navy beans (about 2 cups)
1 large onion, peeled and chopped
1 large boiling potato, peeled and coarsely chopped
1 teaspoon baking soda
2 celery stalks, cut into 3-inch lengths
One 14½-ounce can diced tomatoes, with liquid
1 teaspoon sugar
½ cup extra virgin olive oil, plus extra for topping
Salt and freshly ground pepper
⅓ pound festoncini (square-shaped pasta) or broken tagliatelle pieces
Pinch hot pepper flakes
⅓ cup finely chopped Italian parsley
Freshly grated Parmesan cheese (optional)

Palline di Patate in Brodo (Potato Balls in Broth)

SERVES 4

1 pound potatoes, boiled, peeled, thinly sliced, and cooled

4 tablespoons melted unsalted butter

¼ cup freshly grated Parmesan cheese, plus extra for topping

3 large eggs, separated

Pinch freshly grated nutmeg

⅓ cup freshly chopped Italian parsley

Salt and freshly ground pepper

3 carrots, thinly sliced

3 celery stalks, cut into 1-inch lengths

1 large onion, chopped

1 medium tomato, chopped

1 cup chopped fresh spinach leaves

1 medium potato, peeled and cubed

Sunflower oil, for deep-frying

Pass the cooked potatoes through a food mill or ricer. Place in a large bowl, add the butter, Parmesan cheese, egg yolks, nutmeg, parsley, and salt and pepper to taste, and combine well. Beat the egg whites until peaks form and fold them into the mixture. Shape into a large ball and let rest in a clean bowl, covered with a dish towel, in a cool spot for 2 hours.

In a 5-quart pot, combine the vegetables. Season with salt and pepper. Add water to cover them by 2 inches (about 10 cups). Bring to a boil. Reduce the heat to medium and cook for 1 hour.

Drain and discard the vegetables, saving the vegetable broth. Strain the broth through a fine mesh strainer. Transfer broth to a large, clean saucepan and bring to a simmer.

Form the potato mixture into small balls, each about the size of half a walnut.

Heat 3 to 4 cups of oil in a frying pan with high sides or in a fryer. When oil is hot but not smoking, fry the potato balls, in batches, until golden brown. Drain on paper towels.

Pour the broth into a tureen or large serving bowl. Add the fried potato balls. Pass the Parmesan cheese.

Minestra di Funghi e Patate (Mushroom and Potato Soup)

SERVES 4

½ cup olive oil

1 pound portabello mushrooms, cleaned and coarsely chopped

1 pound potatoes, peeled and cut into ½-inch cubes

1 small onion, chopped

1 garlic clove, minced

6 cups water

Heat the oil in a large saucepan. Add the mushrooms, potatoes, onion, and garlic and simmer for 10 minutes. Add water and bring to a boil. Stir in the Parmesan rind, bouillon cube, and hot pepper flakes and season to taste with salt and pepper. Simmer for 1 hour, stirring occasionally. This soup should be thick and creamy, but add extra water if desired.

Stir in the parsley, butter, and grated Parmesan cheese. Serve hot with grilled bread. Pass the grated Parmesan cheese and the pepper mill.

2-ounce piece Parmesan cheese
   rind, end scraped
1 vegetable bouillon cube
Pinch hot pepper flakes
Salt and freshly ground pepper
½ cup freshly chopped Italian
   parsley
1½ tablespoons unsalted butter
⅓ cup freshly grated Parmesan
   cheese, plus extra for topping
8–12 slices grilled Italian bread
   (optional)

Minestrone Rustico Siciliano (Sicilian Rustic Soup)

SERVES 6

In a large saucepan, heat the butter with the onion on low heat for 1 minute. Stir in the celery, carrots, and garlic. Simmer for 10 minutes. Add the ham and cook 2 more minutes, stirring occasionally. Add the tomatoes and parsley. Cook 5 minutes.

Add water and season with salt. Bring the mixture to a boil. Stir in the zucchini and rice. Cook for 40 minutes or until the rice is cooked, stirring occasionally. Add more water if necessary.

Add the peppers and remove the pan from the heat. Stir in the Parmesan cheese and basil.

2 tablespoons unsalted butter
1 small onion, finely chopped
1 celery stalk, diced
1 carrot, peeled and diced
1 garlic clove, minced
¼ cup diced boiled ham
4 medium tomatoes, peeled and
   cubed
1 tablespoon freshly chopped
   Italian parsley
6 cups water
Salt
4 small zucchini, cubed
¾ cup Vialone Nano, Carnaroli,
   or Arborio rice
2 yellow bell peppers, roasted
   under the broiler, cored,
   seeded, skinned, and cut into
   thin strips (for roasting
   instructions, see page 39)
3 tablespoons freshly grated
   Parmesan cheese
6 fresh basil leaves, chopped

Dadi (Bouillon Cubes)

Bouillon cubes are greatly valued in our kitchen for flavoring broths, soups, sauces, stews, and meat and fish dishes, even risottos. They are so convenient.

In America, as we traveled across the country, we were often questioned about the use of bouillon cubes in our recipes. We were told that they are scorned by serious cooks. This surprised us. We can't think of any serious Italian home cook who doesn't use them. It's a practical consideration. In Sicily, indeed in all of Italy, there are no canned broths available in supermarkets. Why should there be, when good-quality bouillon cubes, dissolved in liquid, are packed with flavor, enhancing any dish they are used in? We stress "good-quality," because there are some dreadful ones on the market. The only test is in the tasting.

There is one precaution one must take when using bouillon cubes: taste the dish for salt content. It may still be necessary to add salt to a dish in which one bouillon cube is used, because one cube used in two quarts of liquid might not release enough salt flavor.

Today we have a variety of bouillon cubes to choose from: chicken, beef, vegetable, mushroom, rosemary, basil, and garlic and parsley. The recently introduced herb-flavored cubes are wonderful, especially in winter.

Regrettably, we have no fish-flavored bouillon cubes here in Sicily, so every time Michele comes to Gangivecchio, she brings us some.

American cooks can substitute quality canned broths for bouillon cubes, if desired—many of these broths come in low-sodium varieties, which is helpful if you have dietary concerns. Of course, if you have the time, the best broth is always homemade, filled with pure natural flavors. But we urge you to try good-quality bouillon cubes. Perhaps you will come to rely on them and regard them, as we always have, as instant tiny bouquets of flavor.

Minestra di Broccoletti (Broccoli Soup)

SERVES 6

Bring 8 cups of water to a boil in a large saucepan. Add the broccoli and cook until tender, about 10 minutes. Over a heatproof bowl, drain the broccoli, saving the cooking water.

In the same pan, cook the olive oil and anchovies over medium heat, stirring constantly, for 3 to 4 minutes, until the anchovies almost melt. Return the reserved cooking liquid to the pan. Add the broccoli, parsley, bouillon cubes, garlic, marjoram, and thyme. Gently combine and bring to a boil. Stir in the pasta and cook over medium heat at a low boil until the pasta is al dente. Season to taste with salt and pepper. Serve with freshly grated cheese.

2 pounds broccoli, stems peeled and cut into small pieces, tops cut into florets
3 tablespoons olive oil
4 anchovy fillets, chopped
2 tablespoons freshly chopped Italian parsley
2 vegetable bouillon cubes
2 garlic cloves, minced
¼ teaspoon dried marjoram
¼ teaspoon dried thyme
¼ pound broken spaghetti
Salt and freshly ground pepper
Freshly grated pecorino or Parmesan cheese

Minestra di Cime di Rapa (Broccoli Rabe Soup)

When my former daughter-in-law, Betty, arrived at Gangivecchio, she brought with her recipes from Apulia, where her father was born. I learned just how delicious the food of this region can be.

Apulia is a region in the south of Italy, on the heel of the boot. It is sunny, and the land is very dry. Water is precious here. Famous for its Baroque architecture, Apulia has some of the most beautiful monuments in the country, in shocking contrast to the extreme poverty here. The region produces an enormous amount of olive oil, around which many of its dishes are based. It also harvests wild greens and other vegetables, which are featured in Apulia's excellent cuisine. *Le orecchiette con cime di rape* (ear-shaped pasta with broccoli rabe), fragrant fava bean purees and soups, and pizza bianca are among the region's most praised dishes. Apulian cooking is simple and straightforward, but it's really tasty.

Here is my adaptation of a wonderful Apulian soup.

3 tablespoons olive oil, plus
  extra for topping
3 garlic cloves, chopped
¾ pound broccoli rabe, tough
  ends and stalks trimmed,
  coarsely chopped
8 cups water
2 vegetable bouillon cubes
⅓ pound ditali (see box below)
  or broken spaghetti
Salt and freshly ground pepper
Pinch hot pepper flakes
Grated ricotta salata cheese

SERVES 4

In a large saucepan, heat the oil and garlic over medium heat for 3 minutes, stirring often. Add the broccoli rabe and cook for about 10 minutes over medium-low heat. Add the water and bring to a boil. Add the bouillon cubes, ditali, and salt and pepper to taste and cook until the pasta is al dente. Stir in the hot pepper flakes. Serve hot. Pass olive oil for each person to drizzle lightly over soup, then pass the ricotta salata cheese.

Ditali

Ditali are very small tube-shaped pasta pieces, less than half an inch long. Because they are hollow they are wonderful used in soups and sauces, since the inside of each piece of pasta fills with the flavor of the liquid or sauce. Ditalini—pasta pieces about half the size of ditali—are also available. We think of using ditalini mainly in soups or other dishes for children.

Ditali means "thimbles" in Italian. Ditali really don't resemble thimbles at all, but the name is charming.

Minestra di Ditali con Lattuga

(Ditali and Lettuce Soup)

This recipe always reminds me of an old family friend who was the administrator of Gangivecchio. Niccolo ("Coco" to friends and family) was enormous, as tall and wide as an armoire. We found it ironic and sweet that this giant of a man loved lettuce, especially Mamma's lettuce soup. He never asked for seconds, and would protest "No, no!" each time Mamma ladled more soup into his bowl, but he would continue to eat until the tureen was empty.

SERVES 6

In a large saucepan, cook the oil, onion, garlic, and pancetta over medium heat until onions begin to turn golden brown. Add ½ cup of the water and tomato paste and combine well. Simmer for 10 minutes, stirring often.

Add the lettuce, parsley, and basil. Season to taste with salt and pepper and simmer for 10 minutes. Add a few additional tablespoons of water if necessary.

Add the remaining 6 cups of water and bring to a boil. Stir in the ditali and cook until done, about 12 minutes. (If you prefer a thinner soup, add 8 cups of water.) Taste again for seasoning. Transfer to a tureen or soup bowl and sprinkle with the cheese and hot pepper flakes. Drizzle with olive oil and serve at once.

3 tablespoons olive oil, plus extra for topping
1 medium onion, finely chopped
4 garlic cloves, chopped
½ cup cubed pancetta
6½ cups water
1 tablespoon tomato paste
2 heads romaine lettuce, coarsely chopped
2 tablespoons freshly chopped Italian parsley
2 tablespoons freshly chopped basil
Salt and freshly ground pepper
1½ cups ditali (see box on page 56) or broken spaghetti
About ⅓ cup freshly grated pecorino cheese, to taste
Pinch hot pepper flakes

Zuppa di Pesce di Maria (Maria's Fish Soup)

My *zia* Maria used to live in a beautiful villa in Mondello, a seaside resort town north of Palermo. We always looked forward to dinners at her home, especially if she had prepared her wonderful fish soup. She and her husband eventually sold the villa, because it was too far from Palermo, where their business is, and because it was quite deserted in the winter. We did not participate in the move back to their apartment in Palermo and weren't served her fish soup or any other food in their home for almost seven years. Our family became separated over a stupid quarrel between the two sisters. Mamma and Maria wouldn't speak to each other, even if they were dining in the same restaurant at the same time. I can tell you, they both suffered tremendously. To the great relief of everyone in the family, this feud ended a few months ago. To celebrate the armistice, Zia Maria cooked her Zuppa di Pesce for our first dinner back together. It has become a symbol of peace.

To make up for lost time, Mamma and Zia Maria see each other as often as possible; when apart, they speak on the phone for hours and have even taken two trips to America together.

SERVES 6

1½-pound lobster
One 1-pound piece of grouper
2 grouper or other fish heads
4 whole red mullets
3 garlic cloves, peeled, and left whole
½ cup olive oil, plus extra for topping
1½ pounds medium shrimp, shelled and deveined
1 pound squid, thinly sliced
1 pound mussels
1½ pounds fresh tomatoes,

Place the lobster, grouper, fish heads, and mullets in a large pot and cover with cool water. Bring to a boil and cook for 18 minutes or until the lobster is done. Remove the lobster, grouper, fish heads, and mullets.

Strain the fish broth through 2 pieces of cheesecloth. Reserve 4 cups of it in a large clean bowl.

When cool enough to handle, remove the lobster meat from the shells, and the bones and skin from the fish. Cut the lobster and fish into small pieces and set aside.

In a large frying pan, cook the garlic in the oil over low heat for 2 minutes. Add the shrimp, squid, and mussels. Cover and simmer for 5 minutes, stirring often. (If you like, remove the mussels, discard their shells, and add the mussel meat back to the pan.) Stir

in the tomatoes, salt and pepper, and hot pepper flakes. Simmer for 10 minutes, stirring occasionally. Add the wine and cook over high heat for 5 minutes.

Add the lobster and fish pieces and a few cups of the broth, as desired. Heat thoroughly.

Serve in individual bowls with the bread cubes. Drizzle the tops with olive oil and sprinkle with equal amounts of the parsley.

cubed and peeled, or two
16-ounce cans diced tomatoes
Salt and freshly ground pepper
Pinch hot pepper flakes
½ cup dry white wine
1½ cups toasted or fried bread
cubes
2–3 tablespoons freshly chopped
Italian parsley

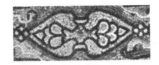

Zuppa d'Inverno di Carne di Wanda

(Wanda's Winter Meat Soup)

SERVES 4

Place the water and all the meat in a large saucepan. Bring to a boil, then reduce the heat and simmer for 30 minutes, skimming the surface occasionally.

Meanwhile, simmer the peas and onion in the butter in a small saucepan, until tender.

Add the peas, onion, and rosemary to the soup and season to taste with salt. Simmer over very low heat, stirring occasionally.

Heat the olive oil in a frying pan until hot but not smoking. Fry the bread cubes until golden brown all over, stirring often. Drain on paper towels.

Discard the rosemary. Serve the soup with the toasted bread cubes and pass the Parmesan cheese.

5 cups cold water
⅓ cup diced raw chicken breast
⅓ cup diced raw turkey breast
⅓ cup diced raw beef tenderloin
or sirloin
⅓ cup diced raw pork loin
½ cup diced boiled ham
1 cup frozen green peas, thawed
1 medium onion, chopped
4 tablespoons unsalted butter
2 sprigs fresh rosemary
Salt
½ cup olive oil
1 cup toasted bread cubes
Freshly grated Parmesan cheese

I Tenerumi (Cucuza Tendrils and Leaves)

In Sicily, we have a thin, long, pale-green squash called *cucuzza*. It can grow up to five feet long. The squash has a very mild flavor; it is peeled and cooked like zucchini, either boiled or steamed. Sicilians really prize the runners and leaves that the squash produces, the *tenerumi*. When it is time, in the early summer, we send Peppe to the garden to collect the *tenerumi* for soup, and he returns with a full basket. Cleaning them is tedious work, because only the tender leaves, tendrils, and buds are edible. So the big basket gives us only enough for one pot of soup. The stems and hard leaves are chopped and fed to the chickens.

Tenerumi have a mild taste, with the distinctive flavors of young zucchini, celery, and lemon. In season, *tenerumi* can be found in some Italian markets in America, especially if the farmers are Sicilian descendants. There is no real substitute for *tenerumi,* but a pleasant soup can be made using baby spinach instead.

Minestra di Tenerumi (Tenerumi Soup)

SERVES 4

5 cups cold water
1 quart (loosely packed) *tenerumi,* cleaned, stemmed, and coarsely chopped (or substitute fresh baby spinach leaves)
Salt and freshly ground pepper
½ cup olive oil
4 large garlic cloves, minced
1 cup chopped canned tomatoes
Pinch sugar
¼ pound broken spaghetti
Pinch hot pepper flakes

Bring water to a boil in a large saucepan. Add the *tenerumi* or spinach, season well with salt and pepper, and cook over medium heat for 5 minutes. Drain well and reserve the liquid.

Heat the oil and garlic in a saucepan. Cook over medium heat for 3 minutes, stirring often. Add the *tenerumi* or spinach, 1 cup of the liquid it cooked in, the tomatoes, and sugar. Simmer for 15 minutes.

Add 3 cups of the remaining liquid and bring to a boil. Stir in the pasta and cook at a slow boil for about 30 minutes or until the pasta is cooked. Stir in the hot pepper flakes. Taste for salt and pepper. Serve hot.

Piatti di Uova

(Egg Dishes)

Uova ad Occhio in Salsa Fresca
  (Eggs Poached in Fresh Tomato Sauce)

Uova Fritte con Mollica e Pecorino alla Siciliana
  (Sicilian Fried Eggs with Bread Crumbs and Pecorino)

Frittata con Zucchine e Menta
  (Omelette Stuffed with Zucchini and Mint)

Quadrettoni di Frittata con Spinaci e Formaggio
  (Square Omelettes Stuffed with Spinach and Cheese)

Frittata con Patate per Paolo *(Potato Omelette for Paolo)*

Frittata con la Marmellata a Portafoglio
  (Wallet-Shaped Jam Omelette)

Frittata al Forno *(Baked Frittata)*

Assassinio nel Pollaio *(Murder in the Henhouse)*

Uova Ripiene di Tonno e Capperi
  (Eggs Stuffed with Tuna and Capers)

Le Uova della Monaca *(Nun's Eggs)*

Uova Sode Ripiene al Gratin
  (Au Gratin of Eggs Stuffed with Cheese)

Perle dal Pollaio

(Pearls from the Henhouse)

*Un mondo senza uova?
Immaginate il dilemma
del cuoco!*

(A world without eggs?
Imagine the cook's
dilemma!)

I n an eastern courtyard of Gangivecchio, about two hundred meters of fenced-in open space and twenty-five meters of covered space house our rooster and hens. Like most farmers, we are privileged to have fresh eggs every day. These beautiful, big, oval pearls, each with a perfect round yellow heart, are indispensable in the kitchen. Beyond typical egg dishes like frittatas (omelettes) or poached, fried, or stuffed hard-boiled eggs, eggs are a vital ingredient in a countless number of dishes such as homemade pasta, mayonnaise, *pasta frolla,* cakes and tarts, cookies, pastry cream, and soufflés. A world without eggs? Imagine the cook's dilemma!

Eggs can save a lunch or dinner when there is no meat in the house and unexpected guests knock at the door, which often happens here. Any kind of frittata can be made with eggs and some vegetables—mushrooms, potatoes, asparagus, peppers, tomatoes, zucchini, artichokes, onions, and greens—herbs, and cheeses. Mamma's omelette lasagne (Frittata della Mamma), featured in our first book, is a baked creation of layered strips of cooked frittatas, with tomato sauce, pecorino cheese, and fresh basil. We also like to stuff eggs, especially for picnics, and we have included several recipes for them here.

My favorite eggs are poached in fresh tomato sauce (Uova ad Occhio in Salsa Fresca, page 65). Mamma, who loves eggs, thinks the best of all possible egg dishes is to simply fry very fresh eggs, while they still possess a distinct sweetness, leaving the yolks warm and runny, and dunking bread sticks into the *liquido dorato* [liquid gold] or sprinkling them with toasted bread crumbs—tampering with one of nature's most glorious foods as little as possible.

Because people usually consider eggs home food, we rarely serve them in our restaurant or at Paolo's, in the *albergo.* But nothing makes my mother happier than when Peppe tells her that a vegetarian guest has requested eggs—"Perhaps a frit-

tata?" Mamma appears before this person and begins describing her repertory of egg dishes. Finally the guest surrenders: "Madame, choose whatever you like. I will eat it."

The most unusual egg invention that we know is one my grandmother Giovanna gave to her son Enzo (my father) when he was a child. Each day she fed her reluctant boy a fresh, raw egg yolk (still warm from the henhouse) in a silver spoon, sprinkled with a few drops of Marsala wine, as a natural remedy to protect him from potential diseases of the day. While it's true that my father was rarely ill in his youth, we do not recommend this prescription.

Uova ad Occhio in Salsa Fresca

(Eggs Poached in Fresh Tomato Sauce)

SERVES 4

Pour the Salsa di Pomodoro into a large nonstick frying pan and bring to a boil, stirring often.

Lower the heat until the sauce is slowly bubbling, and break the eggs, one by one, into the sauce, spaced as far apart as possible but at equal distances. With a fork, gently mix the white of each of the eggs with the tomato sauce surrounding them, taking care not to break the egg yolks.

When the yolks are still soft but not completely runny, sprinkle the top of the eggs and sauce lightly with salt, pepper, and Parmesan cheese. Turn heat off.

Gently spoon 2 of the eggs and sauce onto each of 4 dinner plates in equal amounts. Garnish each dish with 2 slices of the grilled bread. You can also spoon the eggs and sauce over the grilled slices of bread. It's up to you.

2 cups fresh tomato sauce (Salsa di Pomodoro, page 95)
8 large eggs
Salt and freshly ground pepper
Freshly grated Parmesan cheese
Eight ¾-inch-thick slices grilled Italian bread

Uova Fritte con Mollica e Pecorino alla Siciliana

(Sicilian Fried Eggs with Bread Crumbs and Pecorino)

This simple fried-egg dish, with bread crumbs, pecorino cheese, and tomato sauce, is often served in the homes of the region in the Madonie Mountains around the town of Gangi.

SERVES 4

Combine the bread crumbs and cheese in a bowl.

Heat the Salsa di Pomodoro in a saucepan and keep at a very low simmer, stirring often.

In a 12-inch nonstick frying pan with curved sides, heat enough

¾ cup freshly grated dried bread crumbs
⅓ cup freshly grated pecorino cheese, plus extra for topping

1½ cups fresh tomato sauce (Salsa
   di Pomodoro, page 95)
Olive oil
8 large eggs
Salt
Freshly grated pecorino cheese
   (optional)
Freshly ground pepper

olive oil to just coat the bottom of the pan. Break the eggs, side by side, into the pan. Sprinkle with salt and the bread crumb mixture. Cook over low heat until the eggs are set. Separate the eggs with the end of a spatula and gently turn over, one by one. Cook only 2 minutes.

Invert two of the eggs, separately, onto each of four dinner plates. Spoon equal amounts of the tomato sauce over the eggs and serve at once. If you like, you can sprinkle a little grated pecorino cheese on top, and pass the pepper mill. We always serve these eggs with pan-fried potatoes and bread.

Frittata con Zucchine e Menta

(Omelette Stuffed with Zucchini and Mint)

8 large eggs
¼ cup freshly grated pecorino
   cheese
1 tablespoon finely chopped fresh
   mint leaves
Salt and freshly ground pepper
1 tablespoon olive oil
2 tablespoons unsalted butter
3 small zucchini, very thinly sliced

SERVES 4

Beat the eggs in a large bowl. Add the pecorino, mint, and salt and pepper to taste. Mix well and let rest at room temperature for 10 minutes.

Meanwhile, in a 12-inch nonstick frying pan with curved sides, heat the olive oil with 1 tablespoon of the butter. Cook the zucchini slices over medium-high heat, turning often, until just cooked, about 5 minutes.

Add the remaining tablespoon of butter. Stir the egg mixture and pour it over the zucchini. Stir for a few seconds over medium heat. When the eggs begin to set, smooth the mixture evenly across the pan and cook over very low heat until the eggs are no longer runny.

Place a large plate or flat pan lid over it and quickly and carefully invert the pan so that the frittata falls onto the plate or lid. Slide the frittata back into the pan and cook the other side for only a minute. Serve immediately, cut into wedges. A green salad and bread are perfect accompaniments.

Quadrettoni di Frittata con Spinaci e Formaggio

(Square Omelettes Stuffed with Spinach and Cheese)

There are nine portions of this dish—of the six people it will serve, certainly three will want second helpings.

SERVES 6

In a large saucepan, bring the spinach and water to a boil. Reduce to a medium boil and cook until done, about 5 minutes, stirring occasionally. Drain the spinach well and squeeze it dry in a clean dish towel. Finely chop the spinach. Heat the butter and oil in a frying pan and add the spinach. Season well with salt and pepper and cook over low heat for 10 minutes, stirring often.

Preheat the oven to 350 degrees.

In a bowl, beat together the eggs, pecorino, Parmesan, parsley, and salt and pepper to taste.

Generously butter a 10-inch square nonstick baking pan. Add the fontina cheese to the spinach and quickly toss. Mix well with the egg mixture. Pour into the baking pan and bake until golden brown on top, about 30 minutes.

Let the frittata cool for 5 minutes, then invert it onto a cool platter. Let it cool for an additional 15 minutes. Cut into 9 squares and garnish each piece with 2 cherry tomatoes and 2 fresh basil leaves.

1 pound baby spinach leaves
½ cup water
3 tablespoons unsalted butter
1½ tablespoons olive oil
Salt and freshly ground pepper
6 large eggs
1 tablespoon freshly grated pecorino cheese
1 tablespoon freshly grated Parmesan cheese
2 tablespoons freshly chopped Italian parsley
⅔ cup (about 5 ounces) Italian fontina cheese, diced
18 cherry tomatoes
18 basil leaves

Frittata con Patate per Paolo

(Potato Omelette for Paolo)

When my brother was a child, the only food he ate willingly (other than spaghetti) was potatoes. Mamma, who feared having a malnourished son, discovered that he would eat *anything* that contained potatoes. This is one of the dishes she invented for Paolo, but one that I also like very much.

SERVES 6

1¼ pounds boiling potatoes, peeled and cooked
2 large eggs
2 tablespoons freshly grated Parmesan cheese
2 tablespoons freshly grated dried bread crumbs
Salt and freshly ground pepper
Pinch freshly grated nutmeg
2 tablespoons whole milk
Olive oil

Grate the potatoes. In a large bowl, combine them with the eggs, Parmesan, bread crumbs, salt, pepper, nutmeg, and milk. Mix well.

Heat enough oil to cover the bottom of a large frying pan. Drop 12 slightly rounded tablespoons of the mixture into the pan, pressing each down to form little pancake-shaped potato omelettes. Cook on both sides until light golden brown. Serve hot.

Frittata con la Marmellata a Portafoglio

(Wallet-Shaped Jam Omelette)

SERVES 6

12 large eggs
3 tablespoons freshly grated Parmesan cheese
Salt

Break the eggs into a large bowl and beat with a whisk for 1 minute. Add the cheese, salt, and sugar and continue beating for 3 or 4 minutes, until foamy.

Heat a teaspoon of oil in a small omelette pan over medium

heat. Ladle ⅙ of the mixture into the pan. Cook frittata on both sides until lightly browned. Drain on paper towels. Cook the 5 remaining omelettes in the same manner.

Lightly butter a 9-by-13-inch nonstick baking pan. Heat broiler.

Spoon 1 tablespoon of the preserves onto the center of each omelette and spread it across the surface evenly. Fold each omelette in half and place, side by side, in slightly overlapping layers in the pan. Brush the tops with the melted butter and sprinkle with the brown sugar. Place under broiler until the sugar has melted. Serve immediately.

1 teaspoon sugar

Sunflower oil

6 tablespoons fruit preserves (quince, cherry, strawberry, peach, orange, or any fruit you wish)

2 tablespoons melted unsalted butter

3 tablespoons brown sugar

Frittata al Forno (Baked Frittata)

SERVES 6

Preheat the oven to 350 degrees.

Generously butter the bottom and sides of a 10-inch round nonstick baking dish or pan.

Beat the eggs in a large bowl. Add the remaining ingredients and combine well.

Pour the egg mixture into the prepared pan. Cook on the middle shelf of the oven for 30 minutes or until the sharp point of a knife comes out clean. Remove from oven and let rest for 5 minutes.

Invert the frittata onto a round serving dish. Serve hot.

Unsalted butter

10 large eggs

⅓ cup freshly grated pecorino cheese

⅓ freshly grated Parmesan cheese

¾ cup finely diced provolone cheese

1 cup diced boiled or other cooked ham

¾ cup diced fresh tomatoes, well drained

¼ cup freshly chopped basil

Salt and freshly ground pepper

Assassinio nel Pollaio (Murder in the Henhouse)

Among the dogs who live at Gangivecchio, there is Ciccio, my brother's favorite. Ciccio was born, I believe, from the happy union of a dog and a sausage. His abnormally short legs support a long, fat, muscular body with a curled, pointy tail on one end and an intelligent, expressive face on the other. Nothing escapes his eyes and ears.

A present from our stonemason, Ciccio arrived when he was only a few weeks old, looking like a tiny honey-colored hair ball. Immediately demonstrating great energy and a vivid personality, he raced back and forth around our large courtyard. He jumped in front of me, again and again, wanting to be picked up. I took him in my arms and he cuddled against my chest, lovingly licking my neck and face lavishly. Then, he bit my hand, drawing blood.

Throughout his history, Ciccio has played the protagonist of many a catastrophe. We refer to one memorable disaster as "Ciccio's Lunch for Twenty." Smelling something agreeable on a table in the abbey, he pulled off the tablecloth with a few yanks of his teeth—and everything on top of it as well. The platters and bowls were filled with food that had been prepared in advance for twenty guests who were about to arrive for lunch in our restaurant for a feast of veal *involtini*, caponata, roasted peppers, three fruit tarts, a *budino* (pudding), and a large bowl of barlotti beans. We discovered Ciccio in the middle of a sea of spilled food, gobbling up all he could and carefully avoiding any bits of broken china. He'd eaten almost all the beans, which gave him such terrible indigestion that he spent the rest of the day outdoors lying on his back releasing profoundly rude noises.

Ciccio has been permanently banned from the restaurant since he tried to bite some boisterous guests. He also must be locked in the stable when anyone wants to use the swimming pool, because he insists on jumping in the water and wildly splashing about.

But Ciccio's masterpiece was "*Assassinio nel Pollaio* [Murder in the Henhouse]." On a quiet afternoon, I woke from a nap to Mamma's piercing screams. Terrified, I quickly ran to find her. She was leaning against the wall of a second-story outside balcony,

speechless, an expression of tragedy on her face. One of her hands gripped the metal railing; the other pointed down below with a frantic motion at Ciccio, who was sitting in the middle of the henhouse yard, panting excitedly, among the motionless bodies of fifteen hens and a rooster—a war zone after the battle. He looked up at us as if expecting praise: after all, he had proved himself a brave hunting dog. All Mamma could think of was the loss of her precious fresh eggs.

As punishment, my brother had a serious confrontation with Ciccio, who never even glances toward the henhouse anymore.

The next day, we bought new hens and a black rooster. In a couple of weeks, we had fresh eggs again. We never found out who left the henhouse gate open. But ever since this calamity, Ciccio's movements are announced twenty-four hours a day by a little bell attached to his collar.

Uova Ripiene di Tonno e Capperi
(Eggs Stuffed with Tuna and Capers)

SERVES 12 AS A FIRST COURSE OR 6 AS A MAIN COURSE

Remove the yolks from the cold cooked eggs and place in a large bowl. Arrange egg whites on platter or work surface, cut side up. Add the remaining ingredients to the bowl of yolks and mix well. Taste for seasoning. If it's too dry, add a little more mayonnaise.

Spoon equal amounts of the mixture into each egg-white half and shape into smooth domes.

Serve as an appetizer or a light meal with sliced tomatoes or a green salad.

12 hard-boiled eggs, cooled, shelled, and cut in half lengthwise

Two 6⅛-ounce cans white-meat tuna packed in oil, well drained

2 tablespoons capers, rinsed and patted dry

2 tablespoons freshly chopped Italian parsley

About ½ cup mayonnaise

1 tablespoon melted unsalted butter

Juice of 1 lemon

Salt and freshly ground pepper

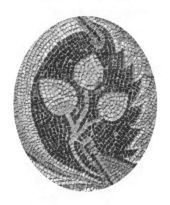

Le Uova della Monaca

(Nun's Eggs)

Here is another version of stuffed eggs—slightly unusual, since they are stuffed, breaded, and fried.

SERVES 12 AS A FIRST COURSE OR 6 AS A MAIN COURSE

12 hard-boiled eggs, cooled,
   shelled, and cut in half
   lengthwise
¼ cup ricotta cheese
2 tablespoons freshly grated
   Parmesan cheese
2 tablespoons freshly chopped
   Italian parsley
Salt and pepper
All-purpose flour
3 large egg whites, lightly beaten
Dried bread crumbs
Sunflower oil, for deep-frying
Salt

Remove the yolks from the cold cooked eggs and place them in a large bowl. Thoroughly mix the egg yolks with the ricotta, Parmesan cheese, parsley, and salt and pepper to taste. Spoon equal amounts of the mixture into 12 of the egg-white halves, rounding the tops into domes. Fit an empty egg white half over each of the filled ones, and press lightly to form perfectly shaped whole eggs.

Dust the stuffed whole eggs with flour, dip them in egg white, and coat thoroughly with bread crumbs.

Heat 3 inches of oil in a deep pan and fry the breaded, stuffed eggs in batches until golden brown all over. Remove with a slotted spoon and drain on paper towels. Season with salt, if desired. Eat while hot.

Uova Sode Ripiene al Gratin

(Au Gratin of Eggs Stuffed with Cheese)

SERVES 4

First, prepare the Salsa Besciamella. When cooked, remove from heat and cover to keep warm.

Preheat the oven to 350 degrees.

Remove the yolks from the cold cooked eggs and place in a large bowl. Add the pecorino, gorgonzola, Parmesan cheese, and parsley and combine by mashing them together with a fork. Season to taste with salt and pepper. Fill the egg whites with equal amounts of the mixture.

Spoon 1½ cups of the Salsa Besciamella into a shallow 9-inch round baking dish. Arrange the stuffed eggs, stuffed side down, over the sauce. Spoon the remaining sauce over the top. Drizzle with melted butter and sprinkle with the Parmesan cheese. Bake for 15 minutes, remove from oven, then place under heated broiler until golden brown. Serve warm with plenty of Italian bread.

3 cups Salsa Besciamella (page 37)
8 large hard-boiled eggs, cooled, shelled, and cut in half lengthwise
¼ cup freshly grated pecorino cheese
¼ cup crumbled gorgonzola cheese
2 tablespoons freshly grated Parmesan cheese
⅓ cup freshly chopped Italian parsley
Salt and freshly ground pepper
2 tablespoons melted unsalted butter
¼ cup freshly grated Parmesan cheese

Pizza e Focacce

(Pizza and Focaccia)

Paste Base per la Pizza *(Basic Pizza Dough)*

Sfincione *(Sicilian Pizza)*

Sei Condimenti per la Pizza *(Six Pizza Variations)*

  Margherita *(Mozzarella, Tomatoes, and Basil)*

  Quattro Formaggio *(Four Cheeses)*

  Pizza con Pomodori, Caciocavallo, e Cipolla Rossa
    (Tomato Sauce, Caciocavallo, and Red Onion)

  Melanzane e Basilico *(Eggplant and Basil)*

  Zucchine e Timo *(Zucchini and Thyme)*

  Patate, Salsiccia, e Rosmarino *(Potatoes, Sausage, and
    Rosemary)*

Le Focacce e la Rivoluzione *(Focaccia and the Revolution)*

Paste Base per Focacce *(Basic Focaccia Dough)*

Focacce con Broccoletti *(Broccoli Focaccia)*

Focacce con Cipolle e Pomodori
  (Focaccia with Onions and Tomatoes)

Focacce di Spinaci di Kery *(Kery's Spinach Focaccia)*

Schiacciata Ripiena *(Stuffed Focaccia with Anchovies and Pecorino)*

Schiacciata di Rucola e Pomodori Secchi *(Focaccia Stuffed with
  Arugula and Sun-Dried Tomatoes)*

Schiacciatine *(Crisp Focaccia Topped with Olive Oil and Oregano)*

I Trionfi della Pasta di Pane

(The Triumphs of Bread Dough)

Pizza: l'umile e deliziosa ambasciatrice d'Italia.

(Pizza: Italy's humble and delicious ambassador.)

I cannot think about the Sicilian kitchen—indeed, the Italian kitchen—today without a grateful nod to pizza and her sister, focaccia—for me, the two triumphs of bread dough.

Pizza probably came to Italy in the middle or late nineteenth century, when some ingenious Italians duplicated our Arabian neighbors' flatbreads. (After all, pizza is simply flattened bread dough with toppings.)

Naples has always claimed that pizza was invented there. We will not quarrel with this assumption. When we went to Naples last year to cook on Italian television, the first thing Mamma, Paolo, and I did was to go out and *facciamo la pizza* [eat a pizza]. Naturally, it was superb. The most basic, famous, and well-loved pizza was named Margherita, in honor of Queen Margherita di Savoia's visit to Naples in the early part of the last century. The colors of a Margherita pizza represent the colors of the Italian flag: the red of the tomatoes, the white of the mozzarella cheese, and the green of the fresh basil. This is my mother's favorite pizza, only she likes to add chopped anchovies to the classic *condimenti* (toppings).

My favorite is Quatro Formaggio (page 82)—usually mozzarella, pecorino, caciocavallo, and gorgonzola, though sometimes other cheeses are used. After consuming all this cheese, I will drink all the red wine on the table and all the spring water in the refrigerator. But it is just too delicious to give up.

In America we learned that many home cooks there use a special heated stone in the oven on which to cook their pizzas. We do not. The best pizzas are cooked in a very hot wood-burning oven until a good crust is formed. In a hot oven, they take less than ten minutes to cook. In a normal home oven, at a temperature of 425 degrees, pizza requires 25 to 35 minutes. Anyone who eats pizza has burned the roof of their mouth at least once or twice because they are in such a hurry to savor

it. When you make pizza at home, warn everyone to wait five minutes before devouring.

Years ago, when the first pizzeria opened in Gangi, a town of about eighty-six hundred, two and a half miles from the abbey, my brother immediately exclaimed, "Finally, civilization has arrived in this town." My father called it barbaric: "Imagine, bringing me to a restaurant to eat pizza for dinner!" For my mother, the opening was a blessing. Going out for pizza meant she did not have to cook dinner for us after preparing a large lunch for our restaurant guests.

Eventually, long after my father died, having a pizza at home became a Sunday-night ritual for my mother and me. It still is today. Mamma drops into her old, ugly chair, puts up her feet, watches television, plays and converses with her beloved little animals, and then comes to the table for pizza. Very soon afterward, she falls into bed.

There must be hundreds of toppings for pizza today. In fancy restaurants, we now see incredibly silly inventions—combinations of sliced fruit, cream, and far too many ingredients. As you will see from the recipes that follow, our pizzas are not complicated. They are made with our favorite ingredients: vegetables, arugula, tomatoes, and a variety of cheeses.

Beyond our Sunday-night pizza, we occasionally like to eat pizza in a restaurant; it's great fun. The pizza party means a collection of friends laughing together at a long table. If there are twelve people, there will be twelve different toppings. While we wait for the pizzas to arrive, two or three at a time, the main topic of conversation will almost certainly be how disgusting it is to have Coca-Cola with pizza. It should be ice-cold beer—or, even better, red wine.

When I was sixteen, my first boyfriend invited me to go out for pizza, just the two of us. Though I was thoroughly infatuated, I ate my pizza in five minutes. Roberto, watching me suspiciously, observed, "You must not be very much in love with me if you have such an appetite." I suppose he was right. Although I suspect that even true love wouldn't stop me from eating pizza.

We also have recipes here for *focacce,* a delicious bread that we often associate with childhood. I was given *focacce* in the afternoons as a *merenda* (snack). It's basically the same dough as pizza, but more yeasty and versatile, so we can be more creative with it—splitting it open and adding delectable fillings, or baking *condimenti* inside double layers of dough.

Pizza, a worldwide phenomenon, is Italy's humble and delicious ambassador. So say to your family, *"Andiamo a mangiare una pizza* [Let's eat a pizza]," and surprise them by making it yourself.

Paste Base per la Pizza (Basic Pizza Dough)

Put the yeast, sugar, and water into a small bowl. Stir and let rest for 10 minutes.

Mix the flour and salt in a large bowl and make a well in the center. Add the melted lard or olive oil to the yeast mixture and pour into the well. Work into a dough with a wooden spoon.

On a lightly floured board, knead the dough, folding it over and over until it is smooth and silky. Add a little flour as needed until the dough is no longer sticky. Shape the dough into a ball and, with olive oil on your hands, lightly coat the dough. Put it into a bowl and cover it with a dish towel. Let the dough double in size in a warm place. This takes about 1 hour.

When the dough has risen, follow instructions in individual pizza recipes.

1 envelope active dry yeast
1 teaspoon sugar
1 cup warm water
3¼ cups all-purpose flour
1 teaspoon salt
¼ cup melted lard or olive oil, plus extra for coating the dough

Sfincione (Sicilian Pizza)

Palermo's famous pizza, *sfincione* (also known as *sfincione di San Vito*), has a thicker, softer, and more bread-like crust than other pizzas. Traditionally *sfincione* is shaped into a rectangle or square, cooked in a special baking pan with 1-inch sides, and served cut into square pieces. The most typical *sfincione* is topped with onions and anchovies; pecorino, caciocavallo, or mozzarella cheese; and tomatoes. The final touch is a dusting of oregano and bread crumbs.

Occasionally we hear from our American guests at Gangivecchio that they are not particularly fond of anchovies. When they ask what ingredients are in a dish they liked, they often are genuinely surprised to hear anchovies were included. Perhaps this is because they don't like it when too many are used or when whole fillets are placed on top of dishes. For this large pizza, we only include four anchovies for the topping. They are chopped up and almost dissolve during the cooking. Anchovies should never over-

whelm any dish, but only suggest a subtle hint of the sea. Before you reject anchovies, try our *sfincione* recipe. And if you ever have the chance to taste *fresh* anchovies, do not miss this extraordinarily delicious experience.

SERVES 6

1 recipe Paste Base per la Pizza
  (page 79)
¾ cup olive oil
2 large yellow onions, thinly
  sliced and separated into rings
8 peeled and seeded fresh or
  canned tomatoes, finely
  chopped
Salt and freshly ground pepper
1 teaspoon sugar
1 pound pecorino, caciocavallo, or
  mozzarella cheese, shaved
4 anchovies, finely chopped
1 teaspoon dried oregano, or to
  taste
Dried bread crumbs

Cover the prepared dough and let it rise while making the topping.

Heat the olive oil in a large frying pan and stir in the onions. Cook over low heat for about 20 minutes, stirring often, until onions are soft. Add the tomatoes, salt and pepper to taste, and the sugar. Cook for 3 minutes, stirring every 30 seconds. Then remove mixture from the heat and set aside to cool.

When the dough has doubled in size, punch it down. Shape or roll the dough into a rough 12-by-16-inch rectangle or a 14-by-14-inch square. The crust will be thicker than other pizzas, and you should use a baking pan with 1-inch sides. Oil the pan lightly on the bottom and sides. Fit the dough into the pan.

Spread the cheese and anchovies evenly over the top of the dough, then cover with the sauce to within a little less than an inch of the sides. Now sprinkle with the oregano and a light covering of bread crumbs. Let the *sfincione* rise for 30 minutes. Preheat oven to 400 degrees for 15 minutes. Cook *sfincione* for 20 to 25 minutes or until the edges of the dough are golden brown and the top sizzling. Let the *sfincione* rest for 10 minutes, then cut it into squares and enjoy the wonderful taste of classic Sicilian street food.

Wanda Tornabene gives "an invitation to all those wanting to enter Gangivecchio's Sicilian kitchen and dining rooms. Be sure to bring along your appetites."

"At our restaurant at Gangivecchio, we typically serve three or four of an assortment of our *antipasti rustici*."

"When risotto, Italy's most elegant rice dish, is on the menu at Gangivecchio, there is great excitement."

Risotto con Zucchini, Patate e Pesto, page 132

"I tasted my first couscous when I was a teenager. I fell in love with it at first taste." – G.T.

Cuscus con Vitello e Verdura, page 126

"In 1992, Paolo built and opened a small nine-room inn, which we call Tenuta Gangivecchio, with his own restaurant."

"In the eastern courtyard of Gangivecchio, about two hundred meters of fenced-in open space and twenty-five meters of covered space house our rooster and hens. Like most farmers, we are privileged to have fresh eggs every day."

Wanda in the
kitchen:
"Never surrender
to a difficult
mayonnaise *or* the
tax collector."

Freshly grated *parmigiano reggiano* cheese

Hot peppers in Gangivecchio's vegetable garden

"The people who live in Mediterranean regions have always believed that fresh vegetables in the kitchen means healthy nourishment and a delicious dinner."

Fried eggplant for *Spaghetti con Melanzane,* page 105

"Seasonal fruits satisfy our craving for sweets."

Sei Condimenti per la Pizza (Six Pizza Variations)

Prepare the basic pizza dough according to the recipe on page 79.

Preheat the oven to 425 degrees at least 10 minutes before preparing the pizza.

Punch the dough down and flatten or roll it into one large pizza or two to four individual pizzas. Make whatever size or shape you want to—round, rectangle, oval, oblong, or square. Though we have never seen one, you could even make a triangular pizza, which would be symbolic of triangular-shaped Sicily. Anyway, the shape doesn't matter, although at Gangivecchio we normally make traditional round pizzas and prefer individual ones to sharing one big pizza.

Place the shaped dough on a lightly oiled baking sheet.

Top the flattened dough with any of the suggested toppings below. There are countless pizza possibilities: all sorts of vegetables and herbs, olives, anchovies, capers, meats, fish and seafood, tomato sauce, tomatoes, and a huge array of cheeses. We like the basic Margherita pizza, which is made by putting thin slices of mozzarella over the dough and covering it with thin tomato slices and a drizzle of olive oil. After the pizza is baked, it is sprinkled with small, fresh basil leaves. We also sprinkle this simple tomato and cheese pizza with young arugula leaves if we have some from the garden. Try it, it's delicious. The five variations we give below are only a handful of the many we like.

The amounts of ingredients for the toppings given are for 1 large round pizza, about sixteen to eighteen inches in diameter, or two to four smaller pizzas. However, if you love cheese, add a little more. If you want more vegetables than cheese, increase the amount of vegetables and reduce the amount of cheese. There are no strict rules. The one thing we do suggest is not to overpower the pizza with too much topping. After all, the crust is important. Use a small amount of tomato or tomato sauce—no more than 1½ cups for a large sixteen-inch pizza; the sauce should just lightly carpet the dough—and use no more than 1 to 1½ pounds of

cheese. Resist adding large amounts of topping ingredients, or the pizza will turn into a casserole. It is like shopping in a market when you are hungry: you buy too much, and you regret it later.

The cooking time for pizza is about 20 to 25 minutes, depending on the size of the pizza and the amount of ingredients, so keep your eye on it.

Here are five more pizza topping suggestions.

Quattro Formaggio (Four Cheeses) Top ¼ of the shaped dough to within an inch of its edge with about ⅓ pound each of thinly sliced mozzarella, Swiss, provolone, and crumbled gorgonzola cheese. Drizzle the cheeses lightly with olive oil. Bake until cheeses have melted and the crust is golden. Season with freshly ground pepper.

Pizza con Pomodori, Caciocavallo, e Cipolla Rossa (Tomato Sauce, Caciocavallo, and Red Onion) Spread 1 to 1½ cups of tomato sauce over the shaped dough to within an inch of the edge. Sprinkle with ¾ pound of diced caciocavallo (or provolone) cheese and 3 medium-sized red onions cut in half crosswise and then into thin slivers. Drizzle the top lightly with olive oil. Bake until the crust is golden.

Melanzane e Basilico (Eggplant and Basil) Top the shaped dough to within an inch of the edge with 2 peeled, seeded, and cubed medium tomatoes, ¾ pound diced mozzarella, 2 thinly sliced and grilled small eggplants, or 3 cups fried cubed eggplant. (To fry cubed eggplant, heat 1½ cups olive oil in a large frying pan. Fry until golden, stirring often. Drain.) Drizzle lightly with olive oil. Bake until the crust is golden. After it comes out of the oven, sprinkle with salt and pepper and a handful of small fresh basil leaves.

Zucchine e Timo (Zucchini and Thyme) Heat ¼ cup olive oil in a saucepan. Dice 4 small zucchini and put them in the saucepan with 2 minced garlic cloves. Season to taste with salt and pepper and stir. Cook over high heat for 3 minutes, then transfer the mixture into a shallow bowl to cool.

Stir 1 tablespoon of chopped fresh thyme into the mixture.

Spread the mixture on top of the shaped pizza dough. Top with ½ pound of shredded provolone or Swiss cheese. Bake until the crust is golden brown.

Patate, Salsiccia, e Rosmarino (Potatoes, Sausage, and Rosemary) Boil 4 small new potatoes until tender. Cool the potatoes completely. Peel and cut the potatoes into thin slices. Meanwhile, cook ¾ pound of crumbled sweet or hot sausage in a frying pan until no longer pink. Drain and let cool.

Spread 1 cup of tomato sauce over the shaped dough to within an inch of the edge. Top with a single layer of the potatoes. Sprinkle the sausage and 2 teaspoons of fresh rosemary over the top. Drizzle the pizza lightly with olive oil. Bake until the crust is golden brown. Season lightly with salt and pepper.

Le Focacce e la Rivoluzione
(Focaccia and the Revolution)

When I was eighteen years old, a student movement exploded in Palermo, like in many other European cities. To us, it was known as "Il '68." As news arrived from Paris and Munich, young people in Sicily's universities began protesting against the system too. Even I, normally content to be quiet, was in the crowd screaming for freedom of speech. *Libertà! Libertà!* When I think of that time now, I remember crazy, exciting days, unlike any since.

Many of my friends let their hair grow long and spent most of their time at the university, reading and writing about philosophy and politics, certain they could change a troubled world. In long dresses and clogs, we girls marched through the streets of Palermo with candles in our hands and excruciating pain in our feet.

One of our favorite late-afternoon retreats was Antica Focacceria San Francesco on the Piazza San Francesco in old Palermo. The Piazza San Francesco was and still is beautiful, although cradled by dilapidated, crumbling old *palazzi,* silent witnesses of past splendor. Many old shops open onto the piazza's pavement of large, shiny gray stones. In 1968, it was still the leather workers' district. An intoxicating mix of baking *focacce* and tanning leather permeated the air. The focacceria was a small, dark place with marble tables and uncomfortable iron chairs. It was famous for *guastelle* (focaccia stuffed with spleen and ricotta), hot and oily, a mighty attack on the body. The owner, sad and gray but alert, always watched us suspiciously.

We found daily rest around a table piled with *panini* (little sandwiches) and other savory foods like *sfincione con broccoletti fritti* (Sicilian pizza with fried broccoletti). Wine was too bourgeois (and also too expensive) for us. Big glasses of beer were the right drink. How many stories and secrets were heard by the old walls of the focacceria? Hundreds and hundreds. No—thousands.

My friends and I were drunk with the enormous, fearless power of youth. Sergio was a law student with an insane passion for India and fried potatoes. Focacceria San Francesco's fried potatoes were fantastic, it's true, but one day, Sergio angrily threat-

ened to kill Silvia, another in our group, who had curly short hair and was forever on a diet, and usually the first to arrive and order our food. She almost forced Sergio's death penalty because she refused to recognize that real activists needed not only a philosophy but hearty sustenance for strength.

My boyfriend, Robert, blond and charming, smoking nonstop as if cigarettes were necessary fuel for his engine, always wanted more ricotta than spleen on his *panini.* "Il '68" was a good excuse to delay responding "No" to his proposal of marriage.

Silvana, the angriest and most passionate of all of us, allowed herself no rest; she even wrote protest pamphlets at the table, and would moan, "But I can't drink beer. *Un martini per favore!*" Her pockets always held more lire than ours.

When our revolution ended, something else more dark and bloody in Italy took the place of the youths of '68. Life led each of us on individual paths. One person really went to India and never came back. Someone else married and moved to a northern town. Another got very fat. Another became exactly like those she claimed to be so enraged at. I went to England to study and to learn English and get on with my life. I don't complain about those days; we tried to give birth to a new vision of the world, to a better future for us and our children. The world listened, a little, at least for a while.

Sometimes I go back to the Antica Focacceria San Francesco for *guastelle,* but the restaurant has changed. There are new elegant tables with comfortable chairs. The new owner is friendly and cheerful but has no good stories in his eyes. And the smell is not the same. Aromas include hamburgers and wurst with ketchup and mustard. The leather shops have been replaced by stores selling plastic objects that hang outside. Young people still come to this popular restaurant, but they seem to be more concerned with personal style, cell phones, and cars than philosophy or changing the world.

Paste Base per Focacce (Basic Focaccia Dough)

The dough for *focacce* is prepared exactly as given in the instructions for the basic pizza dough, but the recipe includes a bit more yeast, salt, and melted lard or olive oil.

ENOUGH DOUGH FOR A LARGE *FOCACCE,* STUFFED
OR UNSTUFFED, TO SERVE 6 TO 8 PEOPLE

1 envelope plus 1 teaspoon active
   dry yeast
1 teaspoon sugar
1 cup warm water
3¼ cups all-purpose flour
1½ teaspoons salt
⅓ cup melted lard or olive oil,
   plus extra for coating the
   dough

Put the yeast, sugar, and water into a small bowl. Stir and let rest for 10 minutes.

Mix the flour and salt in a large bowl and make a well in the center. Add the melted lard or olive oil to the yeast mixture and pour into the well. Work into a dough with a wooden spoon.

On a lightly floured board, knead the dough, folding it over and over until it is smooth and silky. Add a little flour as needed until the dough is no longer sticky. Shape the dough into a ball and, with olive oil on your hands, lightly coat the dough. Put the dough into a bowl and cover it with a dish towel. Let the dough double in size in a warm place. This takes about 1 hour.

When the dough has risen, follow instructions in individual recipes for using the dough.

Focacce con Broccoletti (Broccoli Focaccia)

Here is a tasty stuffed *focacce* that is also healthy and filling.

SERVES 8

1 recipe for Paste Base per Focacce
   (above)
2 pounds fresh broccoli spears,
   stem parts peeled
½ cup olive oil, plus extra for
   topping
¾ pound sweet Italian sausage,

Prepare the recipe for Paste Base per Focacce and let it double in size in a large bowl. Meanwhile, boil the broccoli spears in lightly salted water for about 5 minutes or until just tender but still al dente. Drain the broccoli and let it cool. When the broccoli is about room temperature, chop it into small, coarse pieces and put it into a big bowl.

Sprinkle the olive oil over the broccoli and toss. Add the

sausage, cheese, cayenne, and salt and pepper to taste (don't add much salt, because the cheese and sausage are already quite salty). Gently combine these ingredients and set aside.

When the dough has risen, preheat the oven to 375 degrees. Grease a 14-inch (or larger) round pizza pan with olive oil.

Punch the dough down and divide it into 2 equal portions.

Shape or roll half of the dough into a circle about 14 inches in diameter and fit it into the oiled pan. Toss the broccoli mixture and spoon it evenly over the dough.

Shape or roll the other half of the dough into another 14-inch circle and place it evenly over the lower half. Pinch the edges of the dough together, sealing the edges well. Cut a few slits into the top of the dough with a small sharp knife.

Bake the *focacce* for 30 minutes or until golden brown. Immediately brush the top of the cooked *focacce* with olive oil after you remove it from the oven. Let it rest for 10 minutes, then cut into wedges and serve.

crumbled, sautéed, and well drained

2 cups grated caciocavallo or pecorino cheese

Pinch cayenne pepper

Salt and freshly ground pepper

Focacce di Spinaci di Kery (Kery's Spinach Focaccia)

SERVES 4

Prepare the dough and put it into a bowl to double in size.

While the dough is rising, prepare the filling. Boil the spinach in a small amount of lightly salted water for 4 or 5 minutes, until it has wilted. Drain the spinach well and coarsely chop it.

Heat olive oil in a saucepan and add the spinach and garlic. Let this mixture simmer for 10 minutes, stirring occasionally. Remove the pan from the heat and stir in the remaining ingredients. Put the mixture into a bowl and set it aside to rest at room temperature.

When the dough has risen, preheat the oven to 425 degrees. Punch the dough down and divide in half. Roll each half into a rough 9-inch circle.

Lightly oil a baking sheet. Put 1 circle of dough onto the baking

½ recipe for Paste Base per Focacce (page 86)

3 pounds fresh baby spinach, stem ends removed

½ cup olive oil, plus extra for topping

4 cloves garlic, minced

¾ cup chopped black olives

⅓ cup currants

Pinch cayenne pepper

sheet. Evenly spoon the spinach mixture over the dough to within about an inch of the edge.

Cut a small hole in the center of the other circle of dough. Carefully place the circle over the filled half of dough. Seal the edges securely by pinching them together or rolling them toward the center a little. Brush the top of the *focacce* lightly with oil and bake for 15 minutes or until golden brown. Cut into wedges and serve.

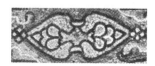

Focacce con Cipolle e Pomodori

(Focaccia with Onions and Tomatoes)

This is another stuffed *focacce,* but the shape is a little different. This time you roll it out into a large oblong shape and fill one side. The other half is brought over the filled side, like a blanket.

SERVES 6

1 recipe for Paste Base per Focacce
 (page 86)
2 large onions, thinly sliced and
 separated into rings
½ cup water
½ cup olive oil, plus extra for
 topping
Salt and freshly ground pepper
4 large tomatoes, peeled, seeded,
 and chopped
Pinch cayenne pepper

Prepare the dough and put it into a bowl to double in size.

Meanwhile, make the filling by combining the onions with the water in a large frying pan. Stirring constantly, bring the mixture to a boil and cook until the water has just about evaporated.

Immediately add the olive oil, salt, pepper, and tomatoes to the mixture. Mix these ingredients together thoroughly and simmer about 5 minutes. Add the cayenne and stir the mixture, then set it aside to cool.

When the dough has risen, preheat the oven to 375 degrees.

Punch the dough down and shape or roll it into a very large oblong shape about 2 feet long and 12 inches wide.

Spread the filling over half the dough on the long side to within an inch of the edge. Bring the other half of the dough gently over

the other half and press the edges together. Cut a few slits in the top of the dough with a small sharp knife.

Bake the *focacce* for 30 minutes or until golden brown. Immediately brush the top of the cooked *focacce* with olive oil when you remove it from the oven. Let it rest for 10 minutes, then cut into pieces and serve.

Schiacciata Ripiena
(Stuffed Focaccia with Anchovies and Pecorino)

SERVES 6

Prepare the dough and put it into a bowl to double in size.

After the dough has risen, punch it down and shape it into 2 rectangles about 6 inches wide and 14 inches long. Combine the cheese and anchovies and sprinkle half the mixture over half of the dough from the center to from 1 inch from the edge of the dough along one side lengthwise. Fold the other side of the dough over the filling and press the 3 sides gently but securely together at the edges. Repeat with the other rectangle of dough and remaining filling.

Lightly oil a large baking sheet and transfer the *schiacciati* to it. Let them rise for 30 minutes.

Preheat the oven to 400 degrees.

Cut several little slits in the top of each *schiacciati*. Brush the tops lightly with olive oil and bake on the middle shelf in the oven for 45 minutes or until golden brown. Cut into crosswise slices and serve hot.

1 recipe for Paste Base per Focacce (page 86)
3 cups grated pecorino or provolone cheese
10 anchovies, chopped
Olive oil

Schiacciata di Rucola e Pomodori Secchi
(Focaccia Stuffed with Arugula and Sun-Dried Tomatoes)

1 recipe for Paste Base per Focacce (page 86)
1 large bunch fresh arugula, finely chopped
⅓ cup olive oil, plus extra for topping
Pinch cayenne pepper
10 sun-dried tomatoes packed in oil, coarsely chopped

SERVES 4

Prepare the dough and put it into a bowl to double in size.

While the dough is rising, prepare the filling. Combine the arugula, olive oil, cayenne, and sun-dried tomatoes in a large bowl and toss well. Let this mixture rest at room temperature.

When the dough has risen, preheat the oven to 400 degrees. Punch the dough down and divide it in half. Roll each half into a rough 9-inch circle.

Lightly grease a round pizza pan and put 1 circle of dough onto it. Evenly spoon the sun-dried tomato and arugula mixture over the dough to within about an inch of the edge.

Cut a little hole in the center of the other circle of dough. Fit the circle over the filled dough. Seal the edges together well. Brush the top of the *schiacciata* lightly with olive oil. Bake on the middle shelf of the oven for 30 minutes or until golden brown.

Schiacciatine (Crisp Focaccia Topped with Olive Oil and Oregano)

This crisp, cracker-like focaccia is characteristic of the area we live in in the Madonie Mountains. We always begin a meal with it at our favorite pizza restaurant, to soothe our appetites as we wait for our pizzas to arrive. This recipe is easily doubled.

½ recipe for Paste Base per Focacce (page 86)
Olive oil
Oregano
Salt and freshly ground pepper

SERVES 4 TO 6

Prepare the dough and put it into a bowl to double in size. When it has doubled, preheat the oven to 400 degrees.

Punch down the dough and roll into a large circle until it is quite thin, about ⅛th of an inch. Lightly oil a round pizza pan and put the *schiacciatine* on it.

With a fork, prick the surface all over. Brush the dough with a generous amount of olive oil and sprinkle with oregano, salt, and pepper. Bake on the lower shelf of the oven for 12 minutes or until golden brown. Cut into triangles and serve immediately.

Pasta

(Pasta)

Salsa di Pomodoro *(Fresh Tomato Sauce)*

Salsa di Concentrato di Pomodoro
(Concentrated Tomato Sauce)

Pasta Fatta in Casa *(Homemade Pasta)*

Spaghetti con Cipolla e Finocchietto di Kery
(Kery's Spaghetti with Onions and Fennel)

Bucatini con Fagiolini, Pomodori Secchi, e
Patate *(Bucatini with Green Beans,
Sun-Dried Tomatoes, and Potatoes)*

Fettuccine Carbonara di Verdure
(Fettuccine Carbonara with Vegetables)

I Cassetti della Pasta *(The Pasta Drawers)*

Pappardelle alle Erbe e Ricotta
(Pappardelle with Herbs and Ricotta)

Lasagne Vegetariane *(Vegetable Lasagne)*

Spaghetti di Mezzanotte
(Midnight Spaghetti)

Spaghetti Aglio, Olio, e Peperoncino
(Spaghetti with Garlic, Oil, and Hot Pepper)

Gli Spaghetti al Limone di Giovanna
(Giovanna's Lemon Spaghetti)

Ruote al Radicchio e Gorgonzola
(Ruote with Radicchio and Gorgonzola)

Penne con Asparagi e Prosciutto
(Penne with Asparagus and Ham)

Melanzane Ripiene di Anelletti
(Eggplant Stuffed with Anelletti)

Spaghetti con Melanzane
(Spaghetti with Eggplant)

Fettucine ai Peperoni Gialli
(Fettucine with Yellow Peppers)

Il Timballo Maritato *(The Wedding Timbale)*

Gemelli alla Zingara *(Gypsy's Gemelli)*

Ravioli con Ricotta in Ragù di Verdure
(Ravioli with Ricotta and Vegetable Filling)

Pennette con Fichi e Pancetta di Paolo
(Paolo's Pennette with Fresh Figs and Pancetta)

Digestione Compromessa in una Serata
Estiva—una Discussione sulla Bottarga
*(Compromising Digestion on a Summer's
Night—a Discussion of* Bottarga*)*

Spaghetti con Bottarga *(Spaghetti with* Bottarga*)*

La Pasta con le Sarde di Nonna Giulia
(Granny Giulia's Pasta with Sardines)

Tagliatelle con Pomodorini, Cozze, e Capperi
*(Tagliatelle with Cherry Tomatoes, Mussels, and
Capers)*

Pappardelle ai Gamberi e Limone di Paolo
(Paolo's Pappardelle with Shrimp and Lemon)

Penne con Gamberi e Sambuca di Capo San
Vito *(Capo San Vito's Penne with Shrimp and
Sambuca)*

I Veri Rigatoni all'Amatriciana
(The True Rigatoni in the Style of Amatrice)

La Pasta del Priore *(The Prior's Pasta)*

Fusilli del Pastore *(Shepherd's Fusilli)*

Pennette con Pancetta e Vodka
(Pennette with Pancetta and Vodka)

Spaghetti con Sapone *(Spaghetti with Soap)*

L'Eredità della Pasta

(A Legacy of Pasta)

Io posso controllare la pasta, ma non i miei figli.

(I can control the pasta, but not my children.)

—Wanda Tornabene

For Sicilians, the discussion of pasta, the pride of our country and our table, is an endless dialogue. Directions for cooking pasta appear in every recipe, but creating and cooking recipes for good taste and for variety—as well as replicating those precious ones handed down to us, designing a well-balanced menu around the pasta, and eating, commenting on, and even arguing about, the result—brings tremendous enjoyment to our daily lives. As a family of cooks running two restaurants, meals are our work, but they are also the work of the providers of food for every family in every home.

In Sicilian cuisine, pasta is the most important dish of each and every meal. For Sunday's special lunch in the abbey, our main restaurant, we always serve two pastas: one with a sauce of green vegetables, the other with a tomato sauce, with or without meat. So here at Gangivecchio, every morning we hold a little summit to select the ingredients and condiments for the day's pasta. There may be only four seasons, but hunger is born at dawn 365 days a year.

Let's say it's summer, and we must use up all the zucchini, tomatoes, basil, and arugula; they are all ripe, crying to be picked from our garden. But what other foods, herbs, and spices shall we include? We must work with these same ingredients over and over yet prepare a different pasta dish and menu for guests in the *albergo* each day. Menus require variation for our guests, and for us, too. So the daily summit begins.

Paolo might suggest the addition of sweet sausage and red onion; Giovanna prefers a combination of yellow, green, and red peppers cut into strips and cooked in olive oil with anchovies and capers. And even Peppe listening to what we say, as always, tells us he would add potatoes to the sauce. After everyone has expressed his or her own opinion, I make the final decision; the Sicilian mamma is endowed

with this special privilege. And my reward is satisfying the appetites of our friends and restaurant guests, and, most importantly to me, satisfying my family. To appease everyone, I might elect to stuff the zucchini with tomatoes and seasoned bread crumbs and serve it as a vegetable, and make a basil and arugula pesto sauce with crumbled sausage, red peppers, and sautéed potatoes. If I'm not in a compromising mood, I'll consider the variables—the quality of the ingredients, yesterday's menu, the fact that one of our guests is a vegetarian—and then I might use sliced zucchini fried in olive oil in a tomato sauce tossed with grated ricotta salata. We'll make a big refreshing salad of arugula with orange slices, toasted pine nuts, and red onions. Enormous bushes of basil can be transformed into a pesto sauce, preserving the herb for another day. The balance of the meal—the soup, meat or seafood, vegetables, and dessert—are then chosen to complement the pasta.

In the Sicilian home, I believe there is a potent connection between *la mamma* and *la pasta*. For a child, there is no emotional substitute in this world stronger than the profound security of eternal love and unequivocal acceptance. That feeling of safety coupled with the nourishment of a soothing bowl of pasta, perhaps replacing mother's milk, produces an unbreakable, powerful bond between a mother and her child.

Many years ago, I returned home to Palermo from Rome, where I had stayed for two long years during the war. After a weary seven-day journey, I remember with tenderness my mother's happy expression, her kisses and warm embrace, and I recall sitting down at the table where an immense bowl of steaming spaghetti with *salsa di pomodoro con melanzane* was placed in front of me. The joy of Mamma's embrace accompanied by the delicious pasta was a beautiful expression of love. We Sicilian mammas nourish those to whom we have given birth—and we nourish them as long as we live.

In this new cookbook we offer more than two dozen of our favorite pasta dishes from Giovanna, Paolo, and myself plus recently discovered recipes from my mother-in-law, Giulia, and some outstanding ones from friends and acquaintances who are very talented cooks.

My only advice for making good pasta is to pay close attention while cooking it. We call this "controlling the pasta." Overcooked pasta is useless. As for the sauce, use only the best and freshest ingredients available that harmonize with each other and with the season. Never oversauce pasta.

Finally, I urge you to cook pasta for your children, from the moment they can hold a fork. And cook it as often as possible.

Salsa di Pomodoro (Fresh Tomato Sauce)

Our basic fresh tomato sauce is used in hundreds of recipes. We like to prepare huge amounts of it in late summer, when tomatoes are delicious and plentiful. With many bottles stored in the pantry, we know that on the worst day of a winter's blizzard, we can appreciate—and be cheered by—the tastes and smells of summer.

MAKES ABOUT 4 CUPS

Combine the tomatoes, onion, and basil together in a large pot. Season to taste with salt. Cook over medium heat for about 15 minutes, stirring often.

A few cups at a time, pass the mixture through a food mill. Return the sauce to a clean pot with the olive oil, basil leaves, sugar, and salt and pepper to taste. Simmer for 30 minutes, stirring occasionally.

Variations A clove of garlic and 2 tablespoons of freshly chopped Italian parsley can be added to the tomatoes, onion, and chopped basil.

5 pounds ripe tomatoes, stem ends removed, coarsely chopped
1 large onion, chopped
½ cup freshly chopped basil leaves, plus 6 whole fresh basil leaves
Salt
½ cup olive oil
1 teaspoon sugar
Freshly ground pepper

Salsa di Concentrato di Pomodoro
(Concentrated Tomato Sauce)

Concentrated tomato sauce, as the name suggests, is a thick, rich tomato reduction. In Sicily, we use *estratto* (extract of tomatoes) made by a tedious process of drying tomatoes and stirring them on a wooden board in the sun for several days. Very few people make *estratto* from scratch nowadays, because we can buy delicious commercially produced *estratto* in Sicily. A few specialty food shops in America, especially Italian food stores, carry it. You will find our own recipe for *estratto* in our first book, *La Cucina Siciliana di Gangivecchio*. Meanwhile, this concentrated tomato sauce is an excellent substitute.

Salsa di Concentrato di Pomodoro *(continued)*

MAKES ABOUT 3 CUPS

1 cup olive oil
1 medium onion, finely chopped
3 cups tomato paste
1 teaspoon sugar
Salt and freshly ground pepper

Heat the olive oil in a heavy-bottomed saucepan. Add the onion and cook for 5 minutes over medium heat, stirring often. Stir in the remaining ingredients, seasoning to taste with salt and pepper. Simmer over low heat for 1 hour, stirring frequently.

Pasta Fatta in Casa (Homemade Pasta)

MAKES ABOUT 1 POUND OF PASTA TO SERVE 6
AS A FIRST COURSE OR 4 AS A MAIN COURSE

4 cups all-purpose flour
4 large eggs
1 tablespoon olive oil
½ teaspoon salt

To make the pasta dough, mound the flour in a little hill on a work surface or in a large, shallow bowl. Make a well in the center about 4 inches in diameter. Put the eggs, oil, and salt into the well and mix them together with a fork in a circular motion. Slowly work the flour in from the side walls. Continue mixing until all the flour is incorporated into the dough. On a lightly floured work surface, shape the dough into a ball and knead it until smooth and silky. This should take about 10 minutes. If the dough is sticky, work in a small amount of flour. Divide the dough in half. Cover the pieces with plastic wrap or a damp cloth and let rest for 1 hour.

Then the dough is ready to use. Instructions are in individual recipes, but generally speaking, you pass each flattened piece of dough through the widest opening in a manual pasta machine twice. Dust lightly with flour, if necessary. Adjust the machine to a narrower opening and pass through 2 more times. Reduce to the next narrower setting, and pass through twice again. Reduce to the next narrower setting, and pass through again, if desired.

Pasta should be lightly floured and then cut into the desired shapes. It can then be covered with towels and kept in the refrigerator for up to 2 hours, or it can be frozen in plastic.

Cook fresh pasta in 4 quarts of boiling water with 1½ tablespoons of salt. Depending on the size, shape, and thickness of the pasta, it will take from 3 to 6 minutes to cook.

Drain the pasta, saving 1 cup of hot pasta water. Transfer the pasta to a bowl and top with approximately 2 cups of desired sauce, adding hot pasta water if too dry. Toss and serve immediately.

Note For a richer "egg" pasta, add 1 or 2 extra egg yolks.

Spaghetti con Cipolla e Finocchietto di Kery

(Kery's Spaghetti with Onions and Fennel)

SERVES 6 AS A FIRST COURSE OR 4 AS A MAIN COURSE

Cook the fennel in lightly salted water for 5 minutes. Drain and chop finely.

In a large frying pan, heat the oil and butter. Add water and onions and cook over medium heat for 10 minutes, stirring often.

Add the anchovies and wine. Cook for 10 minutes, stirring occasionally.

Stir in the fennel and cream. Combine well and season to taste with salt. Set aside.

Bring 4 quarts of water to a boil in a large pot. Add 1½ tablespoons of salt. Stir in the pasta and cook until al dente. Drain the pasta, saving a cup of the pasta water.

Transfer the pasta to a bowl. Spoon the sauce over it and toss well. Add a little pasta water if the mixture is too dry. Serve immediately.

1 cup feathery green fennel tops
¼ cup olive oil
1 tablespoon unsalted butter
2 tablespoons water
2 large yellow onions, chopped
4 anchovies, chopped
½ cup dry white wine
3 tablespoons heavy cream
Salt
1 pound spaghetti

Bucatini con Fagiolini, Pomodori Secchi, e Patate

(Bucatini with Green Beans, Sun-Dried Tomatoes, and Potatoes)

½ pound fresh green beans, ends trimmed, cut into 1-inch pieces
½ cup olive oil
2 large garlic cloves, minced
2 tablespoons water
½ cup pitted black olives
8 sun-dried tomatoes packed in oil, coarsely chopped
¼ cup pine nuts
¼ teaspoon dried oregano
1 pound bucatini or perciatelli
1 cup peeled potatoes, cut into ½-inch cubes
Pinch of powdered saffron
Salt and freshly ground pepper

SERVES 6 AS A FIRST COURSE OR 4 AS A MAIN COURSE

Boil the green beans in 3 cups of lightly salted water for 5 minutes. Drain.

In a large frying pan, heat the oil with the garlic and cook over medium heat until the garlic just begins to turn golden. Add the green beans and water. Simmer for 10 minutes.

In the meantime, chop the olives, sun-dried tomatoes, pine nuts, and oregano together. Add the mixture to the pan. Cook over medium heat for 5 minutes. Remove from the heat and set aside.

Bring 4 quarts of water to a boil. Add 1½ tablespoons of salt. Stir in the pasta, potatoes, and saffron and cook until the pasta is well done—not al dente. Add ½ cup of the hot pasta water to the pan with the green beans. Cook over high heat for 5 minutes. Season to taste with salt and pepper.

Drain the pasta and potatoes thoroughly. Transfer them to a bowl, spoon the sauce over them, and toss well. Serve hot.

Fettuccine Carbonara di Verdure

(Fettuccine Carbonara with Vegetables)

2 stalks broccoli, ends trimmed, stems peeled, cut into small pieces and florets
½ cup olive oil

SERVES 6 AS A FIRST COURSE OR 4 AS A MAIN COURSE

Cook the broccoli in 3 cups of lightly salted boiling water until just tender, about 8 minutes. Drain.

In a frying pan, heat the oil until hot but not smoking. Add the zucchini, leek, carrots, and yellow pepper. Cook over low heat for

12 minutes or until just tender, stirring occasionally. Stir in the basil and cooked broccoli and season to taste with salt. Remove from heat.

Bring 4 quarts of water to a boil. Add 1½ tablespoons of salt. Stir in the fettuccine and cook until al dente, stirring often.

Meanwhile, in a large bowl, beat the eggs with the cream and pecorino.

Drain the pasta, reserving 1 cup of hot pasta water. Transfer the pasta to the bowl with the egg mixture and toss. Add the vegetables and toss well. Sprinkle with pepper and toss again. If too dry, add a little hot pasta water and toss. Taste for seasoning. If desired, add more cheese or pass a bowl of it at the table.

2 small zucchini, cubed

1 leek, white part only, sliced

2 small carrots, peeled and diced

1 yellow bell pepper, cut into thin strips

8 fresh basil leaves, torn into small pieces

Salt

1 pound fettuccine

2 large eggs

¼ cup heavy cream

⅓ cup freshly grated pecorino cheese, or to taste

Freshly ground pepper

Pappardelle alle Erbe e Ricotta

(Pappardelle with Herbs and Ricotta)

SERVES 4

Bring 4 quarts of water to a boil in a large pot. Add 1 tablespoon of salt. Stir in the pasta. Cook until al dente, stirring often.

Meanwhile, combine the chives, parsley, fennel, arugula, and oil in a bowl. Put the ricotta in another bowl.

Drain the pasta well, saving 1 cup of hot pasta water. Transfer the pasta to a large bowl. Add ½ cup of the hot pasta water to the ricotta and combine well. Spoon ricotta and pecorino over the pasta and add the mixed herbs and oil. Toss. If too dry, add a little more pasta water. Season to taste with salt and pepper. Serve hot.

½ pound pappardelle

¼ cup freshly snipped chives

¼ cup finely chopped fresh Italian parsley

¼ cup finely chopped feathery green fennel tops

¼ cup finely chopped fresh arugula

½ cup olive oil

½ cup ricotta cheese

¼ cup freshly grated pecorino cheese

Freshly ground pepper

I Cassetti della Pasta (The Pasta Drawers)

At Gangivecchio, as in all old Sicilian houses, there is at least one *cassettone* (chest of drawers) in every room. As a child, I remember the large walnut *cassettone* in my grandfather's apartment. We were forbidden to look inside. After Grandfather's death, we discovered the chest contained ancient documents about our family and Gangivecchio, which we read with fascination. Today I keep these documents locked safely in my own room in an armoire.

Grandfather's *cassettone* stood useless in an empty room for about forty years, until Mamma decided to give it a new life as custodian of a more prosaic treasure.

I love to restore old furniture, and I immediately began sanding, staining, varnishing, and waxing the *cassettone*. The refurbished chest was then moved to a dining room off the kitchen. Today the chest's drawers are filled with pasta—kilos and kilos of spaghetti, linguine, tagliatelle, rigatoni, farfalle, gemelli, pasta of every conceivable shape and size. Dried pasta now dwells in the place of family history. It must have been quite a shock *cadendo dalle stelle alla stalle* (falling from the stars to the stables), as we used to say.

The new storage space was created because my mother needed to have control over the exact amount of pasta we have in the house. Mamma has an excellent memory for inventory of any kind, and had noticed for some time that the spaghetti and its brothers and sisters had been mysteriously disappearing from our regular pantry shelves. Mamma, the house detective, also observed that as the days and weeks passed, and the pasta continued to disappear, our kitchen workers steadily gained weight. In silent retribution, the pasta was transferred from the *dispensa* (pantry) to the drawers of the *cassettone*. No one is permitted to open these drawers but Mamma and me.

Lasagne Vegetariane (Vegetable Lasagne)

SERVES 6 AS A FIRST COURSE OR 4 AS A MAIN COURSE

⅔ cup olive oil
1 large onion, chopped
4 cups peeled and diced fresh or
  canned tomatoes

In a frying pan, heat the oil and cook the onion for 10 minutes over medium-low heat, stirring often. Add the tomatoes, parsley, basil, and salt and pepper to taste. Combine well and simmer for about 30 minutes, stirring often.

Pass the tomato mixture through a food mill.

Preheat the oven to 400 degrees.

Bring 4 quarts of water to a boil. Add 1½ tablespoons of salt. Stir in the lasagne and cook until al dente. Drain.

Butter the bottom of a shallow 9-by-13-inch baking pan. Spoon a little of the tomato sauce over the bottom. Cover with a single layer of lasagne. Spoon half of the sauce over the lasagne and top evenly with half of the ricotta and half of the pecorino. Repeat with a second layer in the same manner. Sprinkle the bread crumbs over the top. Bake for about 20 minutes.

3 tablespoons freshly chopped Italian parsley
12 basil leaves, finely chopped
Salt and freshly ground pepper
1 pound lasagne
1¾ cups ricotta cheese
¾ cup freshly grated pecorino cheese
½ cup dried bread crumbs

Melanzane Ripiene di Anelletti

(Eggplant Stuffed with Anelletti)

SERVES 6

Cut the eggplants in half. Heat the oil in a large frying pan and fry the eggplants over medium-low heat for about 15 minutes on each side.

Scoop out the pulp of the eggplant from each half, taking care not to break the shells. Let cool and reserve the shells.

Bring 4 quarts of water to a boil. Add 1 tablespoon of salt. Stir in the pasta and cook until al dente. Drain.

Preheat the oven to 400 degrees. Heat broiler.

Meanwhile, finely chop the eggplant pulp and put into a bowl. Add the tomato sauce, basil, and pecorino. Season to taste with salt and pepper and combine thoroughly. Stir the pasta into the mixture. Taste for seasoning.

Spoon equal amounts of the mixture into each eggplant shell. Sprinkle the top liberally with Parmesan cheese. Place in a large shallow baking pan and bake for 20 minutes, then place under a hot broiler until golden brown on top. Garnish each serving with the whole basil leaves. Serve hot or at room temperature.

3 medium-sized eggplants
1 cup olive oil
½ pound anelletti (small ring-shaped pasta)
1½ cups fresh tomato sauce (Salsa di Pomodoro, page 95)
12 basil leaves, freshly chopped, plus extra leaves for garnish
¾ cup diced pecorino cheese
Salt and freshly ground pepper
Freshly grated Parmesan cheese

Spaghetti di Mezzanotte (Midnight Spaghetti)

The first time I felt like I was an adult was when I was given permission to participate in a *Spaghetti di Mezzanotte* (Midnight Spaghetti), after a date at the cinema in Palermo. Many Sicilians enjoy Midnight Spaghetti after a party, the theater, or for whatever reason one has for returning home late. Night people of all ages stay up together, listen to music, talk, and have a little light pasta and white wine. No other food is required. The group usually consists of four to six close friends, and everyone does something to help: open the wine, boil the pasta, chop the garlic, grate the cheese, set the table, wash the dishes, and so on.

My first Midnight Spaghetti party was a highly emotional occasion. At the time, I was madly in love with a young man who claimed to be a wonderful cook. The party was at his parents' apartment; the other guests were his friends. I wanted to impress everyone, of course. I was in charge of setting the table. I remember suffering in new high heels, walking around and around the table to get everything right. I felt like a heroine in a movie. As I circled the table, I imagined what a brilliant married couple we would be. He would cook dinner every night, and I would set the table with beautiful flowers and candles and serve our four children, two boys and two girls—such a typical fantasy for a seventeen-year-old Sicilian girl. In reality, my prince was an awful cook. He burned the garlic and overcooked the spaghetti. And he never asked me out again, breaking my heart—temporarily.

Much later I learned he had grown very fat and married a woman with a mustache.

The most common Midnight Spaghetti is with garlic, olive oil, and hot peppers.

Spaghetti Aglio, Olio, e Peperoncino
(Spaghetti with Garlic, Oil, and Hot Pepper)

For Four: Boil half a pound of spaghetti.

While the pasta is cooking, heat ½ cup of olive oil slowly with 2 or 3 minced garlic cloves. After 5 minutes, season the mixture with salt, freshly ground pepper, and a pinch of hot pepper flakes.

Drain the spaghetti, saving 1 cup of pasta water. Transfer the pasta to a bowl and toss with the garlic sauce. If it's dry, add a little hot pasta water. Pass freshly grated Parmesan or pecorino cheese.

Variations Add 4 chopped anchovies to the oil with the garlic. Just before serving, sprinkle with 1 tablespoon of freshly chopped Italian parsley.

Here are three other typical recipes for Midnight Spaghetti.

Gli Spaghetti al Limone di Giovanna (Giovanna's Lemon Spaghetti)

SERVES 4

2 tablespoons olive oil
¼ pound sliced boiled ham, cut into thin strips
1 tablespoon cognac
¾ cup heavy cream
Grated zest of 1 lemon
1 tablespoon freshly squeezed lemon juice
2 tablespoons freshly chopped basil
Salt and freshly ground pepper
½ pound spaghetti
¼ cup freshly grated Parmesan cheese, plus extra for topping

In a large frying pan, heat the oil until hot but not smoking. Add the ham and cognac. Cook over medium heat for 2 minutes. Remove from heat and set aside.

In a small saucepan, heat the heavy cream with the lemon zest, lemon juice, and basil. Season to taste with salt and pepper and bring to a boil. Reduce the heat and simmer for 5 minutes. Stir the sauce into the ham and cognac mixture.

Meanwhile, bring 4 quarts of water to a boil. Add 1 tablespoon of salt. Stir in the spaghetti and cook until al dente, stirring often.

Drain the spaghetti, reserving 1 cup of hot pasta water. Add the pasta and Parmesan to the sauce in the pan and toss well, adding a little hot pasta water if it's too dry. Taste for seasoning. Serve hot and pass the Parmesan cheese.

Ruote al Radicchio e Gorgonzola (Ruote with Radicchio and Gorgonzola)

SERVES 6

2 cups freshly chopped radicchio
6 tablespoons unsalted butter
2 tablespoons olive oil
5 ounces gorgonzola cheese, crumbled
1 pound ruote
⅓ cup freshly grated Parmesan cheese
Salt and freshly ground pepper

Bring 1 quart of water to a boil in a small saucepan. Add 1 teaspoon of salt. Stir in the radicchio and boil for 4 minutes, stirring often. Lightly drain.

Heat the butter and oil in a large frying pan with the gorgonzola, stirring continuously until the cheese has melted. Stir in the radicchio. Simmer over very low heat for 10 minutes.

Meanwhile, bring 4 quarts of water to a boil in a pot. Add 1½ tablespoons of salt. Stir in the pasta and cook until al dente, stirring often.

Drain the pasta, reserving 1 cup of hot pasta water. Add the pasta to the radicchio and gorgonzola sauce in the frying pan. Toss well. Sprinkle with the Parmesan and season to taste with salt and pepper, adding a little hot pasta water if necessary. Toss again and serve immediately.

Penne con Asparagi e Prosciutto (Penne with Asparagus and Ham)

If a Midnight Spaghetti party is organized at the last minute—as it is likely to be if it's a true Midnight Spaghetti—you might not have fresh asparagus on hand. So you must improvise with whatever vegetables you can find in your pantry, refrigerator, or freezer. (For example, two ten-ounce packages of frozen green peas can be substituted for the asparagus. Just cook the peas in three cups of lightly salted water for five minutes and drain them.

SERVES 6

1 pound asparagus, ends trimmed, stalks peeled with vegetable peeler, cut into 1-inch lengths

¼ cup olive oil

4 tablespoons unsalted butter

4 scallions, white parts and 1½ inches of green, thinly sliced

¼ pound thinly sliced boiled ham, cut into small, thin strips

3 tablespoons fresh tomato sauce (Salsa di Pomodoro, page 95)

Salt and freshly ground pepper

1 pound penne

Freshly grated Parmesan cheese

Bring 1 quart of water to a boil in a medium saucepan. Stir in 1 teaspoon of salt. Add the asparagus and cook at a low boil for 5 minutes or until just tender. Drain and set aside.

Heat the olive oil and butter in a large frying pan. Stir in the scallions and cook over medium heat for 3 minutes. Stir in the ham and tomato sauce and season to taste with salt and pepper. Simmer for 5 minutes, stirring occasionally. Turn off the heat and add the asparagus to the sauce.

Meanwhile, bring 4 quarts of water to boil in a pot. Add 1½ tablespoons of salt. Stir in the pasta and cook until al dente, stirring often. Drain the pasta, reserving 1 cup of hot pasta water. Add the pasta to the sauce in the frying pan and toss, adding a little hot pasta water if necessary. Taste for seasoning. Serve immediately and pass the Parmesan cheese.

Spaghetti con Melanzane (Spaghetti with Eggplant)

My son's favorite pasta dish is also Sicily's most favored pasta dish—spaghetti with eggplant. We have a version in our first book, also known as Spaghetti alla Norma, that is traditionally sprinkled with ricotta salata cheese. I could not leave out a spaghetti with eggplant from this book, for fear of the wrath of my son, so here is another fragrant variation.

SERVES 6 AS A FIRST COURSE OR 4 AS A MAIN COURSE

Heat 3 inches of olive oil in a deep-sided frying pan until the oil is hot but not smoking. Fry the eggplant pieces, in batches, until golden brown. Drain on paper towels and let rest.

Put the tomato sauce in a saucepan. Stir in the pepper flakes and chopped basil. While slowly heating the sauce, bring 4 quarts of water to a boil in a large pot. Stir in 1½ tablespoons of salt and add the spaghetti. Cook until al dente.

Stir the eggplant into the sauce. Heat thoroughly and season to taste with salt and pepper.

Reserve 1 cup of the pasta water. Drain the spaghetti and return it to the pot. Add half the sauce and toss. Turn the rest over the pasta and toss, and drizzle with a little olive oil. Toss well. Garnish with basil sprigs.

Serve immediately and pass the grated cheese.

Olive oil for deep-frying, plus extra for topping

2 medium eggplants, cut into pieces ½ inch thick, 1 inch wide, and about 2½ inches long

2½ cups fresh tomato sauce (Salsa di Pomodoro, page 95)

Pinch hot pepper flakes

3 tablespoons freshly chopped basil, plus 2 or 3 sprigs for garnish

Salt

1 pound spaghetti

Freshly ground pepper

Freshly grated pecorino or Parmesan cheese

Fettucine ai Peperoni Gialli

(Fettucine with Yellow Peppers)

SERVES 4

2 large yellow bell peppers
3 fresh tomatoes, peeled and
    cubed
1 tablespoon capers
⅓ cup freshly chopped basil
½ teaspoon fennel seeds
½ cup diced smoked pecorino
    cheese
½ cup olive oil
Salt and freshly ground pepper
½ pound fettucine

Heat the broiler. Broil the peppers on a piece of aluminum foil on rack about 5 inches from the heat source, turning occasionally, until the skin has blackened all over.

Place the peppers in a brown paper bag. Close the bag securely and let the peppers rest for 5 minutes.

Remove the peppers. When cool enough to handle, remove the stem ends, seeds, and any white membrane. Cut the peppers into thin strips and put into a large bowl. Add the tomatoes, capers, basil, fennel, pecorino, and olive oil. Season with salt and pepper and toss. Set aside.

Bring 4 quarts of water to a boil. Add 1 tablespoon of salt. Stir in the fettucine and cook until al dente, stirring often.

Drain the pasta, reserving 1 cup of hot pasta water. Add the pasta to the sauce in the bowl and toss, adding a little hot pasta water if necessary. Taste for seasoning. Serve hot.

> The appearance of those monumental dishes of macaroni was worthy of the quivers of admiration they evoked. The burnished gold of the crusts, the fragrance of sugar and cinnamon they exuded, were but preludes to the delights released from the interior when the knife broke the crust; first came a mist laden with aromas, then chicken livers, hard-boiled eggs, sliced ham, chicken, and truffles in masses of piping-hot, glistening macaroni, to which the meat juice gave an exquisite hue of suede.
>
> —From *The Leopard,* by
> Giuseppe Tomasi di Lampedusa

Il Timballo Maritato (The Wedding Timbale)

In a large saucepan, combine the oil, onions, tomato paste, tomato sauce, bouillon cubes, and water. Combine thoroughly and bring to a boil. Season to taste with salt. Stir in the meat and return to a boil. Immediately reduce the heat and simmer for 1 to 1½ hours, until the meat is very tender, stirring every 15 minutes. If the sauce becomes too thick, add more hot water. The meat should always be just covered with the sauce.

Meanwhile, bring 4 cups of water to a boil in a saucepan. Stir in ½ teaspoon of salt and the rice. Cover and cook the rice until al dente, about 25 minutes over medium-high heat, stirring occasionally. Drain the rice.

Transfer the rice to a large shallow bowl and let cool for at least 30 minutes.

When the meat ragù is done, stir the beaten eggs into the rice. Blend well. Stir ¾ cup of the ragù, ½ cup freshly grated pecorino or Parmesan cheese, and parsley into the rice. Season to taste with salt and pepper. Combine thoroughly and set aside.

Bring 4 quarts of water to a boil in a pot. Add 1½ tablespoons of salt. Stir in the sedanini or penne and cook until al dente, stirring often. Drain the pasta, reserving 1 cup of hot pasta water.

Meanwhile, melt 6 tablespoons of butter.

Transfer the pasta to a bowl. Add 1 cup of the meat ragù, remaining ½ cup grated pecorino or Parmesan cheese, the melted butter, hot pepper flakes, and ½ cup bread crumbs. Season to taste with salt and pepper. Combine well.

Preheat the oven to 375 degrees.

Generously butter the sides and bottom of a round 12- to 14-inch baking dish with 4-inch sides. Add remaining ¾ cup of bread crumbs to the pan, and coat the bottom and sides of the pan evenly by tipping and rotating the pan.

Spoon one-third of the rice evenly over the bottom of the pan. Top with half of the pasta. Smooth evenly with the back of a spoon. Spoon half of the ragù sauce over the pasta. Top with a

½ cup olive oil

2 medium onions, chopped

¾ cup tomato paste

1½ cups fresh tomato sauce (Salsa di Pomodoro, page 95)

2 vegetable bouillon cubes

3 cups hot water

Salt

2 pounds pork shoulder, cut into 1-inch pieces

1 pound vialone nano, carnaroli, or arborio rice

3 large eggs, lightly beaten

1 cup freshly grated pecorino or Parmesan cheese

⅓ cup freshly chopped parsley

Freshly ground pepper

1 pound sedanini or penne

8 tablespoons unsalted butter

Pinch hot pepper flakes

1¼ cups fresh bread crumbs, plus extra for topping

layer of the rice and a layer of the remaining pasta, then a layer of the remaining ragù sauce. Cover the top with the last third of the rice and smooth evenly. Sprinkle the top of the rice with bread crumbs and dot with 2 tablespoons of butter. Bake for 30 minutes. Let cool for 10 minutes.

Run the thin blade of a knife around the inside edge of the pan to release any sticking particles of food. Place a round serving platter 4 to 6 inches wider than the baking pan over the timbale. Holding both sides of the platter and pan, carefully invert the pan over the platter. Gently remove the pan. If the timbale does not release easily, don't force it. First, place a hot pad on the center of the bottom of the pan and tap it with several slaps of the hand. Then, holding the pan and platter securely, shake them up and down 2 or 3 times. The pan should release easily now. Allow the timbale to rest 10 minutes on the platter before serving it. You can either cut it into wedges or serve it with a spoon.

This is a meal in 1 dish, so serve just a fresh salad or vegetable with it.

Gemelli alla Zingara (Gypsy's Gemelli)

SERVES 6 AS A FIRST COURSE OR 4 AS A MAIN COURSE

½ cup lentils
1 medium carrot, peeled and diced
1 bay leaf
2 Italian sweet sausages
½ cup olive oil
1 medium onion, finely chopped
1 yellow bell pepper, cored, seeded, and cut into thin strips
1¼ cups peeled, diced tomatoes (fresh or canned)

In a saucepan, bring 4 cups of water to a boil. Add the lentils, carrot, and bay leaf. Cook at a low boil until the lentils are tender, about 35 minutes. Drain, discard the bay leaf, and set aside.

Meanwhile, bring 3 cups of water to a boil in a small frying pan. Prick the sausages all over with the sharp point of a knife. Cook the sausages in slowly boiling water for about 15 minutes, turning them often. Drain and let cool.

In a large frying pan, heat the oil. Stir in the onion and yellow pepper. Cook over medium-low heat for about 10 minutes, stirring occasionally. Stir in the tomatoes, parsley, and hot pepper flakes. Season to taste with salt and pepper.

Cut the sausages into thin slices. Add the sausages and lentils to the frying pan. Combine well. Simmer over very low heat for 5 minutes. Set aside.

Meanwhile, bring 4 quarts of water to a boil in a pot. Add 1½ tablespoons of salt. Stir in the pasta and cook until al dente, stirring often.

Drain the pasta, reserving 1 cup of the hot pasta water. Add the pasta to the sauce in the frying pan and toss well, adding a little hot pasta water if necessary. Taste for seasoning. Serve immediately and pass the pecorino cheese.

1 tablespoon freshly chopped
   Italian parsley
Pinch hot pepper flakes
Salt and freshly ground pepper
1 pound gemelli
Freshly grated pecorino cheese

Ravioli con Ricotta in Ragù di Verdure
(Ravioli with Ricotta and Vegetable Filling)

SERVES 6

Make the filling: In a large frying pan, heat the oil and butter. Stir in the eggplant, leeks, peas, and tomatoes and cook over low heat for 10 minutes, stirring occasionally.

Meanwhile, puree the zucchini, carrot, celery, and parsley in a food processor for 35 to 40 seconds, scraping down sides of container after 20 seconds of pureeing.

Add the puree to the frying pan and combine ingredients well. Season with salt and pepper. Simmer for 10 minutes over low heat, stirring often. Transfer the mixture to a colander and let liquid drain into a bowl underneath to collect it. Let cool for 30 minutes.

Reserve the drained liquid. Stir the ricotta into the vegetable mixture.

On a floured work surface, roll each half of the Pasta Fatta in Casa dough out into a long, ⅟₁₆- to ⅛-inch-thick rectangle, about 20 inches by 5 inches. Place rounded teaspoonfuls of the vegetable and ricotta mixture 1 inch from the long edge of 1 of the sheets of dough in 2 parallel rows the length of the dough. Place the other

FILLING

½ cup olive oil
2 tablespoons butter
1 small eggplant, peeled and
   cubed
2 leeks, white parts only, finely
   chopped
1 cup cooked fresh or thawed
   frozen green peas
4 small Italian tomatoes, peeled,
   seeded, and chopped
2 small zucchini, cubed
1 carrot, peeled and cubed
1 celery stalk, cubed
⅓ cup freshly chopped Italian
   parsley, plus extra for topping
Salt and freshly ground pepper
1 cup ricotta cheese

RAVIOLI

1 recipe for Pasta Fatta in Casa
   (page 96), divided in half
All-purpose flour
Salt
4 tablespoons unsalted butter
¼ cup freshly grated caciocavallo
   or pecorino cheese, plus extra
   for topping

sheet of dough on top of the first. Make the ravioli by cutting the dough into 2-inch circles or squares around the filling with the wheel of a serrated pastry cutter or a round or square ravioli cutter. Lightly press the edges to seal. Place the ravioli on a baking sheet lightly dusted with flour.

Bring 4 quarts of water to a boil in a large pot. Stir in 1½ tablespoons of salt. One by one, gently release the ravioli into the water and gently stir. Cook the pasta until done, stirring gently and frequently. The ravioli cook in 4 to 5 minutes.

In a small saucepan, heat the reserved vegetable liquid with the 4 tablespoons of butter. Season to taste with salt and pepper.

Gently drain the ravioli and arrange on a serving platter. Spoon the sauce over the ravioli and sprinkle with the caciocavallo or pecorino cheese and parsley. Pass extra cheese.

Pennette con Fichi e Pancetta di Paolo

(Paolo's Pennette with Fresh Figs and Pancetta)

Paolo at the door of Tenuta Gangivecchio, his country inn and restaurant. He too has become a formidable presence in front of the stove.

This recipe was born on a September afternoon, while my brother was standing in the abbey courtyard, his hands on his hips, contemplating an enormous fig tree. Its branches were laden with fruit. Mamma, watching him from the second-floor kitchen window, thought he was wondering what new dish could be made with those beautiful figs. Since Paolo rarely makes desserts, Mamma said, nothing would come of his standing there. But Paolo surprised her. Recalling the pairing of figs and pancetta, that night he prepared this refreshing, unusual pasta for some American guests. The simple dish was a tremendous success with our guests—and with Mamma and me.

SERVES 6 AS A FIRST COURSE OR 4 AS A MAIN COURSE

In a large frying pan, heat the oil until hot but not smoking. Add the onion and pancetta and cook over medium heat for 10 minutes or until golden brown.

Gently stir in the figs and add the wine. Cook for 5 minutes. Season to taste with salt and pepper. Remove the pan from the heat.

Bring 4 quarts of water to a boil. Add 1½ tablespoons of salt. Stir in the pasta and cook until al dente, stirring often. Drain, reserving 1 cup of hot pasta water.

Add the pasta to the sauce and gently toss, adding hot pasta water if too dry. Simmer for 3 minutes over high heat. Taste for seasoning. Serve hot.

½ cup olive oil

1 medium onion, finely chopped

½ cup cubed pancetta

2 pounds fresh figs, peeled and diced

½ cup dry red wine

Salt and freshly ground pepper

1 pound pennette

Digestione Compromessa in Una Serata Estiva—una Discussione sulla Bottarga

(Compromising Digestion on a Summer's Night— a Discussion of *Bottarga*)

One evening after dinner last summer, we lingered outside in the garden having a pleasant conversation with some of our guests. It was a sweltering night, which is unusual at Gangivecchio since we are so high up in the mountains. We stayed outside as long as possible to avoid a hot, sleepless night.

Among the guests were two young American couples, and a husband and wife, Tanino and Sofia, who had become our friends after several stays at the *albergo*. Tanino, a former president of the high Sicilian court, is a quiet, gentle man with a sweet voice and sharp mind. His elegant, beautiful, and spirited wife, Sofia, possesses a wonderful sense of humor. After forty years of marriage, she is still wildly in love with her husband and jealous of every woman in his presence.

Our dinner that evening included a fantastic spaghetti with *bottarga*. Tanino had brought the *bottarga* from Palermo as a gift. Highly appreciated in Sicily, *bottarga* is salted, pressed, and dried tuna roe. It comes shaped in a small, reddish-brown brick. It's a brick of gold, Mamma says, because *bottarga* is expensive like caviar. However, it is packed with such powerful flavor that only a very small amount produces a strong taste of the sea. (It is comparable in strength to white truffles.) *Bottarga* is quite salty, so caution must be taken when using it.

Most Sicilians love *bottarga*. That night in our garden, the Sicilians present began

giving their views on the best ways of serving it, apart from its being grated and tossed with hot pasta, which was everyone's favorite. Ideas ranged from grating it over risotto or grilled slices of bread with a drizzle of olive oil and lemon juice, to sprinkling it over mashed potatoes, poached eggs, or mozzarella, to being shaved over tomatoes spread lightly with mayonnaise. In the middle of this conversation, we heard one of the American women ask Tanino to tell her more about *bottarga*. Tanino's tender voice began, "I tasted my first *bottarga* many, many years ago, when I was a boy. I will never forget it. My family was living in Porticello [a small seaside village near Palermo]. My father worked aboard a ship. During one of his many journeys he met my mother, Josefa Cortazar. She was an enchanting Spanish angel from a small town on the northern coast of Spain." As he spoke, describing his mother, we could easily see the happy, smiling, blond Sicilian sailor and the young Spanish beauty.

Tanino continued, "When my father offered us *bottarga* for the first time, he told us that it was a sac of eggs from a huge tuna fish, and that tuna live most of their lives deep in the sea. But during migration to spawn, they can meet their worst fate, the *tonnara:* the terrible fishing nets, for the tuna, a tunnel of death with no exit. Using an ancient method, *la mattanza,* a cadre of expert fishermen, catch the tuna in a series of giant connected nets, where they are killed with hooks and harpoons. The water turns red. The tuna's bellies are slashed open and the eggs extracted from the tuna's dead bodies. The eggs are quickly preserved in salt, pressed, and air-dried."

Sophia cried, "Tanino, we have all just enjoyed this magnificent delicacy and now you are compromising our digestion with this horrible and tragic story. And don't say that your mother was a Spanish angel—she was a dragon. My beloved Casanova, it's time to say *buona notte.* I'm sure we will all have nightmares."

Bottarga isn't easily found in America, but some specialty food stores carry it. If you visit Sicily, buy this treasure and bring it home. Serve it as suggested above, or try the following recipe for *bottarga* with spaghetti.

Spaghetti con Bottarga

SERVES 6 AS A FIRST COURSE OR 4 AS A MAIN COURSE

1 cup olive oil, or as
   needed
3 garlic cloves, minced
½ cup grated *bottarga*,
   plus extra for topping
½ cup freshly chopped
   Italian parsley
Freshly ground pepper
1 pound spaghetti

Heat the olive oil with the garlic in a large frying pan over medium-low heat for 5 minutes, stirring frequently. Don't let the garlic brown. Stir in the *bottarga* and cook over low heat for 1 minute. Add the parsley and season to taste with pepper. Do not add salt, as the *bottarga* is very salty. Set aside.

Bring 4 quarts of water to a boil. Add 1½ tablespoons of salt. Stir in the spaghetti and cook until al dente, stirring often.

Drain the pasta, reserving 1 cup of hot pasta water. Add the pasta to the sauce. Toss and cook over high heat for 1 minute, adding a little pasta water if necessary. Transfer the spaghetti to a serving dish and sprinkle with a little grated or shaved *bottarga*. Serve immediately.

La Pasta con le Sarde di Nonna Giulia

(Granny Giulia's Pasta with Sardines)

Pasta with sardines is one of Sicily's most beloved and well-known dishes. As classic as this dish is, every Sicilian woman has perfected her own version. In our first book we gave you our preferred rendition. Now we'd like to give Granny Giulia's old-fashioned travel recipe.

At the beginning of the twentieth century, travel from Gangivecchio to Palermo was a three- to four-day adventure in horse-drawn carriages. For this trip it was necessary to prepare food in advance to eat along the way. There was a particular place where our ancestors liked to make their first stop and have a picnic under the shade of trees. Some of the servants left a few hours before the family in order to chase away any animals,

clean the area, and arrange the meal—the tablecloth was laid out on the grass, weighted at each corner, and covered with napkins, dishes, cutlery, and glasses. When a scout saw the family approaching, the wine was opened and the food was placed in the center of the tablecloth. Among many other foods, like cheese, salami, bread, and fruit, this version of pasta with sardines was often included, because it, unlike most pasta dishes, liked to travel.

Of course, you don't have to go on a picnic or travel to enjoy this dish; you can eat it at home, hot from the stove. But it's also delicious at room temperature. Mamma, who detests all airline food, always thinks we should take it along on our flights to America.

SERVES 8

2 large fennel bulbs, white parts only, finely chopped

1 cup finely chopped feathery green fennel tops

1½ cups olive oil

2 medium onions, finely chopped

6 anchovy fillets

2½ pounds whole fresh sardines or thawed frozen sardines, scaled, cleaned, boned, finned, and deheaded. (After cleaning, only 1 pound of fillets remain. Ask your fishmonger to prepare them for you—order 1 pound filleted sardines.) Reserve 8 whole fillets and cut the remaining fillets into bite-sized pieces

½ cup water

1¾ cups concentrated tomato sauce (Salsa di Concentrato di Pomodoro, page 95)

Place the fennel and tops in a saucepan with 5 cups of water and bring to a boil. Reduce to a low boil and cook the fennel until tender, about 10 minutes. Drain the fennel through a fine sieve into a saucepan or bowl, saving the cooking water. Set aside the fennel and tops.

In a large saucepan, heat 1 cup of the olive oil with the onions and anchovies and cook over medium heat for 5 minutes, stirring often. Add the sardine pieces and water. Stir in the fennel, tomato sauce, drained currants, pine nuts, and salt and pepper to taste and simmer for 20 minutes, stirring every 5 minutes. If sauce is too thick, add a little water.

Bring 5 quarts of water and the reserved quart of fennel cooking water to a boil in a large pot.

Meanwhile, break the bucatini or perciatelli in half (this makes them much more manageable to eat). Stir the saffron and 2 tablespoons of salt into the boiling water, add the pasta, and cook until pasta is al dente, stirring often.

While the pasta is cooking, pat the remaining 8 sardine fillets dry with a clean dish towel or paper towels. Season lightly with salt and pepper. Heat the remaining ½ cup of olive oil in a large frying pan and fry the sardines over medium-high heat until golden on each side, about 4 minutes per side; carefully turn the

fillets with a spatula to keep them whole. Drain the cooked sardines on paper towels.

Preheat the oven to 375 degrees.

Drain the pasta. Return it to the pot and add the sardine sauce. Mix well and taste for seasoning.

Grease the bottoms and side of a 12- to 14-inch round baking pan with 4-inch sides. Put ½ cup of the bread crumbs into the pan and tilt to coat the bottom and sides of the pan. Spoon the pasta into the pan. Arrange the whole sardine fillets on top in a circle from the center to the outside edge of the pan. Sprinkle the remaining ½ cup of bread crumbs over the top. Cover with a piece of aluminum foil and bake for 20 to 30 minutes or until the sides of the pasta are golden brown. Remove from the oven and let rest 10 minutes before serving. Serve hot or at room temperature.

½ cup currants, soaked in ½ cup lukewarm water for 10 minutes, then drained
½ cup pine nuts
Salt and freshly ground pepper
1½ pounds bucatini or perciatelli
½ teaspoon ground saffron
1 cup toasted bread crumbs

Tagliatelle con Pomodorini, Cozze, e Capperi

(Tagliatelle with Cherry Tomatoes, Mussels, and Capers)

SERVES 4

Heat the oil in a large frying pan until hot but not smoking. Add the garlic and cherry tomatoes. Sauté over medium-low heat for 10 minutes. Stir in the mussels, capers, and basil. Season with salt. Cover and simmer for about 10 minutes, until the mussels open, stirring once during cooking time.

Meanwhile, bring 4 quarts of water to a boil. Add 1 tablespoon of salt. Stir in the pasta and cook until al dente, stirring often.

Drain the pasta, reserving 1 cup of hot pasta water. Transfer the pasta to a large shallow bowl. Top with the sauce and gently toss, adding a little hot pasta water if dry. Taste for seasoning.

¾ cup olive oil
2 garlic cloves, minced
1 pound cherry tomatoes, cut in half
2 dozen mussels, well scrubbed and debearded
2 tablespoons capers
8 fresh basil leaves, torn apart into small pieces
Salt
½ pound tagliatelle or linguine

Pappardelle ai Gamberi e Limone di Paolo

(Paolo's Pappardelle with Shrimp and Lemon)

SERVES 4

12 tablespoons (1½ sticks)
    unsalted butter
1 medium onion, finely chopped
Grated zest of 1 lemon
½ cup heavy cream
1 pound small shrimp, shelled
    and deveined
Salt
½ pound pappardelle
Freshly ground pepper
2 tablespoons freshly chopped
    Italian parsley
Freshly grated Parmesan cheese

In a large frying pan, melt the butter. Add the onion, lemon zest, cream, shrimp, and salt to taste. Bring to a boil. Immediately reduce the heat, and simmer for 10 minutes, stirring occasionally.

Meanwhile, bring 4 quarts of water to a boil. Add 1½ tablespoons of salt. Stir in the pasta and cook until al dente, stirring often. Drain, reserving 1 cup of hot pasta water.

Add the pappardelle to the pan with the sauce and toss well. Add a little hot pasta water if too dry. Cook over medium-low heat for 3 or 4 minutes. Sprinkle with pepper and parsley and toss well. Serve immediately. Pass the Parmesan cheese.

Penne con Gamberi e Sambuca di Capo San Vito

(Capo San Vito's Penne with Shrimp and Sambuca)

A couple of years ago, Mamma and I took four days off from work at Gangivecchio for a holiday at a beautiful seaside resort on Sicily's northwestern coast, a charming place called Capo San Vito. Paolo had just returned from his two-week vacation in the Aeolian Islands. In his absence, we had run both restaurants at Gangivecchio and looked after his *albergo*. Mamma said it wasn't fair that our vacation was shorter than his, but that was women's lot. Anyway, it was not possible for us to be away for two weeks.

American guests were arriving at the *albergo,* and my brother speaks twelve words of English, four of which are "I don't speak English." So we settled happily for the four days. For us it was a most precious time. We did absolutely no work. We swam, walked on the beautiful, long beach, read, slept, and ate every meal out in the charming little restaurants of Capo San Vito.

On the drive back home, we each selected the favorite pasta dish we'd sampled. It was the same one: an unusual combination of penne with shrimp and Sambuca. Sadly, we can't remember the name of the restaurant, and were given no recipe, so here is our adaptation of that delicious dish. But we want to honor one of Sicily's most charming villages by naming the recipe after it.

SERVES 4

In a large frying pan, heat the oil and garlic over low heat for 5 minutes, stirring often. Discard the garlic pieces. Add the tomatoes and season to taste with salt and pepper. Simmer for 20 minutes, stirring often.

Add the shrimp and simmer for 10 minutes. Stir in the Sambuca and cook over medium-high heat for 2 minutes.

Meanwhile, bring 4 quarts of water to a boil. Add 1½ tablespoons of salt. Stir in the pasta and cook until al dente, stirring often.

Drain the pasta and transfer to a bowl. Pour the sauce over the top, add the parsley, and toss well. Season to taste with salt and pepper. Serve hot and, if you like, pass the Parmesan cheese.

½ cup olive oil
2 large garlic cloves, halved
2 cups peeled, chopped fresh or canned tomatoes
Salt and freshly ground pepper
1 pound medium shrimp, shelled and deveined
¼ cup Sambuca
1 pound penne
3 tablespoons freshly chopped parsley
Freshly grated Parmesan cheese (optional)

I Veri Rigatoni all'Amatriciana

(The True Rigatoni in the Style of Amatrice)

Amatrice, where this dish originated, is a town near Rome.

SERVES 4

2 tablespoons olive oil
¾ cup pancetta, cut into
    ½-inch cubes
1 tablespoon dry white wine
Pinch hot pepper flakes
2 cups peeled, diced fresh
    tomatoes
Salt
½ pound rigatoni
Freshly grated pecorino cheese

In a frying pan, heat the oil and cook the pancetta until golden, stirring occasionally. Stir in the wine, pepper flakes, tomatoes, and salt to taste. Simmer for about 15 minutes, stirring occasionally.

Meanwhile, bring 4 quarts of water to a boil. Add 1 tablespoon of salt. Stir in the pasta and cook until al dente, stirring occasionally.

Drain the pasta and add to the sauce in the frying pan. Cook over medium heat for 30 seconds, tossing once. Serve hot and pass the pecorino cheese.

La Pasta del Priore (The Prior's Pasta)

SERVES 6 AS A FIRST COURSE OR 4 AS A MAIN COURSE

2 tablespoons olive oil
4 tablespoons unsalted butter
1 medium onion, finely chopped
2 small zucchini, diced
1 tablespoon water
2 cups ricotta cheese
Pinch powdered saffron
⅓ cup currants
½ cup diced boiled ham
Salt and freshly ground pepper
1 pound rigatoni
Freshly grated Parmesan cheese

In a large frying pan, heat the oil with the butter, onion, and zucchini. Add water. Cook over low heat, stirring often, until the onion and zucchini are just cooked.

Add the ricotta and mix well with a wooden spoon. Sprinkle a little hot water over the mixture to produce a creamy consistency. Do not bring to a boil.

Add the saffron, currants, ham, and salt and pepper to taste. Cook over very low heat for 5 minutes.

Bring 4 quarts of water to a boil. Add 1½ tablespoons of salt. Stir in the rigatoni and cook until al dente, stirring occasionally. Drain the pasta, saving 1 cup of hot pasta water. Transfer the pasta to a bowl. Add the sauce to the pasta and mix well, adding a little pasta water, if necessary. Serve immediately and pass the Parmesan cheese.

Fusilli del Pastore (Shepherd's Fusilli)

SERVES 6 AS A FIRST COURSE OR 4 AS A MAIN COURSE

In a large saucepan, heat the oil, add the onion, and cook over medium heat, stirring often, until it just begins to turn gold. Stir in the peppers and cook over medium heat, stirring often, until the peppers have softened, about 10 minutes.

Stir in the veal, pork, and wine. Cook over high heat, stirring often, for 3 minutes. Add the tomato paste, tomato sauce, hot pepper flakes if desired, and salt and pepper to taste. Simmer for 20 minutes, stirring occasionally.

Meanwhile, bring 4 quarts of water to a boil. Add 1½ tablespoons of salt. Stir in the fusilli and cook until al dente, stirring often.

Drain the pasta, saving 1 cup of the hot pasta water. Return the fusilli to the saucepan and add the sauce. Add a little pasta water if too dry. Toss well and adjust seasoning. Serve with the pecorino.

1 cup olive oil

1 medium onion, thinly sliced

2 pounds mixed red, yellow, and green peppers, cut into thin strips

¼ pound ground veal

¼ pound ground pork

½ cup dry red wine

½ cup tomato paste

1 cup fresh tomato sauce (Salsa di Pomodoro, page 95)

Pinch hot pepper flakes (optional)

Salt and freshly ground pepper

1 pound fusilli

Freshly grated pecorino cheese

Pennette con Pancetta e Vodka

(Pennette with Pancetta and Vodka)

SERVES 4

In a large frying pan, heat the oil until hot but not smoking. Add the scallions and pancetta. Sauté for 3 minutes. Stir in the tomatoes and heavy cream and season with salt. Simmer for 15 minutes, stirring often.

Meanwhile, bring 4 quarts of water to a boil. Add 1 tablespoon of salt. Stir in the pasta and cook until al dente, stirring occasionally.

Stir the vodka into the sauce. Cook over high heat for 2 minutes, stirring a few times. Season with salt and pepper to taste.

½ cup olive oil

3 scallions, white parts and 2 inches of green, thinly sliced

½ cup cubed pancetta

¼ cup cubed smoked pancetta

1 cup diced fresh or canned tomatoes

¾ cup heavy cream

Salt

½ pound pennette
¼ cup vodka
Freshly ground pepper

Drain the pasta, reserving 1 cup of the hot pasta water.

Add the pasta to the pan with the sauce and toss well, adding a little pasta water if too dry.

Spaghetti con Sapone (Spaghetti with Soap)

When I was a child, meals in our home were served punctually. My strict parents accepted absolutely no excuse for being even one minute late to the table. Punishment meant no food, and isolation in our room for hours—for my brother and sister and me, these were the worst possible penalties, because we were always hungry and hated being alone. So we were always watching the clock, or pestering everyone, asking, *"Che ora è?"* In opposition to this rigid regimen, I never imposed such a rule on my own children—five or ten minutes, what does it matter?

Anyway, my brother and sister and I used to wait for the time when Mamma's meal wasn't ready on time, or for my father to arrive late. It finally happened.

Mamma was cooking pasta. The water had come to a boil—she removed the lid, added the salt and the pasta to boiling water, and put the lid back on the pot to bring the water back to a boil. Unknowingly, she had set the hot, moist lid over a cake of soap on the counter, and it had stuck to the lid. When she replaced the lid, the soap fell into the pasta. When the pasta boiled again, she removed the lid. Soon the kitchen reeked of soap, and bubbles began foaming, rapidly overflowing from the pot. Mamma began screaming. We all raced to the kitchen. She told Papa what had happened. He began to laugh. Eventually, she did too. We all laughed so hard, tears filled our eyes. Once in a while after that, when Mamma would ask Papa what kind of pasta he wanted for dinner, he would look very serious and say, *"Oggi, spaghetti con sapone."*

—Wanda Tornabene

Cuscus

(Couscous)

Cuscus con Vitello e Verdure *(Couscous with Veal and Vegetables)*
Cuscus alla Trapanese *(Couscous with Fish)*
Cuscus Estivo *(Summer Couscous with Herbs)*

Un Sontuoso Ricordo Arabo

(A Sumptuous Arabian Souvenir)

I nostri invasori sono diventati nostri fratelli nei gusti.

(Our conquerors became our brothers in taste.)

Years ago, a friend made couscous at Gangivecchio and we served it in our restaurant for dinner. Some local Sicilian guests rejected it, calling it "food for chickens." We had to cook some pasta for them instead. To be fair, they were not familiar with this unusual and wonderful dish, which is so popular in western Sicily, particularly along the coast where there had been strong Arabian domination (from there it's less than one hundred miles to Tunisia). Every woman from Trapani to Mazara del Vallo is able to "*incocciare*" millions of raw semolina grains, a process of rolling them in circles in a pan while gradually sprinkling them with water to rehydrate them. The technique is as old as the food itself. We will speak more about this later.

I tasted my first couscous when I was a teenager, while my parents and I were guests of friends in Marsala. I fell in love with it at first taste, but my parents declared it was something they could avoid for life.

Recently, we had the good fortune to renew an old friendship with Fiorenzo De Santis, a close friend of my father's when they were young. Fiorenzo has been happily married to his Tunisian wife, Angela, for nearly thirty years. Angela, we learned, is a master maker of couscous. When I decided that couscous should be in our book, I invited them both to Gangivecchio so that we could learn the ancient proper method of cooking it.

Fiorenzo, now a retired philosophy, Italian, and Greek professor, met my father during World War II. When the De Santis family was evacuated from Palermo, they took refuge near us in the Madonie Mountains. Fiorenzo's mother, Camilla, became a dear friend of my granny Giovanna, and the De Santis family became frequent dinner guests at Gangivecchio.

When the war ended, the De Santis family returned to Palermo, and, as some-

times happens, we fell out of touch. But since our reunion, Fiorenzo has brought us up to date.

When he was in his early fifties, he met Angela, who was twenty years his junior. She was a very smart student in one of his Italian classes. When he first saw her, he thought: "I could teach Italian to this stunning jewel for the rest of my life." And although the two have very different temperaments, the marriage has lovingly endured. Fiorenzo is engaging, exuberant, and a bit restless. He never stops moving. Angela is always calm, but never stops talking.

For our couscous party, Fiorenzo and Angela arrived early in the morning by bus from Palermo, laden with an enormous bag of special semolina. Angela, Michele, and I set up everything we needed in the abbey's restaurant kitchen. Michele, always the paparazza with her camera, captured images of Angela in a cloud of semolina and took notes on the technique and recipe. Angela instructed us slowly and calmly; it was nonstop conversation, with comments on anything that came into her head. "Where is Fiorentino? . . . Chase those birds away from the window before they become *spiedini* . . . Giovanna, how many dogs do you have now? . . . What is Wanda doing? . . ." (Wanda was hiding, so she wouldn't have to listen to all the chatter.)

Amid the chatter Angela gave us a wonderful couscous lesson. She placed about three cups of the semolina in a large round pan. She wet the fingers of her left hand with salted water and sprinkled the water over the grains. With her right hand, which she always kept dry, she worked the semolina in a circular motion, around and around, until the grains began to swell. She kept adding more sprinkles of water and turning the semolina until the grains were the right size and separated into individual grains. Then she transferred the rehydrated semolina to a cloth to let it rest. She repeated the same process two or three more times in order to have enough couscous for twelve people. It took a total of forty-five minutes. She said it usually took her only thirty minutes with no people watching or talking.

Then came a moment of panic. Angela had forgotten to bring her *cuscussiera*, the special two-part pan for cooking the couscous. We devised an emer-

gency *cuscussiera* from a big pot that we usually use for cooking meat sauce, topped with a large metal colander. We rolled up a wet dish towel and fit it between the pot and colander to secure them and force the vapors through the semolina, to steam the grains. The classic *cuscussiera* is ceramic, but metal ones are more readily available. You can also construct something like our own emergency *cuscussiera*. After this first steaming, the couscous must cool off, be reconstituted with more water, and cooked again. This ancient process for preparing and cooking the couscous took the entire day.

We gathered with our friends for dinner at eight o'clock. Michele and I were ready for a glass of wine, I can tell you. When Angela entered with a huge dish of her fabulous couscous, everyone applauded. For the first time, she was speechless.

The traditional method of making couscous is time-consuming, and I probably will never have the time to make it again in this way. Fortunately for all of us there is now excellent couscous available that cooks quickly. We give you three recipes using this faster couscous; the authentic savory veal and vegetable stew and the Cuscus alla Trapanese are Angela's. If you speak Italian and have any questions (and have time for a long chat), I'd be happy to give you her telephone number.

Cuscus con Vitello e Verdure

(Couscous with Veal and Vegetables)

CHICKPEAS

2 tablespoons olive oil
1 medium onion, finely chopped
2 stalks celery, diced
1 canned tomato, crushed
Salt
½ pound (about 1 cup) chickpeas,
    soaked overnight, boiled until
    tender, and skins removed,
    or 1 10-ounce can chickpeas,
    skins removed

VEAL STEW

½ cup olive oil
1 medium onion, thinly sliced
2½ pounds veal stew pieces
2 carrots, peeled and diced
2 potatoes, peeled and sliced
2 stalks celery, sliced
One 35-ounce can diced
    tomatoes
1 vegetable bouillon cube
6 cups water

VEGETABLES

4 cups water
1 vegetable bouillon cube
2 stalks celery, sliced
2 tablespoons olive oil
3 medium zucchini, cut in half
    lengthwise, then cut into
    thirds crosswise

SERVES 6

To make the chickpeas, heat the olive oil in a medium saucepan, add the onion and celery, and sauté for 5 minutes, stirring often. Stir in the crushed tomato and season to taste with salt. Simmer for 10 minutes, stirring often. Remove from heat and reserve.

To cook the stew, heat the olive oil in a large, heavy-bottomed pan. And the onion and cook over medium heat for 5 minutes, stirring often. Add the veal and cook for 10 minutes, stirring often. Add the carrots, potatoes, celery, tomatoes, and bouillon cube. Stir in water. Combine well and simmer for 1 hour and 15 minutes, or until the veal is very tender. Stir the chickpea mixture into the simmering stew.

In the meantime, to cook the vegetables, put water, bouillon cube, celery, and olive oil into a large saucepan. Bring to a boil. Add the zucchini pieces and simmer for 10 minutes.

In another saucepan, bring 4 cups of lightly salted water to a boil. Add the carrots and cook until just tender, about 12 minutes.

Drain the cooked zucchini through a strainer into a bowl, reserving the cooking liquid. Set aside the zucchini pieces.

When the carrots are cooked, drain and set them aside with the zucchini.

To cook the couscous, bring water and 2 cups of the zucchini cooking water to a boil in a large saucepan with the salt and butter. Remove the pan from the heat. Stir in the couscous, cover, and let rest for 10 minutes.

Meanwhile, bring the remaining reserved zucchini water to a boil in a large saucepan. Add the cooked zucchini and carrots and reduce the heat to a simmer. Cook for just 1 or 2 minutes until reheated.

Fluff the couscous with a fork and transfer to a large platter. Spoon half of the veal stew mixture and half of the vegetables over the couscous. Ladle a cup of the stew broth over the top of the

dish. Transfer the remaining stew to a bowl and the remaining vegetables to a platter and serve on the side.

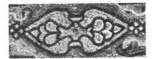

Cuscus alla Trapanese (Couscous with Fish)

SERVES 6

To cook the fish and make the broth, heat the olive oil in a large heavy-bottomed saucepan. Stir in the onions and cook for about 5 minutes over medium-low heat, stirring often. Add the fish pieces, celery, cayenne pepper, bay leaf, tomato paste, and bouillon cube. Stir in water and bring to a boil. Reduce the heat and simmer for 30 minutes, stirring occasionally.

To make the parsley pesto, put the parsley, garlic, and oil into the bowl of a food processor. Season with salt and pepper. Process for about 15 seconds until you have a thick puree. Transfer to a small bowl and set aside.

Prepare the vegetables. In separate saucepans, boil the squash and potatoes in lightly salted water until just tender—about 8 minutes for the squash and 12 minutes for the potatoes. Drain and reserve.

When the fish has cooked for 30 minutes, season it with a pinch of cayenne pepper and salt and pepper to taste. Transfer the fish to a platter. Pass the broth through a fine strainer into a large bowl. Stir the parsley pesto into the broth and transfer 2 cups of the seasoned broth to a large saucepan.

3 large carrots, peeled and cut in half lengthwise

COUSCOUS

2 cups water
1 teaspoon salt
3 tablespoons unsalted butter
Two 10-ounce boxes plain couscous

FISH AND BROTH

½ cup olive oil
1 cup chopped onions
3 pounds boneless pieces of mixed fish, such as grouper, sea bass, red snapper, and red mullet
½ cup diced celery, including some finely chopped top leaves
Cayenne pepper
1 bay leaf
3 tablespoons tomato paste
1 vegetable bouillon cube
6 cups water

PARSLEY PESTO

¾ cup coarsely chopped Italian parsley
4 garlic cloves, halved
⅔ cup olive oil
Salt and freshly ground pepper

VEGETABLES

3 medium yellow squash, cut in
    half lengthwise, then cut into
    thirds crosswise
3 medium potatoes, peeled and
    cut into ½-inch-thick slices

COUSCOUS

2 cups water
2 tablespoons olive oil
Two 10-ounce boxes plain
    couscous

Return the remaining broth to its original saucepan and keep at a simmer on the stove.

To prepare the couscous, add 2 cups of water to the pan with the 2 cups of seasoned broth. Stir in olive oil and bring to a boil. Remove the pan from the heat and stir in the couscous. Cover and let rest for 10 minutes.

Meanwhile, spoon the cooked fish, squash, and potatoes into the broth simmering on the stove. Simmer for 1 minute or just long enough to reheat them. Remove them with a slotted spoon and place on a serving platter.

Fluff the couscous with a fork and taste for seasoning.

Transfer the couscous to a large shallow plate. Arrange half of the fish and half of the vegetables over the couscous. Pass the platter with the remaining fish and vegetables, and serve the reheated broth in a gravy boat.

Cuscus Estivo (Summer Couscous with Herbs)

SERVES 4

2 cups water
Salt
2 tablespoons unsalted butter
One 10-ounce box plain couscous
½ cup freshly chopped mint
    leaves
¼ cup freshly chopped basil
    leaves
12 cherry tomatoes, quartered
3 tablespoons extra virgin olive
    oil
1 tablespoon freshly squeezed
    lemon juice
Freshly ground pepper

In a medium saucepan, bring the water, ½ teaspoon salt, and butter to a boil. Stir in the couscous. Cover the pan, remove from the heat, and let rest for 10 minutes.

Remove the cover and fluff the couscous with a fork. Stir in the mint and basil leaves, cherry tomatoes, oil, and lemon juice. Season to taste with salt and pepper and toss well. Cover and let rest for 30 minutes.

Toss the mixture again and serve at room temperature.

Riso
(Rice)

Eleganza in Chicchi

(Grain of Elegance)

La Pasta, per i Siciliani, è come la moglie: fedele compagna di ogni giorno. Ma riso è come l'amante, benvenuto a tavola solo occasionalmente, ma sempre con emozione e grande affetto.

(Pasta, for Sicilians, is the wife—the loyal companion of everyday life. But rice is the lover, welcome at the table only occasionally, but always with excitement and great affection.)

One of Sicily's most famous foods is based on rice: *arancine. Arancine* (little oranges) are breaded and fried balls, ovals, or cone-shaped portions of basic cooked risotto with a small amount of stuffing inside—béchamel sauce with ham, or mozzarella, or meat ragù with peas. Palermo specializes in *arancine,* and we wrote a lot about them in *La Cucina Siciliana di Gangivecchio.*

In Sicily, rice is also used in soups and stuffings for vegetables like peppers and zucchini, and it is also an important supporting player in timbales, such as Mamma's Timballo Maritato (page 107). But although rice was once cultivated here, it has never been able to compete with our beloved pasta. Pasta, for Sicilians, is the wife—loyal companion of everyday life. But rice is the lover, welcome at the table only occasionally, but always with excitement and great affection.

When risotto, Italy's most elegant rice dish, is on the menu at Gangivecchio, there is great excitement. We usually serve it in the restaurant only for special celebrations or by special request, and only for twenty people or fewer. Like our pastas, our risottos change with the seasons. In summer and spring, the risottos include fresh vegetables like asparagus, fava beans, peas, and zucchini and herbs. In fall and winter, we like heartier risottos, such as mushroom or pumpkin.

For some reason, there is a perception that risotto is a difficult dish to prepare. It's not at all difficult, but as Mamma says, you can't be lazy or impatient. When all the ingredients are ready, the cook must stand in front of the stove constantly stirring and slowly administering the broth to the pan for eighteen to twenty minutes. The exquisite cooked risotto is a great reward for this labor.

Risotto con Gorgonzola e Finocchi

(Risotto with Gorgonzola and Fennel)

6 cups homemade or canned vegetable broth
2 tablespoons olive oil
4 tablespoons unsalted butter
1 small onion, finely chopped
1 large fennel bulb, diced
1 cup chopped feathery green fennel tops
Salt and freshly ground pepper
2 cups Vialone Nano, Carnaroli, or Arborio rice
4 ounces gorgonzola cheese, crumbled
½ cup freshly grated Parmesan cheese, plus extra for topping
Freshly chopped Italian parsley

SERVES 6 AS A FIRST COURSE OR 4 AS A MAIN COURSE

Bring the broth to a boil in a medium saucepan next to the burner where you will cook the risotto. While cooking the risotto, keep the broth at a low boil.

Heat the oil and 2 tablespoons of the butter in a medium heavy-bottomed saucepan. Stir in the onion, fennel, and fennel tops. Cook over medium heat for 5 minutes, stirring often. Season with salt and pepper. Stir in the rice and cook for about 2 minutes, stirring constantly. Add ½ cup of the simmering broth and cook, stirring constantly until the broth has been absorbed. Add another ½ cup of the simmering broth and cook, stirring constantly until the broth has been absorbed by the rice. Continue cooking the risotto in the same manner until only about 1 cup of the broth remains, then stir in ½ cup of the remaining broth with the gorgonzola cheese. Continue cooking until the last of the broth has been absorbed. From the time the rice is added, the whole process should take 18 to 20 minutes.

When the risotto is done, remove it from the heat and stir in the remaining 2 tablespoons of butter and the Parmesan cheese. Sprinkle the top with parsley and serve at once. Pass the Parmesan cheese.

Risotto con Zucchini, Patate, e Pesto

(Risotto with Zucchini, Potatoes, and Pesto)

PESTO SAUCE

1 cup packed fresh basil leaves
2 tablespoons pine nuts
2 tablespoons blanched almonds

SERVES 6 AS FIRST COURSE OR 4 AS MAIN COURSE

To make the pesto sauce, puree the basil leaves, pine nuts, almonds, and garlic in a food processor while pouring the olive oil through the feed tube opening in a slow steady stream. After oil is

incorporated, process for 15 seconds more. Season with salt and pepper and process for another 10 seconds. Set aside.

Bring the broth to a boil in a medium saucepan next to the burner where you will cook the risotto. While cooking the risotto, keep the broth at a low boil.

Heat the oil and 2 tablespoons of the butter in a medium heavy-bottomed saucepan. Stir in the onion and zucchini and cook over medium heat for 5 minutes, stirring often. Season with salt and pepper. Stir in the rice and cook for about 2 minutes, stirring constantly. Add ½ cup of the simmering broth and cook, stirring constantly, until the broth has been absorbed. Add another ½ cup of the simmering broth and cook, stirring constantly, until the broth has been absorbed. Continue cooking the risotto in the same manner until only about 1 cup of the broth remains, then stir in ½ cup of the remaining broth with the pesto and potatoes. Continue cooking until the last of the broth has been absorbed. From the time the rice is added, the whole process should take 18 to 20 minutes.

When the risotto is done, remove it from the heat and stir in the remaining 2 tablespoons of butter and the Parmesan cheese. Serve at once and pass the Parmesan.

2 garlic cloves, halved
½ cup olive oil
Salt and freshly ground pepper

RISOTTO

6 cups homemade or canned chicken broth
2 tablespoons olive oil
4 tablespoons unsalted butter
1 small onion, finely chopped
1 medium zucchini, diced
Salt and freshly ground pepper
2 cups Vialone Nano, Carnaroli, or Arborio rice
⅔ cup pesto sauce
1 cup diced boiled and peeled potatoes
½ cup freshly grated Parmesan cheese, plus extra for topping

Per un Risotto di Successo (For a Successful Risotto)

- Use quality butter, olive oil, rice, broth (homemade or canned), freshly grated cheese, and other ingredients.
- Use only imported Italian short-grain rice: Vialone Nano, Carnaroli, or Arborio.
- The broth for the risotto must be kept at a low boil in a saucepan on a burner next to the one where the risotto is being cooked.
- Keep a ½- to 1-cup ladle in or next to the broth pot.
- Use a heavy-bottomed saucepan (with curved sides if possible) for cooking risotto.
- Stir the risotto constantly with a wooden spoon while it cooks.
- Cooked risotto must be served immediately, so call the diners to the table five minutes before it is done.

Risotto Affumicato con Pistacchi di Paolo

(Paolo's Risotto with Smoked Provolone and Pistachios)

SERVES 6 AS A FIRST COURSE OR 4 AS A MAIN COURSE

6 cups homemade or canned vegetable broth

2 tablespoons olive oil

4 tablespoons unsalted butter

3 scallions, white part and 1 inch of green, thinly sliced

2 cups Vialone Nano, Carnaroli, or Arborio rice

Bring the broth to a boil in a medium saucepan next to the burner where you will cook the risotto. While cooking the risotto, keep the broth at a low boil.

Heat the oil and 2 tablespoons of the butter in a medium heavy-bottomed saucepan. Stir in the scallions and cook for 5 minutes over medium-low heat, stirring often. Stir in the rice and cook for 2 minutes, stirring constantly. Add ½ cup of broth and the saffron. Cook, stirring constantly, until the broth has been

Frutta Secca (Nuts)

Since I've lived at Gangivecchio, we have always had almond, walnut, and hazelnut trees, plus towering pine trees for pine nuts. But it is the hazelnut harvest that I love best. Hazelnuts dropping from the trees in the first week of September announce the arrival of fall, even though it is usually still hot in the Sicilian countryside. When I was a child, the hazelnuts were collected by workers and dried in a single layer on a vast terrace off our private living quarters in the abbey—a delicious sea of brown.

The hard nuts had to be opened by hand, one by one. For this difficult work, my grandfather employed eight young girls from nearby farms or the village of Gangi, or from the more distant Geraci, for a month. The wages were very low, but the girls were always laughing and smiling, even though my grandfather told them that they must each whistle while they worked to prove they weren't eating any of the hazelnuts. He was joking, but this harvest helped support our property, so it was serious business. His stern warning was always taken well. It was only years later that I realized the girls weren't doing the work for money or a keen appetite for hazelnuts; they were searching for husbands. A dozen or so young men were also hired at that time of year to attend to other farmwork. Young girls were watched closely at home, so harvest time at Gangivecchio or other farms was one of the few places they could meet prospective mates. Sometimes I see these same girls today in Gangi or Geraci, grown women now of course, with their harvest husbands and their children.

absorbed by the rice. Add another ½ cup of the broth and cook until the broth has been absorbed, stirring constantly. Continue in this manner until there is 1 cup of broth left. Stir in ½ cup of the remaining broth and the provolone cheese. Continue cooking and stirring until all the broth has been absorbed. From the time the rice is added, the process should take 18 to 20 minutes.

When the risotto is done, remove it from the heat and stir in the remaining 2 tablespoons of butter and the Parmesan cheese. Season to taste with salt and pepper. Sprinkle the top with the pistachios and serve at once. Pass the Parmesan cheese.

Pinch saffron threads
8 ounces smoked provolone
    cheese, diced
½ cup freshly grated Parmesan
    cheese, plus extra for topping
Salt and freshly ground pepper
½ cup chopped pistachios

At Gangivecchio, Peppe now collects our much-reduced hazelnut harvest. They're still dried on our terrace. Peppe cracks them open in his room at night in front of his big television. The amount he eats is his pay.

Even though our personal nut production has diminished significantly, Sicily produces a tremendous amount of superb almonds, walnuts, and pistachios, though not so many hazelnuts—because of the difficult work, I presume. The hazelnuts in the markets these days are from Turkey.

Brought here by our Arabian conquerors, nuts are still a very important part of Sicilian cuisine, especially in pastries and ice creams. Mamma's favorite ice cream is hazelnut; mine is pistachio. Paolo also loves pistachios and uses them often in risottos and salads.

Risotto Affumicato con Radicchio

(Risotto with Radicchio)

SERVES 6 AS A FIRST COURSE OR 4 AS A MAIN COURSE

6 cups homemade or canned
 vegetable broth
2 tablespoons olive oil
4 tablespoons unsalted butter
1 medium onion, finely chopped
1 large head red radicchio, cored
 and shredded
2 cups Vialone Nano, Carnaroli,
 or Arborio rice
½ cup dry white wine
8 ounces smoked scamorza or
 provolone cheese
1 tablespoon freshly chopped
 mixed herbs such as thyme,
 sage, Italian parsley, or
 marjoram
Salt and freshly ground pepper
½ cup freshly grated Parmesan
 cheese, plus extra for topping

Bring the broth to a boil in a medium saucepan next to the burner where you will cook the risotto. While cooking the risotto, keep the broth at a low boil.

Heat the oil and 2 tablespoons of the butter in a medium heavy-bottomed saucepan. Stir in the onion and radicchio. Cook over medium heat for 5 minutes, stirring constantly. Stir in the rice and cook for about 2 minutes, stirring constantly. Stir in the wine and and cook, stirring constantly, until it has been absorbed. Add ½ cup of broth and cook, stirring constantly, until the broth has been absorbed. Repeat until there is 1 cup of broth left. Stir in the cheese and herbs and ½ cup of the remaining broth. Continue stirring until all the broth has been absorbed and the rice is done. Season to taste with salt and pepper. Remove from the heat and stir in the remaining 2 tablespoons of butter and the Parmesan cheese. Serve at once and pass the Parmesan cheese.

Risotto di Mele al Calvados

(Risotto with Apples and Calvados)

Bring the broth to a boil in a medium saucepan next to the burner where you will cook the risotto. While cooking the risotto, keep the broth at a low boil.

Heat the olive oil in a medium saucepan. Add the apples, onion, and scallions and cook over medium heat for 8 minutes, stirring often. Season to taste with salt and pepper. Transfer half of the mixture to a small bowl and reserve.

Stir the rice into the pan with 2 tablespoons of the butter. Cook over medium heat for 2 minutes, stirring constantly. Add ½ cup of the simmering broth and cook, stirring constantly, until the broth has been absorbed. Add another ½ cup of the simmering broth and cook, stirring constantly, until the broth has been absorbed. Continue cooking the risotto in the same manner until about 1 cup of the broth remains. Stir in the Calvados and ½ cup of the broth and continue cooking until the last of the broth has been absorbed. Remove the pan from the heat. Stir in the reserved apple mixture, the remaining 2 tablespoons of butter, and the Parmesan cheese. Taste for seasoning. Serve at once and pass the Parmesan cheese.

6 cups homemade or canned vegetable broth

4 tablespoons olive oil

2 Red Delicious apples, peeled, cored, and diced

1 medium onion, finely chopped

2 scallions, white part and 1 inch of green, thinly sliced

Salt and freshly ground pepper

2 cups Vialone Nano, Carnaroli, or Arborio rice

4 tablespoons unsalted butter

⅓ cup Calvados

½ cup freshly grated Parmesan cheese, plus extra for topping

Secondi di Carne

(Meat Main-Course Dishes)

Costolette Siciliane di Vitello
(Sicilian Oven-Braised Veal Shanks)

Cotolette di Vitello di Wanda *(Wanda's Veal Cutlets)*

Vitello Delizioso con Funghi
(Delicious Veal Rib Roast with Mushrooms)

Pacchettini di Vitello *(Stuffed Packets of Veal)*

Stufato in Casseruola della Mamma
(Mamma's Veal Casserole)

Impanata di Vitello e Maiale
(Veal and Pork Baked in Dough)

Le Cotolette dei Ragazzi *(My Boy's Cutlets)*

Stinco di Maiale al Forno *(Roast Pork Shanks)*

Spezzatino di Maiale con Patate ed Aromi di Sicilia
(Pork Stew with Potatoes and Sicilian Herbs)

Rollò di Maiale Arrostito *(Roasted Rolled Pork Loin)*

Cosciotto di 'Agnello al Forno "Una Mia Idea"
(Roasted Lamb "My Idea")

Pasticcio di Pollo *(Chicken Soufflé)*

La Casa di Annunziata *(Annunziata's House)*

Stemperata di Pollo
(Chicken with Vegetables, Green Olives, Capers, and Mint)

Petto di Tacchino Farcito alla Siciliana
(Sicilian Stuffed Turkey Breast)

Tacchino Impanato
(Fried Herb-Breaded Turkey Breast Cutlets)

Un Sogno da Ricchi

(A Dream of Riches)

Prima di cominciare a litigare, dammi il vitello che hai messo da parte per te!

(Before we start arguing, give me the veal you have saved for yourself!)

There aren't as many recipes for meat in this book as in our previous one, where we gave most of our cherished traditional meat recipes. That's because at home, unless it's for a holiday or other celebration, we prefer soups, vegetables, and pasta. In the restaurant, of course, we must serve a meat main course—Sicilian diners expect and anticipate it. They know very well that Mamma will prepare something wonderful from the superior-quality meats that are now widely available to us in this region. The first question Sicilians ask about our set menus is always: "What is the meat course today?" This is not surprising, because of the ancient social significance of meat in the Sicilian kitchen. In the past, only the rich could afford meat, even though they often opted for fish. But for the poor, meat was a dream of riches. So the clever Sicilians invented dishes that contained no meat but were given names that implied they did. For example, the word *caponata,* our famous sweet-and-sour vegetable stew, comes from the word *capponi* (capons). Cooks liked to serve stewed vegetables with the fowl; since the poor people could not have the capons themselves, they used the name for the vegetable dish to make them feel rich.

There is a story told here about meat and the separation of classes: A young boy was constantly ridiculed by his schoolmates, being the poorest child in the class. When the teacher questioned each pupil about what they had had for dinner the previous night, the boy always answered wild fennel, beet tops, chicory, or some other humble food from the earth. The other children would laugh because he only ate vegetables, and no meat. One day, fed up with this mockery, the boy announced that he had had veal for supper. "How much did you eat?" the teacher asked. "Two bunches," he replied.

For my mother, the subject of meat stirs great conflict in her soul. On the one

hand, she is the cold-hearted expert at the butcher shop, choosing only the best quality and cuts of meat, fighting with our butcher, Pino, at almost every exchange: "How do you dare say that this red roast is the most tender, youngest veal you have? Show me the birth certificate. With all due respect, I will be forced to pay my guest's dentist bill because of your meat. Your prices are already the highest in town. I'll become a vegetarian before I'll buy this. Come, come, Pino, before we start arguing, give me the veal you have saved for yourself."

Mamma not only knows how to choose the best meat, she also loves to eat it, if only occasionally. When we travel in America, she either orders fish or a thick grilled fillet of tenderloin. She believes that America's beef is the finest in the world. We do not have great beef in Sicily, but our veal, pork, and lamb are sublime.

The other half of my mother's personality is that of a passionate animal lover. She has great admiration for vegetarians.

When you live in the country, as we do, being friendly with the animals is a natural instinct. As we have said before, all our animals, including the cows, have names. We love them so much: If they are ill, we send for the veterinarian immediately, far sooner than we would go to a doctor for our own ailments. Once an animal is named, we give up the idea of transforming it into steaks, chops, sausages, or a ragù.

Years ago, a shepherd gave us a little lamb. Mamma named this beautiful white creature Felice. Felice used to walk with Mamma like a dog; he played with the cats like one of them, and he was allowed to jump onto Mamma's bed after he'd been given a bath. When he got bigger, he was banned from the house and slept in the stables. During the day he roamed about freely. In time, Felice became a rather large *mouton* with a handsome pair of horns, and Papa said he was becoming dangerous. As predicted, one day he rudely pushed my mother in the back, sending her to the ground. My father decided it was time for Felice to become a delicious roast surrounded by some roasted potatoes and onions. "It would be like eating a member of my family!" Mamma screamed.

The house was in turmoil. My mother declared that she could not live without Felice. So after a week of tears and pleading, there was a compromise. Felice would become a *stallone* in the nearby mountains. He was welcomed back warmly by the shepherd who had brought him to us.

If you have not become a vegetarian from reading this story, we hope you will enjoy our meat recipes.

Costolette Siciliane di Vitello

(Sicilian Oven-Braised Veal Shanks)

SERVES 6

In a large frying pan, heat ½ cup of oil and 2 tablespoons of the butter. When hot but not smoking, add the veal shanks and cook over medium-high heat until golden brown on each side. Remove the pan from the heat.

Preheat the oven to 375 degrees.

Transfer the veal shanks to a covered, heavy baking dish just large enough to hold the shanks comfortably. Set aside.

In the frying pan, heat 2 tablespoons of olive oil and the remaining 2 tablespoons of butter. Stir in the garlic and cook for 2 minutes over medium heat, stirring occasionally. Stir in the olives, capers, *peperoncini,* tomatoes, oregano, and sugar. Season to taste with salt and pepper. Simmer for 10 minutes, stirring often. Add a little water to the pan if the mixture becomes too dry.

Spoon equal amounts of the sauce over each shank. Cover and cook for 45 minutes or until veal is very tender.

½ cup plus 2 tablespoons olive oil
4 tablespoons unsalted butter
Six 1½-inch-thick veal shanks
4 garlic cloves, minced
⅔ cup pitted and chopped green olives (Sicilian, if possible)
4 tablespoons capers, washed and drained
4 *peperoncini* (peppers in vinegar), well drained and chopped
3 large ripe red tomatoes, cored, peeled, and chopped
½ teaspoon oregano
1 teaspoon sugar
Salt and freshly ground pepper

Cotolette di Vitello di Wanda (Wanda's Veal Cutlets)

SERVES 6

Beat the eggs lightly in a shallow dish with a little salt. In another shallow dish, combine the bread crumbs and Parmesan cheese and season with salt. Put the flour into a shallow bowl.

Dredge each veal cutlet on each side in the flour, eggs, and bread crumb mixture. Press the crumbs lightly onto the meat.

Heat ⅓ cup of olive oil with the butter in a large frying pan and sauté the cutlets until golden on each side, in batches if necessary, adding olive oil when needed. When cooked, drain on paper towels.

After the cutlets are browned, add 3 tablespoons olive oil, the

2 large eggs
Salt
2 cups fresh bread crumbs
2 tablespoons freshly grated Parmesan cheese
1 cup all-purpose flour
Six 6-ounce thin veal scallops
About ⅔ cup olive oil
3 tablespoons unsalted butter
2 garlic cloves, chopped

1 small onion, chopped

1½ pounds ripe tomatoes, peeled and chopped

1 teaspoon sugar

Pinch cayenne pepper

Freshly ground pepper

Freshly chopped Italian parsley

garlic, onion, tomatoes, sugar, and cayenne pepper to the frying pan, and season with salt and pepper to taste. Cook over medium heat for 15 minutes, stirring occasionally. Add a little water if mixture becomes too dry.

Preheat the oven to 350 degrees.

Pass the tomato mixture through a food mill. Wipe out the frying pan with a thick wad of paper towels, and return the mixture to the pan. Simmer for a few minutes until creamy, stirring constantly.

Arrange the veal scallops in a shallow baking dish large enough to hold them all in 1 layer. Spoon the sauce evenly over the top. Cover with aluminum foil and cook in the oven for 10 minutes.

Sprinkle with parsley and serve immediately. Little boiled potatoes seasoned with rosemary, salt, and pepper and tossed with olive oil go very well with this dish.

Vitello Delizioso con Funghi

(Delicious Veal Rib Roast with Mushrooms)

SERVES 4

2½-pound boneless veal rib roast, tied

1 medium onion, coarsely chopped

2 medium carrots, peeled and chopped

1 stalk celery, sliced

¼ cup freshly chopped Italian parsley

½ cup dry white wine

Salt and freshly ground pepper

4 tablespoons olive oil

3 tablespoons unsalted butter

Put the veal roast into a large nonreactive bowl and add the onion, carrots, celery, parsley, and white wine. Season to taste with salt and pepper. Cover and refrigerate overnight, turning occasionally.

Remove the veal from the marinade. Reserve the marinade.

Wipe the veal clean and dry it with paper towels. Heat 2 tablespoons of oil in a large frying pan and brown the veal all over. Transfer the veal to a large saucepan just large enough to hold the roast comfortably.

Heat the remaining 2 tablespoons of oil and the butter in the large frying pan the veal was browned in. Add the onion, all the ham, and the mushrooms. Cook over medium heat for 5 minutes, stirring often. Add the reserved marinade, the water, and the bouillon cube. Bring to a boil. Pour the mixture over the veal.

Simmer for 1 hour, stirring and turning the veal occasionally. Let rest 10 minutes before carving into thin slices. Serve with the mushrooms and sauce. Boiled spinach flavored with lemon juice and salt and pepper is a good side dish.

1 small onion, finely chopped
½ cup diced boiled ham
½ pound crimini or field mushrooms, thinly sliced
2 cups water
1 vegetable bouillon cube

Pacchettini di Vitello (Stuffed Packets of Veal)

SERVES 4

Heat ½ cup of olive oil in a large frying pan. Add the mushrooms, garlic, and parsley and cook over medium heat, stirring often, for about 15 minutes. Transfer to a large bowl to cool for 15 minutes.

Add the pork, Parmesan cheese, cayenne pepper, eggs, and salt and pepper to taste. Mix thoroughly.

Place equal amounts of the mixture in the center of each veal scallop and roll up. Secure each roll with a toothpick. Heat 2 tablespoons of oil in a heavy-bottomed saucepan and brown the veal rolls all over. Add the tomatoes and vegetable broth and bring to a boil. Reduce the heat to a simmer and cook about 1 hour, stirring occasionally and basting rolls with the liquid in the pan.

A fresh cooked green vegetable, such as green beans, and mashed potatoes complete the menu.

½ cup plus 2 tablespoons olive oil
8 ounces crimini or field mushrooms, chopped
1 garlic clove, minced
1 tablespoon freshly chopped Italian parsley
¼ pound ground pork
3 tablespoons freshly grated Parmesan cheese
Pinch cayenne pepper
2 eggs, lightly beaten
Salt and freshly ground pepper
Four 6-ounce veal scallops, flattened as thin as possible without breaking the skin
1 cup peeled, chopped tomatoes
1 cup homemade or canned vegetable broth

Stufato in Casseruola della Mamma

(Mamma's Veal Casserole)

SERVES 6

2 large onions, thinly sliced

2¼ pounds small baking potatoes, peeled and thinly sliced

Six 6-ounce veal cutlets

Salt and freshly ground pepper

2 cups vegetable broth, or as needed

6 tablespoons unsalted butter

Preheat oven to 350 degrees.

In a 9-by-13-inch baking pan, arrange half the onions in a layer. Top evenly with half of the sliced potatoes. Place 3 cutlets on top. Season well with salt and pepper. Repeat another layer of the onions and potatoes and top with the 3 remaining veal cutlets. Add broth. Season with salt and pepper. Dot with butter. Cover and cook for 1 hour. Check after 30 minutes to see if more vegetable broth is needed.

When cooked through, uncover and place under the broiler until golden brown.

Impanata di Vitello e Maiale

(Veal and Pork Baked in Dough)

SERVES 4

¼ pound ground veal

¼ pound ground pork

3 tablespoons finely chopped toasted almonds

1 large egg, separated

1 tablespoon cocoa powder

1 tablespoon sugar

3 tablespoons olive oil

1 medium onion, thinly sliced

Salt and freshly ground pepper

1 recipe for pizza dough (Paste Base per la Pizza, page 79)

In a large bowl, combine the meats, almonds, egg white, cocoa powder, and sugar. Mix well with your hands.

In a large skillet, heat the oil. Cook the onion over medium heat until the slices just begin to turn golden brown, about 5 minutes. Add the meat mixture and cook over medium heat for about 8 minutes, breaking the pieces apart with a fork and stirring frequently, until the meats are no longer pink. Season to taste with salt and pepper. Transfer to a shallow bowl and cool.

Preheat the oven to 400 degrees.

On a lightly floured work surface, divide the pizza dough in half. Roll out each into a 12-inch circle.

Butter and flour the bottom and sides of a 12-inch baking pan. Place 1 piece of dough across the bottom of the pan. Spoon meat mixture over the top to within an inch of the edge and smooth evenly. Cover with the remaining circle of dough. Press the edges

together with your fingers. Brush the top evenly with the egg yolk. Bake for 30 minutes. Serve warm or at room temperature, with a mixed green salad.

Le Cotolette dei Ragazzi (My Boy's Cutlets)

SERVES 6

Preheat the oven to 350 degrees.

Brush the cutlets with olive oil and season with salt, pepper, and oregano. Coat each cutlet with bread crumbs and set aside.

In a large bowl, combine the potatoes and onion and season with salt, pepper, and oregano.

Grease a shallow 9-by-13-inch baking pan. Arrange half of the potato and onion mixture in the pan and top with the breaded cutlets. Cover evenly with the remaining potatoes. Top with the chopped tomatoes. Season with salt, pepper, and oregano.

Heat vegetable cubes with water in a small saucepan. Stir until cubes dissolve. Add vegetable broth to pan and cook for 45 minutes or until golden brown.

Six 6-ounce veal cutlets
3 tablespoons olive oil
Salt and freshly ground pepper
Dried oregano
Dried bread crumbs
3 pounds potatoes, peeled and thinly sliced
1 large onion, thinly sliced
3 medium tomatoes, peeled and chopped
2 vegetable bouillon cubes
2 cups water

Stinco di Maiale al Forno (Roast Pork Shanks)

SERVES 4

Place the shanks in a large nonreactive dish. Add the wine, juniper berries, orange peel, and herbs and season with salt and pepper. Cover and refrigerate overnight or for at least 4 hours, turning occasionally.

Drain the shanks, reserving the marinade, and pat them dry. Discard the orange peel and juniper berries.

Heat ½ cup olive oil in a large frying pan. Thoroughly brown the shanks over medium-high heat. Transfer the shanks to a roasting pan.

Preheat the oven to 350 degrees.

4 pork shanks (back legs)
2 cups dry red wine
6 juniper berries
Peel of 1 orange, cut in 1 long piece
1 tablespoon freshly chopped rosemary
1 tablespoon freshly chopped marjoram
Salt and freshly ground pepper

¾ cup olive oil

2 large onions, thinly sliced

1 bay leaf

1 cup fresh tomato sauce (Salsa di Pomodoro, page 95)

½ cup peeled, chopped tomatoes

2 pounds sliced boiled potatoes (optional)

Add ¼ cup of oil to the frying pan and sauté the onions for about 10 minutes, stirring often. Add the marinade, bay leaf, tomato sauce, and tomatoes and bring to a boil. Cook for 5 minutes, stirring often. Season to taste with salt and pepper. Spoon the mixture over the shanks. Turn the shanks to coat them evenly. Cover with aluminum foil and cook for 1 hour, turning and basting the shanks with the sauce in the pan every 20 minutes. Uncover and cook another 15 minutes or until done. Discard bay leaf.

If desired, add boiled potatoes to the roasting pan during the last 20 minutes of cooking time and coat them in the sauce. Serve them alongside the shanks.

Spezzatino di Maiale con Patate ed Aromi di Sicilia (Pork Stew with Potatoes and Sicilian Herbs)

SERVES 6

½ cup olive oil

1 large onion, chopped

½ cup freshly chopped mint

1 tablespoon each freshly chopped rosemary, Italian parsley, sage, and marjoram, or 1 teaspoon each dried

4 carrots, peeled and cut into ⅛-inch-thick slices

2 large potatoes, peeled and cut into 1-inch cubes

2 tablespoons tomato paste

Salt and freshly ground pepper

1 teaspoon sugar

Pinch hot pepper flakes

One 2½-pound boneless pork shoulder, cut into 1½-inch pieces

In a large saucepan, heat the oil until hot but not smoking. Add the chopped onion and cook over medium heat for 5 minutes, stirring occasionally. Add the mint, herbs, carrots, and potatoes. Cook over medium heat for 20 minutes, stirring occasionally.

Stir in the tomato paste, salt and pepper to taste, sugar, and hot pepper flakes. Add the meat and cook for 5 minutes over medium heat.

Pour enough water into the pan to just cover the ingredients. Cover and simmer for 2 hours, stirring occasionally. Taste for seasoning and serve hot.

Rollò di Maiale Arrostito (Roasted Rolled Pork Loin)

SERVES 6

Preheat the oven to 350 degrees.

Season the inside of the flattened piece of pork with salt and pepper and arrange the sage, cheese, and sausages over it evenly. Roll it up on the long side and tie with string. Dust the roast with flour.

Heat the oil and butter in a frying pan and brown the roast all over. Add the wine and simmer until it is reduced by half. Transfer the roast and liquid to a roasting pan just large enough to comfortably hold it. Add the broth. Roast for 1 hour.

Remove the roast and let cool 10 minutes before cutting into ½-inch-thick slices.

Strain the liquid in the pan and serve with the pork.

One 2½-pound boneless pork loin, butterflied (cut open) lengthwise and flattened until ⅓ inch thick
Salt and freshly ground pepper
4 sage leaves, coarsely chopped
8 ounces scamorza or provolone cheese, thinly sliced
3 cooked Italian sausages, cut into ¼-inch-thick slices
All-purpose flour
2 tablespoons olive oil
2 tablespoons unsalted butter
½ cup dry white wine
1 cup vegetable broth

Cosciotto di 'Agnello al Forno "Una Mia Idea" (Roasted Lamb "My Idea")

SERVES 6

Preheat the oven to 350 degrees.

Heat the olive oil in a deep, heavy pot until hot but not smoking. Season the lamb with salt and pepper, place in the pan, and brown on all sides.

Add the potatoes, garlic, onion, rosemary, and water. Cover and cook for 1 hour, basting occasionally with the liquid in the pan.

Let rest 10 minutes before serving. Cut roast into thin slices.

2 tablespoons olive oil
One 2½-pound boneless leg of lamb, tied
Salt and freshly ground pepper
1½ pounds small baking potatoes, peeled and cubed
3 garlic cloves, chopped
1 large onion, thinly sliced
1 tablespoon fresh rosemary
1 cup water

Pasticcio di Pollo (Chicken Soufflé)

If you like, the chicken can be cooked ahead of time and set aside until you are ready to make the soufflé.

SERVES 6

1 small onion, quartered
1 medium carrot, peeled and
  sliced
1 stalk celery, sliced
One 2½-pound chicken
Salt and freshly ground pepper
2 cups béchamel sauce (Salsa
  Besciamella, page 37)
Pinch freshly grated nutmeg
2 tablespoons unsalted butter
½ cup freshly grated Parmesan
  cheese
6 large eggs, separated

Bring 2 quarts of water to a boil in a large pot with the onion, carrot, and celery. Add the chicken and salt and pepper to taste and return to a boil. Reduce the heat and simmer for 1 hour or until cooked, stirring and turning the chicken occasionally. Remove the pan from the heat and set it aside to cool.

When the chicken is at room temperature, drain it and remove the skin and bones. Finely chop all the meat and set it aside in a large bowl.

Prepare the béchamel sauce and add a pinch of nutmeg. Pour the sauce over the chicken, add the butter and Parmesan cheese, and mix well. Season to taste with salt and pepper. Let cool for 5 minutes, then, 1 by 1, mix in the egg yolks.

Preheat the oven to 350 degrees.

Butter a 2-quart soufflé dish.

Beat the egg whites until firm but not stiff. Carefully fold the egg whites into chicken mixture. Transfer the mixture to the prepared soufflé dish and cook for 40 minutes or until the soufflé has puffed up and is golden brown on top. Serve immediately.

La Casa di Annunziata (Annunziata's House)

On a freezing winter night about forty years ago, Annunziata, a woman who worked for our neighbors, knocked at our door. She was crying, and she hadn't come alone. Behind her, shivering with cold, were her four children and Minico, her husband. They had been cruelly evicted from their home by their master over some trivial matter and had nowhere to go.

Immediately my father ordered that beds, linens, blankets, and pillows be brought

to a little empty house adjacent to the abbey, at the edge of the park. A pile of wood was delivered, a fire lit in the hearth. My grandmother arranged for dried fava beans, lentils, and other foods to be taken to Annunziata so she could prepare a pot of hot, hearty soup.

Annunziata and Minico thanked us and asked permission to stay a few nights until they could find work and a place to live. They stayed for twenty years. Annunziata became our maid, and Minico a gardener and field-worker.

I spent many afternoons of my childhood, especially during the summers and holidays, in that small stone cottage, which we always referred to as La Casa di Annunziata. That house eventually became my refuge. My brother and I played with their children, Nino, Francesco, Gaetano, and Anna. They were the only other children close by, and they were welcome company.

When we weren't playing games, we loved listening, breathlessly, to Annunziata and Minico's ghost stories about the local countryside. And, as time passed, they began to tell tales heard from other servants at Gangivecchio about Gangivecchio itself. One was about a young monk who lived in the abbey long ago. He fell in love with a beautiful young girl in Gangi, but when she married another man, the distraught young monk hanged himself inside Gangivecchio.

Another tale was that after my grandfather died, his ghost began appearing. Grandfather had a passion for English peppermint talcum powder. One night, during a bad storm, a lost man was taken in and spent the night in my grandfather's old bedroom. The next morning, the man discovered peppermint talcum powder sprinkled on the bed. Since we believed every word, stories like these only stretched our already fertile imaginations into the shadows and darkness where the spirits lived.

It was fascinating for me to move from the sophisticated kitchen of my house at Gangivecchio to Annunziata's *cucina povera* kitchen. Annunziata's kitchen was where I had the first occasion to eat the authentic food of *I contadini* (the country people)—simple meatless pasta dishes full of onions and garlic and herbs, indeed, any edible, tasty wild thing that grew in the ground. Annunziata used fresh eggs for plain but delicious *frocia* (omelettes), flavored with cinnamon. Minico planted a home garden. Soon more vegetables materialized. Annunziata's *padella* (frying pan) of simmering potatoes, onions, and sweet and hot peppers produced an irresistible aroma that wafted through

the park all the way to the window of my room, making me long to be there rather than at home.

I learned my great fear of turkeys at Annunziata's house. My granny gave her an enormous turkey for their family's Christmas meal one year. When it arrived, I approached the bird for a closer inspection. The turkey proceeded to chase me around, wildly flapping its wings, ruffling its feathers, squawking, and pecking at my legs. Everyone found this amusing, except for me. I was quite pleased to see this beast silent and roasted in a big pan, unable to chase me.

When I was eighteen, the local *contadini* organized an enormous dinner and dance party to celebrate San Giuseppe (St. Joseph's Day), on March 19. The party was to be held at the

biggest house available among friends of the community. Because I belonged to a different social world, I wasn't invited, but I enthusiastically participated in planning the dishes for the dinner that preceded the dance. Everyone brought dishes for this feast. There can never be too much food at a San Giuseppe celebration. I still remember the menu: pasta with almonds, roast pork with pecorino cheese, salt cod with wild fennel, lamb with beans, and little cakes called *cucchie* (hearts of currants). The *contadini* spent all their combined saved lire for this banquet.

The day after the party, I ran to Annunziata's to hear the report. The food, music, and dancing had been wonderful, but something unexpected had occurred. Annunziata was deeply distressed. For the first time I faced the harsh realities and consequences of the strict rules of the society of the Sicilian *contadini*.

Annunziata's son, Gaetano, then twenty, had danced so energetically that he was sweating like a fountain. He asked a girl named Maria for her handkerchief to dry his face. In such a public place, this action was interpreted as a gesture of deep familiarity. If Gaetano and Maria didn't marry within a year, a big scandal would erupt. So they did marry, and, after a few years, divorced. Later, no one concerned themselves about the private matter of a divorce.

In 1974 Annunziata's family moved to a new apartment in Gangi. They found other jobs, and their children were now adults. A chapter in my life closed. Annunziata died in 1987 at the age of eighty-five.

Ivy and other vines slowly covered the house at the edge of the park. The home garden turned to weeds and wild herbs. The windows became glassless somber black eyes without tears. The house waited patiently to be cheerful again, to hear new stories and laughter—a rebirth that I thought would never come.

In January of 1997, Mamma announced that, for practical purposes of income, we would restore Annunziata's house. She also knew that these plans would please me. Workers appeared and began the task. The house was totally renovated: a new roof and new stonework, including planters and a little terrace with an herb garden. There is a new fireplace, gleaming glass windows and doors, and, for the first time, plumbing and electricity. Mamma, Paolo, and I furnished the house with antiques from Gangivecchio and Palermo.

We had our first guests in April of 1998. Annunziata's house has become a separate part of the *albergo,* Tenuta Gangivecchio, where people can rent the one-bedroom cottage for a week or even a month to enjoy the privacy and evoke the feeling of having their own small home in the Sicilian countryside. A little hand-painted ceramic sign on the outside of the house reads "La Casa di Annunziata," announcing to all that she lives again.

Stemperata di Pollo

(Chicken with Vegetables, Green Olives, Capers, and Mint)

SERVES 4

One 3½-pound chicken, cut into
    8 serving pieces
Salt and freshly ground pepper
Olive oil
½ cup dry red wine
2 medium potatoes, peeled and
    cubed
2 small eggplants, cubed
2 red bell peppers, cored, seeded,
    and cut into thin strips
2 medium carrots, peeled and
    thinly sliced
½ cup pitted green olives, Sicilian
    if possible, quartered
2 tablespoons chopped celery
2 tablespoons capers
2 tablespoons freshly chopped
    mint
6 garlic cloves, minced
2 tablespoons tomato paste
½ cup red wine vinegar
Hot pepper flakes

Pat the chicken dry and season with salt and pepper. In a big frying pan, heat 3 tablespoons of olive oil. Add the chicken and sauté until golden brown on each side, about 5 minutes per side. Add the wine. Turn the chicken pieces. Simmer, partially covered, for 25 minutes, turning once halfway through the cooking time.

Meanwhile, sauté the potatoes, eggplants, red peppers, and carrots, in separate pans with ½ cup of olive oil in each, until tender, stirring often. The potatoes should be golden brown.

Put the vegetables in a large pan with the olives, celery, capers, mint, and garlic. Stir in the tomato paste and vinegar. Season to taste with salt, pepper, and hot pepper flakes. Add the chicken. Combine well. Simmer over low heat for 15 minutes, occasionally stirring gently.

Transfer to a serving dish. Bring to room temperature before serving.

Petto di Tacchino Farcito alla Siciliana

(Sicilian Stuffed Turkey Breast)

SERVES 8

Spread out the boned turkey breast on a work surface.

Soak the bread in the milk for 30 seconds. Squeeze out excess milk. Place the bread in a large bowl with the pork, veal, ham, salami, eggs, Parmesan cheese, basil, salt and pepper to taste, and hot pepper flakes. Mix well.

Stuff the turkey with this mixture and tie the opening in back securely with kitchen string. In a large heavy-bottomed pot heat 1 cup of olive oil. Add the onions and garlic, and cook for 5 minutes, stirring often. Stir in the tomato paste and add 1 cup of hot water. Stir in the bouillon cubes, rosemary, salt and pepper to taste, hot pepper flakes, and the sugar. Stir and cook until the bouillon cubes have dissolved. Add the stuffed turkey breast, breast side up. Cover the turkey with cool water. Sprinkle the surface of the water with the flour, cover and slowly bring to a boil. When a boil is reached, cook over low heat for 2 hours, turning occasionally.

Remove the turkey from the pan to a carving board.

Pass the sauce from the pan through a food mill. Serve it with the sliced turkey.

One 7-to-8-pound turkey breast
Six ½-inch-thick slices Italian bread
1 cup milk
¾ pound ground pork
¾ pound ground veal
¾ cup boiled ham, thinly sliced and cut into thin strips
½ cup diced salami
2 large eggs, lightly beaten
⅔ cup freshly grated Parmesan cheese
2 tablespoons freshly chopped basil
Salt and freshly ground pepper
Pinch hot pepper flakes
Olive oil
2 large onions, thinly sliced
2 large garlic cloves, chopped
2 tablespoons tomato paste
2 vegetable bouillon cubes
2 beef bouillon cubes
1 tablespoon freshly chopped rosemary
Pinch sugar
2 tablespoons all-purpose flour

Tacchino Impanato (Fried Herb-Breaded Turkey Breast Cutlets)

3 cups fresh bread crumbs

¼ cup freshly grated pecorino cheese

¼ cup freshly grated Parmesan cheese

⅓ cup freshly chopped Italian parsley

6 mint leaves, freshly chopped

6 basil leaves, freshly chopped

1 small onion, minced

Pinch hot pepper flakes

Salt and freshly ground pepper

3 large eggs, lightly beaten

Six 6-ounce turkey breast cutlets, flattened to ⅓-inch thickness

4 tablespoons unsalted butter

¼ cup sunflower oil

¼ cup olive oil

In a large bowl, mix together the bread crumbs, two cheeses, herbs, onion, and hot pepper flakes and season with salt and pepper.

Place the eggs in a shallow dish and season with salt and pepper. Coat the turkey cutlets on each side with the egg. Then coat each cutlet with the bread crumb mixture.

Heat the butter and oils in a large frying pan. Fry the breaded cutlets until golden brown on each side—cook over medium heat for the first 5 minutes, then reduce heat to medium-low. Cook in batches if necessary, or use 2 frying pans. Add extra olive oil if needed. Drain on paper towels and serve at once. Mamma says a fresh tomato salad goes very well with this dish.

Secondi di Pesce e Frutti di Mare

(Fish and Seafood Main-Course Dishes)

Involtini di Tonno *(Stuffed Tuna Rolls)*

Spigole alla Salvia *(Sea Bass with Sage)*

Cernia in Umido con Verdure
(Braised Grouper with Vegetables)

Orate Gratinate *(Gratin of Sea Bream)*

Impanata di Pesce Spada e Verdure
(Swordfish and Vegetable Pie)

Salmone Capriccioso *(Capricious Salmon)*

Una Lezione di Pesca *(A Fishing Lesson)*

Sarde Farcite Ripiene *(Fried Stuffed Sardines)*

Pesce di Ischia *(Fish Cooked in the Style of Ischia)*

Gamberi di Wanda *(Wanda's Shrimp)*

Gamberi in Crosta alla Gangivecchio
(Gangivecchio's Shrimp in Pastry)

L'Aragosta del Fidanzato Imaginario
(The Imaginary Fiancé's Lobster)

Tagliatelline con Salsa di Triglie
(Tagliatelline with Red Mullet Sauce)

Un Abbondante Messe dal Mediterraneo

(A Bountiful Mediterranean Harvest)

Una dieta di pesce e' un nutrimento perfetto.

(A diet of fish is the perfect nourishment.)

I can say without reservation that either seafood or fish is my favorite main course at any meal. After years of suffering up here in the mountains with no fresh fish nearby, we now have a proper fish market in Gangi. In the past, it was a big event when the fishmonger arrived in his truck once a week, even though his offerings were very limited. Now we have wonderful, fresh fish every day. Santo, the owner of the market, travels to the coast, to Cefalù or Porticello, every evening except Sunday, to buy the freshest fish from the day's catch. At 9 a.m., when he opens the door to his market, there is already a line.

When I am in Palermo, or any other place by the sea, I must go to the fish market to examine the magnificent fresh seafood. In old Palermo, there's the big old, bustling Vucciria market—not to be missed. But there are also the Capo, Ballaro, and Borgo Vecchio markets. The last is small but conveniently located near the center of town, and it is usually not too crowded. The Borgo Vecchio's fish stalls display only the freshest, finest seafood: shining red mullet, sparkling salmon, dentex, tuna, and grouper, as well as lobsters, shrimp, sea urchins, squid, octopus, mussels, and clams, to name only a few. Whenever I'm there, I can rarely resist spending a healthy sum of lire on a luscious swordfish steak—a fantastic price for a fantastic fish. I truly believe that a diet of fish is the perfect nourishment.

Involtini di Tonno (Stuffed Tuna Rolls)

SERVES 4

½ cup dried bread crumbs
¼ cup freshly grated pecorino
   cheese
¼ cup pine nuts
¼ cup currants
¾ cup olive oil, plus more as
   needed
Salt and freshly ground pepper
2 pounds tuna pieces, approximately 3 inches wide and
   6–7 inches long, cut into
   ¼-inch-thick slices
1 large onion, finely chopped
½ cup dry white wine

In a medium-sized bowl, mix together the bread crumbs, pecorino, pine nuts, and currants. Sprinkle a little olive oil over the
mixture to moisten it. Season with salt and pepper and
combine.

Spread equal amounts of the mixture down the center of each
slice of tuna and smooth evenly. Roll up and secure the end of
each roll with a toothpick.

Heat ½ cup of olive oil in a large frying pan. Sauté the onion
over medium heat until it begins to turn golden brown, stirring
often. Arrange the tuna rolls over the onion in a single layer, seam
side down. Sprinkle with salt and pepper to taste. Add the wine
and simmer for 20 minutes. Carefully transfer tuna rolls and sauce
to a serving dish. Discard toothpicks. Serve hot.

Spigole alla Salvia (Sea Bass with Sage)

SERVES 4

Four 1½-pound sea bass,
   thoroughly cleaned and
   left whole
½ cup olive oil
Salt and freshly ground pepper
2 tablespoons freshly chopped
   sage
2 garlic cloves, quartered
½ cup dried bread crumbs
4 sprigs parsley
2 lemons, cut into wedges
   and seeded

Place the fish in a shallow glass or ceramic dish and sprinkle with
oil, salt and pepper to taste, sage, and garlic. Turn the fish to coat
evenly. Cover and refrigerate for 2 hours.

Preheat the oven to 350 degrees.

Discard the garlic clove quarters. Coat each fish evenly with the
bread crumbs. Arrange the fish in a shallow baking dish, side by
side but not touching. Sprinkle the marinade around the fish.
Cover the pan with aluminum foil and bake for 45 minutes. Garnish each serving with a parsley sprig. Serve hot with the lemon
wedges.

Cernia in Umido con Verdure

(Braised Grouper with Vegetables)

SERVES 4

Heat the olive oil in a large frying pan with the garlic, onion, and carrots. Season to taste with salt and pepper. Cook over medium heat for 5 minutes, stirring often.

Meanwhile, in a small bowl, thoroughly combine the butter, parsley, lemon zest, and lemon juice. Spread equal amounts of this mixture evenly over both sides of each fillet.

Preheat the oven to 350 degrees.

Place the coated fillets in the pan with the chopped vegetables, add the wine, and cook over medium heat for 5 minutes.

With a spatula, transfer the grouper fillets to a shallow baking dish. Spoon the remaining ingredients and sauce over and around the grouper fillets. Top each piece of fish with a bay leaf. Cover with aluminum foil and bake for 20 minutes. Serve hot. We like to serve this dish with hot boiled spinach, well drained and seasoned only with a dash of nutmeg, salt, and pepper.

¼ cup olive oil
2 garlic cloves, minced
1 medium onion, chopped
2 medium carrots, peeled and diced
Salt and freshly ground pepper
4 tablespoons unsalted butter, softened
½ cup freshly minced Italian parsley
2 teaspoons grated lemon zest
Freshly squeezed juice of 1 lemon
Four 6-ounce grouper fillets
½ cup dry white wine
4 bay leaves

Orate Gratinate (Gratin of Sea Bream)

SERVES 4

Preheat the oven to 350 degrees. Heat the broiler.

Heat the oil in a large frying pan and sauté the fillets on each side until they begin to turn golden.

Arrange the onion slices on the bottom of a shallow baking dish. Top with the sautéed fillets. Sprinkle with salt and pepper. Pour in the milk and bake for 30 minutes.

Sprinkle with the Parmesan cheese and briefly place under the broiler until golden brown.

¼ cup olive oil
4 sea bream, porgy, or red snapper, cleaned and filleted
1 large onion, thinly sliced
Salt and freshly ground pepper
1 cup milk
¼ cup freshly grated Parmesan cheese

Impanata di Pesce Spada e Verdure
(Swordfish and Vegetable Pie)

In Sicily, we have many ways of cooking our marvelous swordfish. But Messina, in the straits between the island and the continent, where swordfish are caught in large numbers, is famous for inventive, delectable dishes like this one.

SERVES 6

½ cup olive oil
1 medium onion, chopped
½ cup chopped celery
½ cup pitted and chopped green
   olives (Sicilian, if possible)

In a large frying pan, heat the oil and cook the onion until it begins to turn golden brown, about 5 minutes, stirring often. Add the celery and cook over medium heat for 5 minutes. Stir in the olives, capers, and raisins. Season to taste with salt and pepper. Combine well and simmer for 10 minutes.

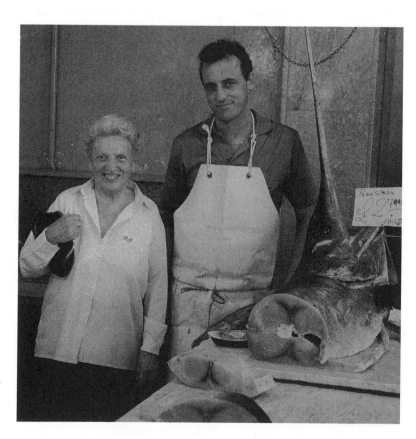

Wanda at the fish market. "I can rarely resist spending a healthy sum of lire on a luscious swordfish steak." – G.T.

Stir in the tomatoes and swordfish. Cook over medium-low heat for 10 minutes, stirring often. Taste for seasoning. Transfer to a shallow bowl and set aside to cool for 15 minutes.

Preheat the oven to 375 degrees.

Butter and flour a 9-inch round baking pan. Set aside.

Divide the Pasta Frolla dough in half. Roll out each half into a 12-inch circle. Fit 1 circle into the pan, letting the extra dough hang over the edge. Spoon the seafood mixture over the dough. Cover with the second piece of dough and seal the edges securely by pinching them together or pressing them with the tines of a fork. With a knife, make several evenly spaced short slashes or little holes in the top of the dough. Brush the top with the egg yolk. Cook for 40 minutes or until the top is golden brown. Remove from oven and let cool. Serve at room temperature.

2 tablespoons capers, rinsed and drained
½ cup raisins, soaked in tepid water for 10 minutes and drained
Salt and freshly ground pepper
1 cup chopped fresh tomatoes
2 pounds swordfish, cut into 1-inch cubes
½ recipe for Pasta Frolla Piccante (page 37), worked with the grated zest of 1 orange
1 large egg yolk, beaten

Salmone Capriccioso (Capricious Salmon)

SERVES 4

In an extra-large frying pan, heat the oil until very hot but not smoking. Lightly sear the fish on each side. Pour in the wine and allow it to evaporate over low heat.

Add the onion, rosemary, and diluted tomato paste and season to taste with salt and pepper. Cover and simmer for 20 minutes, turning once halfway through.

Uncover, and sprinkle the lemon juice over the salmon. Let it cool in the pan.

Transfer the salmon to a serving platter. Pour the sauce onto the platter. Pat the top of the salmon dry and arrange the cucumber slices across it in rows.

¼ cup olive oil
One 2½-pound whole salmon, thoroughly cleaned and skinned, head and tail removed
½ cup dry white wine
1 medium onion, sliced
2 tablespoons chopped fresh rosemary
1 tablespoon tomato paste diluted in 1 cup hot water
Salt and freshly ground pepper
Freshly squeezed juice of 1 lemon
1 medium cucumber, peeled and thinly sliced

Una Lezione di Pesca (A Fishing Lesson)

When I was a girl of fourteen, born and raised by the sea, we lived in a house called Romagnolo, on the outskirts of Palermo. The front of the house faced the sea, and in the back there was a green yard with lemon, orange, and other fruit trees. To me, it was the center of the universe.

At fourteen, I was a strange, lonely creature. The sea was a mysterious source of dreams, adventures, and fantastic tales. Each morning, as I watched the big fishing boats go out to sea, listening to the steady, purposeful, knocking sound of the motors, I had an incredible yearning to accompany them. We often waved to the fishermen, and one day I asked one of them if my brother and I could go out with him on his boat (I was too afraid to go alone). He laughed and said, "*Certo*, ma . . ." Certainly, *but* . . . only if your mother agrees.

The boats left at 5 a.m., so, without telling our mother, my brother and I snuck out of the house late at night and slept in an empty cabin on the shore near the fishing boats. (Actually, I don't think we slept at all, worrying about demons and being late.)

We arrived on time and were given a spot on the boat to sit and keep out of the way. The knocking sound of the motor was much louder onboard. The fishermen yelled out orders to each other and called out cheerfully to men on other boats as they passed. All this blaring noise was music to my ears.

The wind blew on our faces and attacked our hair, and we gleefully drank in the scent of the intoxicating sea. The sun rose and lit up the glistening, watery world. When the fishermen began hauling in the nets, filled with silvery fish of all sizes turning and jumping helplessly in their agony, my joy ceased. I turned away in tears, refusing to watch.

I recovered later when the fishermen brought out a big frying pan and began cooking sardines, shrimp, and anchovies on the bridge of the boat, frying them together, seasoning them only with olive oil and salt and pepper. I watched the pale-blue smoke rising from the pan; I smelled, from the cooking fish, the sensual scent of the sea, and then I ate every morsel heaped on my plate. I was gently told that an end to life also gave the gift of life. At that moment, I felt very grown up, but, of course, I was just a foolish, dreamy adolescent on an adventure, learning a lesson of life. Another lesson of life followed shortly: the harsh reprimand from our mother. But my lifelong love affair with the astonishing fruit of the sea began on that day.

—Wanda Tornabene

Sarde Farcite Ripiene

(Fried Stuffed Sardines)

SERVES 6

Put the bread, tuna, fennel, and parsley into a food processor. Season with salt and pepper and process for 10 seconds. Add a little olive oil through the feed tube until you have a thick, creamy mixture.

Line up half of the sardine fillets on a work surface, skin side down. Spoon equal amounts of the filling evenly across each sardine. Cover each with the remaining fillets, bone side down. Press each sardine sandwich gently together. Coat the sardines with flour.

Heat 3 cups of olive oil in a large, deep frying pan until hot but not smoking. Cook the sardines in batches until golden brown on each side, carefully turning the sardines with tongs or 2 spoons. Drain on paper towels.

To make the sauce, heat the oil with the oregano and wine in a small pan until it just boils. Season with salt and pepper. Serve the sardines hot with the sauce.

Six 1-inch-thick slices Italian bread, torn into small pieces
One 6⅛-ounce can oil-packed tuna, drained
1 fennel bulb, white part, cleaned and chopped, and ½ cup finely chopped feathery green tops
½ cup freshly chopped Italian parsley
Salt and freshly ground pepper
3 cups olive oil, plus a little extra for filling
36 thoroughly cleaned sardine fillets of 18 sardines (see page 114)
All-purpose flour

FOR SAUCE

½ cup extra virgin olive oil
1 teaspoon dried oregano
2 tablespoons dry white wine
Salt and freshly ground pepper

Pesce di Ischia (Fish Cooked in the Style of Ischia)

The small island of Ischia, near Capri, is covered with lemon trees, so it's no surprise that the people of Ischia like to use lemon in cooking. The simple recipe, using lots of lemon juice to braise almost any fish, is *molto gustoso* (very tasty).

SERVES 4

Four 6-ounce fillets of bass, cod, grouper, or salmon
Salt and freshly ground pepper
2 tablespoons freshly chopped Italian parsley
2 garlic cloves, thinly sliced
1 medium-large onion, thinly sliced
⅓ cup freshly squeezed lemon juice

Season the fish fillets with salt and pepper, and put them in a medium frying pan. Sprinkle the parsley, garlic, and onion slices over the fish. Add the lemon juice and just enough water to cover the fish. Slowly bring to a boil over medium heat. When the water boils, reduce the heat and simmer for 10 minutes. Turn each fish fillet. Simmer for 10 more minutes. Serve the fish hot. Spoon 2 tablespoons of the liquid from the pan over each serving.

Gamberi di Wanda (Wanda's Shrimp)

SERVES 4

2 tablespoons dried porcini mushrooms
½ cup olive oil, plus extra for topping
1 medium onion, finely chopped
1 medium carrot, peeled and finely chopped
1 celery stalk with leaves, finely chopped
2 garlic cloves, minced
2 anchovies, chopped
1½ cups fish broth
2 pounds extra-large shrimp, shelled and deveined

Soak the dried mushrooms in ½ cup hot water for 30 minutes. Drain well, finely chop, and set aside.

In a large saucepan, heat the oil until hot but not smoking. Add the onion, carrot, celery, garlic, anchovies, and fish broth. Cook over medium heat for 10 minutes, stirring occasionally.

Add the mushrooms and the shrimp, and combine well. Simmer for 15 minutes, stirring occasionally, adding a little water if necessary.

Preheat the oven to 375 degrees.

Remove the pan from the heat. Season the mixture to taste with salt and pepper.

Spoon equal amounts of the shrimp, vegetable mixture, and liquid into each of 4 individual au gratin dishes. Sprinkle the top of each with equal amounts of pine nuts. Drizzle a little olive oil

over each. Bake for 5 minutes. Sprinkle with equal amounts of the parsley and a pinch of hot pepper flakes and serve hot.

Salt and freshly ground pepper
2 tablespoons coarsely chopped
    pine nuts
4 teaspoons freshly chopped
    Italian parsley
Hot pepper flakes

Gamberi in Crosta alla Gangivecchio
(Gangivecchio's Shrimp in Pastry)

Mamma has fallen in love with frozen puff pastry, because, as she says, "My arms no longer love to roll out dough. And the product is excellent." With this "miracle" dough, she has created countless pastries and tarts with creamy fillings and fruit toppings and many other desserts. And now, she has moved on to seafood dishes, and proudly serves this savory dish at home on special occasions, especially birthdays.

SERVES 4

Heat the oil and 2 tablespoons of the butter in a large frying pan. Stir in the garlic, mushrooms, and parsley and season with salt and pepper. Cook over medium heat for about 10 minutes, stirring often. Add the shrimp and cod and simmer for about 5 minutes until cooked, stirring occasionally.

Meanwhile, mash the flour with the remaining 2 tablespoons of butter. Bring the milk to a boil in a small saucepan. Whisk in the flour and butter mixture and stir until the sauce thickens. Season to taste with salt and pepper. Stir the sauce into the mushroom and seafood mixture. Check for seasoning. Transfer the mixture into a shallow dish and cool for 15 minutes.

Preheat the oven to 375 degrees.

Lightly dust a work area with flour and roll out the pastry sheets to ⅛-inch thickness. Cut eight 5-inch circles out of the pastry sheets. Put 4 of the circles onto a baking sheet several inches apart. Using a slotted spoon, put equal amounts of the seafood

2 tablespoons olive oil
4 tablespoons unsalted butter
1 garlic clove, minced
12 ounces portabello mushrooms,
    cleaned and coarsely chopped
2 tablespoons freshly chopped
    Italian parsley
Salt and freshly ground pepper
⅓ pound raw shrimp, chopped
½ pound cod fillets, cut into
    small pieces
2 tablespoons flour
½ cup milk
2 sheets (1 pound) frozen puff
    pastry, thawed
1 large egg yolk

mixture over the circles. Top each with 1 of the remaining round pieces of puff pastry. Seal the edges of the top and bottom pieces of pastry by pressing them together with your fingers and rolling a serrated pastry cutter around the edges. Brush the tops with egg yolk. Bake for 25 minutes or until golden brown. Serve hot.

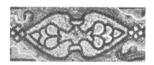

L'Aragosta del Fidanzato Imaginario

(The Imaginary Fiancé's Lobster)

We sampled this lovely dish at a seaside restaurant near Trapani, on Sicily's west coast. Mamma was so enthusiastic about it, she asked the cook for the recipe. The woman who was the custodian of the treasure flatly refused. Undaunted, Mamma invented a story about my beastly imaginary fiancé, who, after five years, still would not set a wedding date. Mamma whispered to the woman, "Surely if Giovanna served him your fantastic dish, he would find the voice to name this important date." I, the accomplice, with an expression of hope and gratitude spread across my face, thanked her profusely as Mamma tucked the cook's recipe into her purse.

It was only when we got home that Mamma realized she'd been caught in her lie. The recipe the cook had given her wasn't for anything remotely resembling the lobster dish. Mamma recalled all the unbelievable stories guests at our restaurant used to tell her to get her to reveal her recipes. (Of course, that was before our first cookbook.) Anyway, Mamma was furious and said we'd never return to that restaurant. Then, with a look of guilt, she admitted she would be too ashamed and embarrassed. But, Mamma, being Mamma, worked hard at re-creating this delicious recipe from memory.

Fill a large pot with enough water to completely cover the lobsters when they are dropped in. Add the carrots, onion, and wine to the water, and bring to a boil. Drop in the lobsters and boil for about 25 minutes. Thoroughly drain the lobsters in a colander and let cool. Extract the meat from the lobsters, taking care to leave the tails in one piece. Cover and refrigerate for at least 2 hours.

Meanwhile, make the mayonnaise. In a small bowl, whisk the egg yolks while adding the combined oils in a slow, steady stream. Whisk in the mustard and vinegar. Season to taste with salt and pepper. Cover and refrigerate until needed.

When ready to assemble the dish, cut the lobster tails into medallions and set aside. Chop the remaining lobster.

Transfer the mayonnaise to a large bowl and add the potatoes, green beans, peas, and chopped lobster. Mix well and season to taste with salt and pepper.

Arrange the radicchio and romaine leaves on the bottom of a large round serving dish. Spoon the lobster salad into the center. Arrange the lobster medallions in a circle around the salad. Garnish with the cherry tomatoes, egg halves, and parsley.

Two 2-pound lobsters
2 medium carrots, peeled and sliced
1 large onion, quartered
1 cup dry white wine
1 cup boiled potatoes, cut into ½-inch cubes and chilled
1 cup boiled green beans, cut into 1-inch lengths and chilled
1 cup boiled peas, chilled
Salt and freshly ground pepper
6 whole radicchio leaves
6 whole romaine lettuce leaves
12 cherry tomatoes
6 hard-boiled eggs, chilled and halved lengthwise
Bouquet of fresh parsley for garnish

MAYONNAISE

2 large egg yolks
½ cup olive oil
½ cup corn oil
1 teaspoon Dijon mustard
1 tablespoon white wine vinegar
Salt and freshly ground pepper

Tagliatelline con Salsa di Triglie

(Tagliatelline with Red Mullet Sauce)

SERVES 4

1¼ cups plus 4 tablespoons olive oil

2½ pounds small whole red mullet, cleaned, with skin left intact

Salt and freshly ground pepper

⅓ cup freshly chopped Italian parsley

⅛ teaspoon ground saffron

1 pound tagliatelline

¾ cup fresh bread crumbs

In a large frying pan, heat 1¼ cups olive oil until hot but not smoking. Fry the mullets on each side until the skin turns golden brown, turning 2 or 3 times. Drain on paper towels. When cool enough to handle, remove the skin from each side of the mullet. Coarsely chop the skin and reserve.

Fillet the fish and discard the bones. Break the cooked fillets into small pieces.

Return the pieces of mullet fillet to the frying pan, season with salt and pepper, and sauté over low heat for 5 minutes. Remove the pan from the heat and stir in the parsley. Transfer the mixture to a bowl.

Bring 4 quarts of water to a boil in a large pot. Add 1½ tablespoons of salt and the saffron. Stir in the pasta and cook until al dente, stirring often.

Meanwhile, heat 2 tablespoons of olive oil in a medium frying pan. Add the chopped fish skin. Cook over high heat, stirring often, until nicely crisp. Remove and drain. Process the fish skins in a food processor for 30 seconds.

Combine the fish skins and bread crumbs in a bowl. Heat 2 tablespoons of olive oil in a clean medium frying pan and toast the combined skin and bread crumbs, stirring often, for about 4 minutes. Remove from heat.

Drain the pasta, reserving 1 cup of cooking liquid. Return the pasta to the pan. Add the fish mixture plus ½ cup of the hot pasta water. Toss well. Season to taste with salt and pepper. Add more hot pasta water if necessary.

Transfer the pasta to a serving bowl. Sprinkle with the skin and bread crumb mixture.

Verdure

(Vegetables)

Sformato di Asparagi, Patate, e Funghi
  (Asparagus, Potato, and Mushroom Cake)

Carciofi al Limone di Lina
  (Lina's Lemon-Flavored Artichokes)

CARDI *(Cardoons)*

Cardi Imbottiti *(Fried Stuffed Cardoons)*

Cardi ed Acciughe al Forno
  (Baked Cardoons with Anchovies)

Cavolfiore alla Pizzaiola *(Cauliflower Pizza)*

Involtini di Melanzane *(Stuffed Eggplant Rolls)*

Tegame di Verdure *(Vegetable Flan)*

Misto di Verdure in Crosta
  (Mixed Vegetables in Pastry)

Patate Siciliane alla Pizzaiola
  (Sicilian-Style Potato Pizza)

Funghi e Patate *(Mushrooms and Potatoes)*

Patate Ripiene *(Stuffed Baked Potatoes)*

Patate con Alloro *(Baked Potatoes with Bay Leaves)*

La Caponata di Peperoni di Wanda
  (Wanda's Pepper Caponata)

Zucca Rossa d'Inverno Marinata
  (Marinated Red Winter Pumpkin)

Refer to the Antipasti chapter for more delicious vegetable dishes.

Regali dall'Orto

(Gifts from the Garden)

Un cesto di verdure in cucina significa un salutare e delizioso pasto.

(A basket of fresh vegetables in the kitchen means a healthy and delicious meal.)

Vegetables have always been the main component of the country table. The *contadini* were too poor to buy meat, and fish, beyond salt cod and preserved sardines, was unknown to them. If they were fortunate enough to own a cow, they made and sold cheese (which they called "fruit").

I arrived at Gangivecchio more than fifty years ago. I went around and visited the local inhabitants, listened to their stories and their complaints, and saw and tasted the humble dishes they made—*la Pietanza*—to survive. I learned how wonderful and comforting the *qualazzi,* a sort of wild *cime di rape* cooked with potatoes, can be. And *cicerchie,* similar to lentils, cooked with wild fennel, made a delicious dish. Winters were hardest for the country people, when many were forced to dig for roots.

Caterina, a small, round, ever-smiling woman, was my confidant. I learned from her that it was possible to be happy in life with only a few ingredients, mostly vegetables, on the table. She never complained. Before Caterina died four years ago, at the age of seventy-six, she told me: "Now that my son can provide me with all the meat I want, I can't eat it. But I've lived a very long life. I believe it's because I ate so many vegetables."

Indeed, the people who live in Mediterranean regions have always believed that fresh vegetables in the kitchen means healthy nourishment and a delicious dinner.

Sformato di Asparagi, Patate, e Funghi

(Asparagus, Potato, and Mushroom Cake)

SERVES 8

1 cup olive oil

4 garlic cloves, minced

2 pounds asparagus, cut into 1-inch lengths

½ cup water

Salt and freshly ground pepper

4 pounds potatoes, peeled and coarsely chopped

1 pound portabello or crimini mushrooms, cleaned and chopped

½ cup dried bread crumbs

6 large eggs, lightly beaten

¾ cup freshly grated pecorino or Parmesan cheese

2 tablespoons freshly chopped mint leaves

In a medium sauté pan, heat ½ cup of olive oil with half the garlic. Cook for 2 minutes over medium heat, stirring often. Add the asparagus and water. Season to taste with salt and pepper. Bring to a boil. Cook over medium heat, stirring occasionally, until asparagus is just tender, about 6 minutes. Set aside.

Meanwhile, bring 4 quarts of water to a boil in a large pot. Add 1 tablespoon of salt and the potatoes and cook until very tender.

While the potatoes are cooking, heat the remaining ½ cup of olive oil in a medium sauté pan with the remaining garlic. Cook for 2 minutes over medium heat, stirring often. Stir in the mushrooms. Season to taste with salt and pepper. Cook over medium heat, stirring often, until the mushrooms are cooked, about 10 minutes. Set aside.

Preheat the oven to 350 degrees.

Butter a 12-inch round baking pan with 3- to 4-inch sides. Coat with the bread crumbs. Set aside.

Drain the boiled potatoes and pass them through a food mill or ricer and into a large bowl. Add the eggs, cheese, and mint and season to taste with salt and pepper. Combine well. Spoon half of the mashed potatoes into the prepared pan and smooth the top evenly. Spoon the asparagus and mushrooms over the potatoes in the pan. Cover with the remaining half of the potatoes and smooth the top evenly. Bake for 40 minutes or until the edges are golden brown. Serve hot or at room temperature.

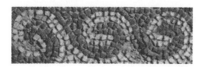

Carciofi al Limone di Lina

(Lina's Lemon-Flavored Artichokes)

This delicious artichoke dish comes from the recipe collection of our dear friend Lina Alberti. Lina is from Polizzi Generosa, a town not far from us in the Madonie Mountains, famous for its good cooking and its beautiful women.

SERVES 6

Put the oil, garlic, and onion into a large frying pan and cook over low heat for 2 minutes. Add the anchovies and stir with a wooden spoon until melted, about 4 minutes.

Add the artichoke hearts and mint leaves to the mixture. Season to taste with salt and pepper. Add water, cover, and simmer until artichokes are cooked—about 20 minutes if fresh or 10 minutes if frozen and thawed. If necessary, add a little extra water.

Sprinkle with the lemon juice and bread crumbs. Toss and cook 2 more minutes. Taste for seasoning and lemon flavor. Add a little extra juice, if desired.

Transfer to a shallow serving dish and cool. Serve at room temperature.

½ cup olive oil
3 garlic cloves, finely chopped
1 medium onion, finely chopped
2 anchovy fillets, chopped
12 fresh artichoke hearts, cleaned and quartered, or two 10-ounce packages frozen artichoke hearts, thawed and quartered
6 mint leaves, chopped
Salt and freshly ground pepper
3 tablespoons water
1 tablespoon freshly squeezed lemon juice, or to taste
½ cup toasted bread crumbs

Cardi (Cardoons)

Cardoons are thistles, each topped with a beautiful fluffy purple flower. They are related to artichokes. Although cardoons' delicate flavor is unique, it has hints of both celery and artichoke. Cardoons can be found in season in markets in America, especially in Italian neighborhoods or specialty shops.

I always look forward to cooking cardoons for family and guests at home or in the restaurant, particularly if foreign guests haven't tasted them before. I always coat the first cardoons of early spring with batter and deep-fry them, because, to me, they are best that way.

It's hard work to clean these silvery, green, meaty *cardi*, which resemble celery stalks but are much larger, some weighing up to four or five pounds. The thorns, leaves, and tough strings on the ribbed stalks must be stripped. Then, before preparing any dish, the cardoons must be boiled to remove their bitter taste. For every two or three pounds of cardoon you discard, you will have only one or two pounds to eat.

When I first came to Gangivecchio, wild vegetables were sold in the streets of the town; they were displayed in big baskets by women who collected them in the countryside. These women were experts at locating any edible plant—a talent passed from generation to generation. Twenty years later, Peppe arrived in our home as an inexperienced worker, but he had great natural talent. He became a superb forager, calling his wisdom simply a gift from God.

In time, I got into the habit of accompanying him by car to collect cardoons when they were in season. As he hunted, I waited for him along the border of country paths, or in the car, reading a book, writing poetry—sometimes for hours. I knew how difficult wild cardoons were to find, but when he was very late, I would be furious, thinking he'd forgotten about me, lost in the lovely sensation that pure nature provides—and knowing that our dear Peppe is distracted by anything. Of course, he always returned, and always with several *cardi*. At the sight of the *cardi* and his smiling face, all was immediately forgiven.

Back at home, Peppe immediately would begin the tedious task of cleaning the cardoons; they do not keep well. Then we would boil them until tender. That evening for dinner, we would all happily feast on the wonderful *cardi selvatici* (wild cardoons).

To Clean and Precook Cardoons

Cut the stalk end off the cardoon and separate the stalks. Throw away any withered or discolored stalks. Trim off the tops and discard the leaves and thorny edges by cutting down each side of the stalk. Remove the tough fiber strings on the outer side of the stalks, as you would remove the strings on celery. Use a vegetable peeler or a small sharp knife.

Cut the cleaned stalks into the size directed in individual recipes. They can also be cut straight or diagonally into small pieces, one to two inches long, for a simple but delicious au gratin (see below).

The cardoons must be boiled to get rid of their bitter taste. Bring 2½ quarts of water to a boil. Stir in 2 teaspoons of salt and add the cardoons. Cook at a low boil for about 20 minutes or until just tender. Taste frequently so you don't overcook them.

Drain the cooked cardoons. They are ready to be used in our recipes.

For a simple au gratin, toss the cardoons in melted butter, salt, and pepper and transfer to a greased au gratin dish. Sprinkle with a tablespoon of lemon juice or 3 tablespoons of heavy cream, and freshly grated Parmesan cheese. Bake in a 350-degree oven for 20 minutes, then briefly place under a hot broiler until golden brown.

You can also dip the prepared cardoon pieces into any batter and deep-fry until golden brown.

Cardi Imbottiti (Fried Stuffed Cardoons)

16 stalks cleaned, boiled, and
   dried cardoons (see box page
   177), cut into 6-inch lengths
8 anchovies, patted dry
¾ cup freshly grated pecorino
   cheese
2 large eggs, lightly beaten
Salt and freshly ground pepper
All-purpose flour
1 cup olive oil

Line up 8 of the cardoons on a work surface, cleaned side down. Put an anchovy down the center of each. Sprinkle equal amounts of the cheese over the top. Cover each with 1 of the remaining 8 cardoons, cleaned side up.

Brush the cardoons with beaten eggs, holding them carefully together as you brush each side. Season with salt and pepper and carefully coat with flour.

Heat the olive oil in a large frying pan and fry the cardoons until golden on each side. Carefully turn each stuffed cardoon to keep the bottom and top halves together. Drain on paper towels. Let rest 5 minutes before serving. Sprinkle with salt if you like.

Cardi ed Acciughe al Forno
(Baked Cardoons with Anchovies)

SERVES 6

20 stalks cleaned, boiled, and
   dried cardoons (see box page
   177), cut into 4-inch lengths
4 anchovy fillets, minced
½ cup diced fresh pecorino or
   provolone cheese
¼ cup freshly grated pecorino
   cheese
½ cup fresh bread crumbs
⅓ cup freshly chopped Italian
   parsley
Salt and freshly ground pepper
3 tablespoons melted unsalted
   butter
Olive oil

Preheat the oven to 350 degrees.

Oil a shallow 9-by-13-inch baking pan. Arrange the cardoon pieces in a single layer in the bottom of the pan. Sprinkle the minced anchovies and diced cheese evenly over the cardoons.

In a bowl, combine the grated cheese, bread crumbs, and parsley. Season with salt and pepper to taste. Sprinkle the mixture with the melted butter and toss well.

Sprinkle the mixture evenly over the cardoons. Drizzle the top with a little olive oil. Bake for 25 minutes or until golden on top. Serve hot.

Cavolfiore alla Pizzaiola (Cauliflower Pizza)

SERVES 6

Bring 1 quart of water to a boil. Stir in 1 teaspoon of salt and add the cauliflower. Cook for 10 minutes or until tender. Drain well.

Preheat the oven to 350 degrees.

Oil the bottom and sides of a 10-inch round baking pan. Line the bottom with half of the tomato slices. Sprinkle the tomatoes with half the bread crumbs, a pinch of hot pepper flakes, half the oregano, and salt to taste. Arrange half of the cauliflower pieces over the top and sprinkle with half of the Parmesan cheese. Repeat another layer, starting with the tomatoes, in the same manner. Drizzle the oil over the top. Bake for 20 minutes. Serve hot.

Salt

2 pounds cauliflower florets, cut into thin slices

1 pound ripe tomatoes, cut into thin slices

½ cup dried bread crumbs

Hot pepper flakes

1 teaspoon dried oregano

½ cup freshly grated Parmesan cheese

½ cup olive oil

Involtini di Melanzane (Stuffed Eggplant Rolls)

SERVES 4

In a medium sauté pan, heat 2 tablespoons of olive oil. Stir in the pork, onion, and celery. Cook over medium heat for 5 minutes, stirring often. Stir in the wine and cook over high heat for 1 minute. Stir in the tomato sauce, peas, and half of the parsley. Season to taste with salt and pepper. Simmer for 10 minutes over very low heat, stirring occasionally.

Dust the eggplant slices with flour. Heat enough oil in a large frying pan to generously cover the bottom. Fry the eggplant slices, in batches, until golden brown on each side. Drain on paper towels as cooked. Add more olive oil as needed.

Spread equal amounts of the ricotta over each fried eggplant slice and sprinkle with equal amounts of the diced ham and pecorino.

Roll up each eggplant slice and secure with a toothpick. Stir the sauce, and arrange eggplant rolls in a single layer in the pan with the sauce. Spoon some of the sauce over the tops of the rolls. Sim-

Olive oil

4 ounces ground pork shoulder

1 medium onion, finely chopped

1 celery stalk, diced

2 tablespoons dry white wine

1¾ cups fresh tomato sauce (Salsa di Pomodoro, page 95)

½ cup fresh or thawed frozen green peas

4 tablespoons freshly chopped Italian parsley

Salt and freshly ground pepper

4 small eggplants, cut into ⅛-inch-thick slices lengthwise

All-purpose flour

1 cup ricotta cheese

¾ cup minced boiled ham slices

¾ cup grated pecorino or
  Parmesan cheese

mer over low heat for 15 minutes, occasionally spooning some of the sauce over the rolls.

Gently transfer the *involtini* to a serving platter. Discard the toothpicks. Spoon sauce over and around the *involtini* and sprinkle the top with the remaining 2 tablespoons of the parsley. Serve hot or at room temperature.

Tegame di Verdure (Vegetable Flan)

½ cup olive oil

1 medium-sized yellow bell
  pepper, diced

1 medium-sized green bell
  pepper, diced

2 small zucchini, diced

1 small eggplant, peeled and diced

1 large ripe tomato, diced and
  blotted between paper towels

1 medium onion, very thinly
  sliced

Salt

6 fresh basil leaves, finely
  chopped, or 1 teaspoon dried

1 teaspoon freshly chopped thyme
  or ½ teaspoon dried

1 teaspoon freshly chopped
  rosemary or ½ teaspoon dried

1 teaspoon freshly chopped
  marjoram or ½ teaspoon dried

Pinch cayenne pepper

6 large eggs

1 tablespoon all-purpose flour

SERVES 4

Heat the olive oil in a large frying pan. Add the vegetables and season to taste with salt. Stir in the herbs and cayenne pepper. Cook for about 20 minutes over medium-low heat, stirring often, until vegetables are just cooked and tender. Remove from the heat and spread out in a shallow dish to cool for 10 minutes.

Preheat the oven to 400 degrees.

In a large bowl, beat the eggs together with the flour and a pinch of salt. Stir in the vegetable mixture.

Generously butter the bottom and sides of a shallow 9-by-13-inch baking dish. Transfer the mixture to the pan and smooth the top evenly. Bake for 20 minutes. Serve hot.

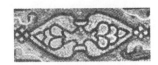

Misto di Verdure in Crosta

(Mixed Vegetables in Pastry)

SERVES 4

To make the dough, combine the flour and a pinch of salt in a bowl. Cut the butter and the olive oil into the flour with a knife or pastry cutter until the mixture has the consistency of crumbs. Add the egg yolk and milk and mix until a soft, but firm, dough forms. Cover and let rest for 1 hour.

Meanwhile, prepare the filling. In a large saucepan, bring 3 quarts of water to a boil. Add 1 tablespoon of salt and all the vegetables. Cook at a low boil for 15 minutes, stirring occasionally, until the vegetables are tender. Drain well.

Preheat the oven to 350 degrees.

Butter the bottom and sides of a 9-inch tart pan with removable bottom. Roll out the dough to a rough 12-inch circle and fit it into the pan. Cut off the extra dough hanging over the edge by rolling a rolling pin across the top of the pan.

Transfer the vegetables into a bowl. Add the herbs and season to taste with salt and pepper. In a small bowl, beat the eggs with the milk and Parmesan cheese and pour over the vegetables. Gently toss. Spoon the vegetables and sauce into the prepared pastry. Bake for 25 minutes or until edges of the dough are golden brown.

Heat the broiler. Sprinkle the top of the pastry with the Swiss cheese. Place under the broiler for 1 minute, or until the cheese is golden brown. Serve hot.

PASTRY

1½ cups all-purpose flour
Salt
6 tablespoons unsalted butter
2 tablespoons olive oil
1 large egg yolk
3 tablespoons milk

FILLING

Salt
3 carrots, peeled and thinly sliced
1½ cups frozen green peas, thawed
3 celery stalks, thinly sliced
2 boiling potatoes, peeled and cut into ¼-inch-thick slices
2 tablespoons each freshly chopped basil, thyme, and parsley
Freshly ground pepper
2 large eggs
½ cup milk
¼ cup freshly grated Parmesan cheese
½ cup shredded Swiss cheese

Patate Siciliane alla Pizzaiola

(Sicilian-Style Potato Pizza)

SERVES 6

1 medium onion, thinly sliced

2 pounds baking potatoes, peeled and thinly sliced

Salt

1½ cups peeled, diced tomatoes

½ teaspoon dried oregano

Freshly ground pepper

⅓ cup olive oil

½ cup freshly grated pecorino or Parmesan cheese

¼ cup dried bread crumbs

Preheat the oven to 400 degrees.

In a shallow 9-by-13-inch baking dish, arrange the onion and potatoes. Pat them down evenly. Season with salt and cover with 2 cups of boiling water. Bake for 25 minutes or until the potatoes are almost done.

Remove the pan from the oven. Spoon the tomatoes evenly over the surface. Sprinkle with oregano, salt, and pepper. Drizzle the olive oil over the top. Combine the cheese and bread crumbs and dust evenly over the top.

Return the pan to the oven and bake for 10 more minutes. Serve hot.

Funghi e Patate (Mushrooms and Potatoes)

SERVES 4

½ cup olive oil

3 garlic cloves, minced

1 pound portabello mushrooms, cleaned and cut into ¼-inch-thick slices, then cut into thirds crosswise

Salt and freshly ground pepper

1 pound new potatoes, boiled, peeled, and cubed

2 large eggs, lightly beaten

¼ cup pecorino or Parmesan cheese

⅓ cup freshly chopped Italian parsley

Heat the oil with the garlic in a large frying pan for 3 minutes over medium heat, stirring often. Stir in the mushrooms, season with salt and pepper, and cook over medium heat for 5 minutes, stirring occasionally.

Add the potatoes and combine. Cook over medium heat, stirring often, for 10 minutes.

Meanwhile, combine the eggs with the pecorino and parsley. Stir this mixture into the mushrooms and potatoes and cook over low heat until the eggs have set.

Patate Ripiene (Stuffed Baked Potatoes)

SERVES 4

Preheat the oven to 400 degrees.

Bake the potatoes until just tender, about 45 minutes.

Meanwhile, cook the carrots, zucchini, and broccoli rabe in separate small saucepans of lightly salted water until just tender. Drain the carrots and zucchini and set aside. Drain the broccoli rabe well, first in a strainer, pressing the back of a spoon against it. Then squeeze dry in a clean dish cloth and set aside.

Make the béchamel sauce. Cover and set aside.

Remove the potatoes and reduce the oven heat to 350 degrees.

Cut the baked potatoes in half lengthwise. When cool enough to handle, taking care not to break the shells, remove the potato pulp with a tablespoon, leaving a layer of about ⅓ inch of pulp attached to the shells. Put potato pulp into a large bowl.

Mash the potatoes with the béchamel sauce and season to taste with salt and pepper. Fold in the reserved vegetables. Spoon equal amounts of the mixture into each of the potato shells, rounding the mounds into little oval domes.

Place each stuffed potato in the center of a large square of aluminum foil. Bring the sides of the foil up around each. Spoon equal amounts of the melted butter over the top of each potato, and fold the top edges of aluminum foil together to enclose the potato.

Cook foil packets on a baking sheet in the oven for 30 minutes. Serve hot.

2 large baking potatoes

2 medium carrots, peeled and diced

2 small zucchini, diced

1 cup finely chopped broccoli rabe

1 recipe béchamel sauce (Salsa Besciamella, page 37)

Salt and freshly ground pepper

3 tablespoons melted unsalted butter

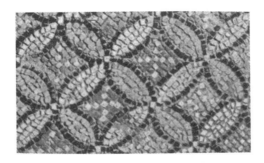

Patate con Alloro (Baked Potatoes with Bay Leaves)

At Gangivecchio we have a large number of bay laurel bushes that line the pathways, so we are always happy when Mamma invents a new dish to use their fragrant leaves.

SERVES 6

2½ pounds small new potatoes
Olive oil
2 medium onions, thinly sliced and separated into rings
Salt and freshly ground pepper
⅔ cup grated pecorino cheese
10 bay leaves

In a large saucepan, bring 3 quarts of water to a boil and boil the potatoes for 10 minutes. Drain the potatoes and run cold tap water over them to stop the cooking. Allow to cool.

Preheat the oven to 375 degrees.

When cool enough to handle, peel the potatoes and cut them into ¼-inch-thick slices.

Spread 2 tablespoons of olive oil on the bottom and sides of a shallow 9-by-13-inch baking pan. Scatter half of the onions over the bottom of the pan evenly and cover with half of the potato slices. Sprinkle the potatoes with salt and pepper and half the pecorino cheese. Drizzle with olive oil. Make another layer with the remaining onions and potatoes, season with salt and pepper, and sprinkle with the remaining cheese. Arrange the bay leaves over the top of the cheese and drizzle lightly with more olive oil. Cover with aluminum foil and bake for 10 minutes. Remove the foil and bake 20 to 25 minutes longer or until top is golden brown. Discard the bay leaves and serve the potatoes hot.

La Caponata di Peperoni di Wanda

(Wanda's Pepper Caponata)

SERVES 10 TO 12

3 (of each) large yellow, red, and green bell peppers
1 large onion, thinly sliced
1 small head of celery, root end

Remove the cores, seeds, and white membrane from the peppers and cut them into 1-inch squares. Set aside.

Put the onion, celery, and water into a large pot. Cook over medium heat until the water has almost evaporated. Add the oil

and cook over high heat for 1 minute. Stir in the capers, olives, raisins, and anchovies. Cook for another minute over high heat. Add the peppers and season to taste with salt and pepper. Mix well, cover, and cook over medium heat, stirring occasionally, for 15 minutes. Stir in the tomatoes and tomato paste and simmer, uncovered, for 10 more minutes, stirring occasionally.

Remove the pan from the heat. Stir in the sugar and vinegar. Taste to check salt and pepper and also the sweet-and-sour balance. If desired, add a little more sugar and/or vinegar.

Transfer the caponata to a bowl and let cool. Serve at room temperature. The caponata will keep up to a week in the refrigerator. Return to room temperature before serving.

cut off, stalks and tender leaves cut into ¼-inch slices
½ cup water
1 cup olive oil
⅔ cup capers, rinsed and drained
1 cup pitted and coarsely chopped green olives (Sicilian, if possible)
¾ cup raisins
3 tablespoons chopped anchovies
Salt and freshly ground pepper
2 pounds fresh tomatoes, peeled and chopped
2 tablespoons tomato paste
1 teaspoon sugar
1 tablespoon vinegar

Zucca Rossa d'Inverno Marinata

(Marinated Red Winter Pumpkin)

SERVES 6

Dust the pumpkin pieces with flour.

Heat the oil in a large frying pan until hot but not smoking. Fry the pumpkin over high heat until tender and golden brown on each side. Drain on paper towels.

Arrange the pumpkin in a shallow serving dish.

Pour out all but 1 cup of oil from the frying pan. Return to the heat and stir in the vinegar, sugar, and olives. Season lightly with salt and cook over medium heat for 3 minutes.

Spoon the sauce over the pumpkin and let cool. Serve at room temperature.

2 pounds fresh calabasa or pumpkin, peeled and cut into pieces about 4 inches long, 1½ inches wide, and ¾ inch thick
All-purpose flour
2 cups olive oil
3 tablespoons red wine vinegar
3 tablespoons sugar
⅔ cup pitted and chopped black olives (Gaeta, if possible)
Salt

Insalate

(Salads)

Insalata di Finocchi Crudi *(Raw Fennel Salad)*

Insalata di Finocchi e Carciofi
  (Fennel and Artichoke Salad)

Insalata di Cetrioli e Capperi *(Cucumber and Caper Salad)*

Insalata di Funghi *(Mushroom Salad)*

I Sanguinelli *(Blood Oranges)*

Insalata di Fagioli Bianchi con Verdure
  (White Bean Salad with Vegetables)

Insalata di Olive Consate *(Dressed Olive Salad)*

Pacchettini di Prosciutto con Rucola e Parmigiano
  (Packets of Prosciutto with Arugula and Parmesan Cheese)

Disastri Naturali *(Natural Disasters)*

Panini di Pomodori e Mozzarella
  (Tomato and Mozzarella Sandwiches)

Insalata di Melone e Prosciutto *(Melon and Ham Salad)*

Insalata di Polipetti *(Baby Octopus Salad)*

Insalata di Riso con Pesto e Gamberi
  (Rice Salad with Pesto and Shrimp)

Una Buona Compagna

(A Good Companion)

Oggi le nostre insalate sono più creative che nel passato.

(Today our salads are more creative than in the past.)

Many types of salad are a regular part of our restaurant menus today. But in the past, our salads were merely a single bowl of greens dressed with extra virgin olive oil, vinegar, and salt and pepper. There was also, of course, the mixed salad, composed of greens, tomatoes, shredded carrot, fennel, and onion, and the same oil and vinegar dressing. There were a few other more exotic combinations that were presented as part of our special holiday menus, like the classic Christmas salad, with oranges, olives, and capers, and another variation with cauliflower, anchovy, and green olive, which was never missing from our Christmas table. (Both recipes appear in our first book.)

Sicilians have long admired potato salads with tomatoes and green beans or potatoes combined with black olives and capers. Sicily is famous for its extraordinary seafood salads, but as for meat, a simple chicken and mayonnaise blend was perfect enough.

The salad revolution appeared at Gangivecchio several years ago when Betty, my former daughter-in-law, arrived. She insisted that we prepare salads for ourselves and for our guests, and we are forever grateful to her for her passionate love of these marvelous, healthy concoctions.

When we traveled throughout America, we were amazed by the variety of wonderful salad combinations. They appeared at the table on huge plates with a tower of ingredients—ingredients we'd never heard of, ingredients we'd never imagined could be served together with success in the same dish. We tasted our first Caesar salad in New York, then tried it all over the country. While we don't serve this salad in our restaurant, we prepare it sometimes for ourselves at home, letting our palates recall our delightful journeys.

Today, our salads are now more creative than they were in the past, but we

remain devoted to Italian ingredients and simplicity. So we often serve arugula salad with Parmesan cheese shavings and pomegranate seeds with a simple dressing. Radicchio and red onion salad with basil is another favorite. Part of the joy of salad making is invention. The following collection includes new creations such as Insalata di Melone e Prosciutto, and traditional Sicilian offerings like mushroom and octopus salads—all good companions to any meal.

Insalata di Finocchi Crudi (Raw Fennel Salad)

We like to serve this wonderfully refreshing salad between courses, perhaps between the pasta and fish or meat, to refresh the palate. But sometimes Mamma puts the fennel salad on the table at the beginning of the meal and suggests that everyone nibble at it whenever they like.

SERVES 4

Cut the ends and hard top off each fennel bulb. Cut each bulb into quarters from the top to the bottom. Trim away any of the remaining core, then cut the pieces into thin strips. Put the fennel strips into a bowl of cold water with a teaspoon of salt and let rest for 1 hour.

Drain and rinse the fennel slices and pat them dry with paper towels.

Put the fennel into a shallow bowl and sprinkle with the lemon juice and olive oil. Add salt to taste and a generous amount of pepper. Toss well and serve.

3 medium-sized fennel bulbs
Salt
2 tablespoons freshly squeezed lemon juice
⅓ cup olive oil
Freshly ground pepper

Insalata di Finocchi e Carciofi

(Fennel and Artichoke Salad)

SERVES 4

Cut the ends and hard top off each fennel bulb. Cut each bulb into quarters from the bottom to the top. Trim away any of the remaining core, then cut the pieces into thin strips.

Put the fennel, artichoke hearts, and raisins into a serving bowl.

In a small bowl, combine well the olive oil, lemon juice, mustard, and yogurt. Season to taste with salt and pepper. Turn out over the salad and toss. Serve immediately.

2 medium-sized fennel bulbs
8 small cleaned and cooked artichoke hearts, fresh or frozen, thinly sliced
1 tablespoon raisins
3 tablespoons olive oil
1 tablespoon freshly squeezed lemon juice
1 teaspoon Dijon mustard
2 teaspoons plain yogurt
Salt and freshly ground pepper

Insalata di Cetrioli e Capperi (Cucumber and Caper Salad)

When my granny Giovanna was still with us, she was always happy when cucumbers ripened in the garden. She said that they were not only refreshingly delicious, but invaluable for the skin. She urged us to place cucumber slices over our faces and eyes for thirty minutes, and see the miracle. Save some leftover slices and try it.

SERVES 4

3 small Kirby cucumbers, peeled and cut into thin slices

2 tablespoons capers, rinsed and dried

½ cup finely shredded romaine lettuce

3 tablespoons olive oil

1 tablespoon white wine vinegar

Salt and freshly ground pepper

2 tablespoons mayonnaise

Place the cucumber slices in a shallow bowl.

Sprinkle the capers and lettuce over the cucumbers.

In a small bowl, combine the oil, vinegar, and salt and pepper to taste. Whisk in the mayonnaise and blend until smooth.

Spoon the sauce over the vegetables and toss well.

Insalata di Funghi (Mushroom Salad)

SERVES 4

4 garlic cloves, peeled and left whole

⅓ cup finely chopped fresh Italian parsley

½ cup extra virgin olive oil

1 tablespoon white wine vinegar

⅓ cup raisins

⅓ cup pomegranate seeds

Salt and freshly ground pepper

1 pound portabello mushrooms, cut into bite-sized pieces, or crimini mushrooms, sliced

Freshly shaved Parmesan cheese

In a bowl, combine the garlic, parsley, oil, vinegar, raisins, and pomegranate seeds. Season with salt and pepper to taste and let rest for 30 minutes. Discard the garlic cloves.

Put the mushrooms into a bowl and drizzle the dressing over the top. Gently toss. Top each serving with a few shavings of Parmesan cheese.

At the market:
baby octopus
and capers

Wanda buys
olives at
Palermo's La
Vucciria market.

Pungent, delicious
garlic sold by the braid

Juicy tomatoes are used
for *Salsa di Pomodoro*,
page 95. "We like to
prepare huge amounts
of it in late summer,
when tomatoes are
delicious and plentiful."

Fresh green almonds: "Sicily produces a tremendous amount of superb almonds, walnuts, and pistachios . . . nuts are still a very important part of Sicilian cuisine."

A flat of Sicilian oranges: "Palermo rests between two mountains, in a large valley called the Conca d'Oro ('the golden shell' or 'horn of plenty'), taking its name from the vast citrus groves that were once cultivated there."

One of Wanda's signature lattice-topped tarts. "Hell, for me, would be Palermo without pastry."

With *Crema Pasticciera*, page 208, and *Pasta Frolla* page 209, you can make "a beautiful mixed fruit tart using fresh fruits and berries of the season."

I Sanguinelli   (Blood Oranges)

Palermo rests between two mountains, in a large valley called the Conca d'Oro ("the golden shell" or "horn of plenty"), taking its name from the vast citrus groves that were once cultivated there. Thousands of orange trees dotted the landscape at the edge of the city, stretching out for miles beyond. In winter, when the fruit was ripe, the oranges glistened under the sun like globes of gold among dense, dark-green leaves. But that was once upon a time. Few trees survive today. During the wild development of the 1960s, ugly, poorly constructed, modern buildings replaced the groves, defacing our town's beautiful perimeter.

Fortunately, oranges and other citrus fruits are still cultivated in great numbers in many other regions of Sicily. Our climate and soil give us spectacular lemons, mandarins, clementines, and two types of oranges: delicious sweet oranges, and dramatic, blood-red oranges.

Our friend Peppino Sillitti has enormous orange groves in the southern part of the island, where he cultivates primarily *sanguinello,* a type of blood orange. The other two varieties of blood oranges are *tarocco* and *moro,* but Sicilians consider *sanguinello* the best because of its sweet/tart, citrus/berry flavor, and because it's the rarest of the three.

Sanguinelli are the size of tennis balls, with orange-colored skins splotched with streaks of red. Inside, the dark-red fruit is filled with glistening juice that's packed with flavor and vitamins. This juice will stain your fingers and shirt like blood if you're not careful.

Nothing is more refreshing than a chilled glass of *sanguinelli* juice. When the oranges are in season, we keep a large carafe of juice in the refrigerator to quench our thirst any time of the day.

We love *sanguinelli* oranges for their unique taste and enchanting ruby-red color, but also because they appear at the end of February as a bright promise of spring.

Blood oranges are now available in some American markets, so in addition to making juice with them, consider using them in other dishes, such as fruit sauces or salads. It's unlikely that you'll be able to find *sanguinelli,* but try any kind of blood orange you can find.

After peeling the blood oranges and removing all the white pith and seeds, combine the sliced or sectioned oranges with arugula, lettuce, shrimp, and raisins and toss with a lemon and olive oil dressing. Or make a single layer of blood orange slices in two or three circles on a big round plate, top them with thin rings of red onion, and drizzle with extra virgin olive oil.

Insalata di Fagioli Bianchi con Verdure

(White Bean Salad with Vegetables)

This salad can be a meal in itself, presented on a bed of greens, or served as a side dish. It pairs very well with cold meat such as thinly sliced chicken, veal, or pork.

SERVES 4 AS A MAIN COURSE OR 6 AS A SIDE DISH

1¼ pounds canellini beans, cooked and cooled

1 large carrot, peeled and shredded

1 cup diced Italian plum tomatoes

½ cup diced red onion

¼ cup freshly chopped Italian parsley

½ cup extra virgin olive oil, or to taste

2 tablespoons white wine vinegar, or to taste

Salt and freshly ground pepper

Put the beans into a large bowl with the carrot, tomatoes, onion, and parsley. Gently combine.

In a small bowl, whisk together the oil, vinegar, and salt and pepper to taste. Drizzle the dressing over the salad and toss. Let rest for 10 minutes. Taste for seasoning, adding a little more vinegar, salt, and pepper, if desired. If too dry, sprinkle with a little extra oil.

Insalata di Olive Consate (Dressed Olive Salad)

This salad must be prepared twenty-four hours in advance. It's wonderful for a picnic.

SERVES 6

1½ pounds pitted green olives

2 garlic cloves, minced

1 cup chopped onion

4 medium carrots, peeled and thinly sliced

In a large bowl, combine the olives, garlic, onion, carrots, parsley, and oregano. Drizzle the olive oil and vinegar over the mixture and season with salt and pepper. Toss thoroughly. Cover and let rest overnight in the refrigerator.

One hour before serving, remove the salad from the refrigera-

tor. Stir in the tomatoes and celery. Bring to room temperature before serving.

⅓ cup freshly chopped
    Italian parsley
½ teaspoon dried oregano
1 cup olive oil
2 tablespoons white wine vinegar
Salt and freshly ground pepper
2 large tomatoes, diced
½ cup diced celery

Pacchettini di Prosciutto con Rucola e Parmigiano

(Packets of Prosciutto with Arugula and Parmesan Cheese)

Paolo often serves this recipe at Tenuta Gangivecchio. He invented it a few years ago for a demanding guest of his who insisted on an elegant, original salad as a first course for a dinner party she was hosting.

SERVES 4

In a small bowl, combine the olive oil, lemon juice, and salt and pepper to taste. If the lemon flavor is too strong, add a little extra olive oil.

    On a work surface, place 4 slices of prosciutto in 1 overlapping layer. Spoon ¼ cup of arugula over the center of the prosciutto slices and top with 2 tablespoons of the shaved Parmesan cheese. Sprinkle the arugula and cheese with ¼ of the dressing. Fold the edges of the prosciutto over each other, making a rectangular-shaped packet about 3 inches by 6 inches. Tie a single piece of fresh chive around the packet's short side, and knot it.

    Assemble the remaining 3 packets in the same manner.

    Serve at once.

⅓ cup extra virgin olive oil,
    or to taste
1 tablespoon freshly squeezed
    lemon juice
Salt and freshly ground pepper
16 (about ½ pound) thin slices
    prosciutto
1 cup chopped arugula
8 tablespoons freshly shaved
    Parmesan cheese
4 long fresh chive stems

Disastri Naturali (Natural Disasters)

Sicily is a land of earthquakes, with at least one sizable quake a year. Thankfully, we haven't had a major earthquake recently—nothing like the awful ones in Messina in 1908 or those on the southwest coast in 1968, which took so many lives. We also have the stupendous Mount Etna, the largest active volcano in Europe. Tremendous eruptions have occurred in the past, and there is always the possibility—or should I say the inevitability—that it will erupt again at any moment. Etna normally erupts three or four times a year, with what we call peaceful outbursts, to release interior pressure. Clouds of white smoke eternally hover over Mount Etna, reminding us of its heart of fire.

We Sicilians also have hearts of fire. We can be volcanoes of love or hate, or earthquakes that shatter lives. My family's most recent earthquake happened when my sister-in-law, Betty, suddenly left my brother and Gangivecchio after only one year of marriage. The first tremor came after only their first few months of marriage. Whatever the crisis, it soon passed. But just before Paolo and Betty would have celebrated their first anniversary, she disappeared, never to return again.

We all suffered, my brother most of all. With the passage of time, Betty vanished from vivid memory. We no longer saw her face in the kitchen or heard her voice calling from the garden.

What happens between two people who once loved each other is always a mystery. Paolo remains stoic on the subject of his marriage. But Mamma and I have discussed this earthquake for many, many hours. Betty had lived at Gangivecchio for seven years before marrying Paolo. She seemed extremely happy in the countryside, as my mother and Mamma's mother-in-law, Giovanna, had been. All three women had spent their youths as "city girls" in Palermo. Although Betty was always ready to go to Palermo or travel abroad at a moment's notice, she also loved to ride horses, to stroll in the pasture and orchards, to plant seeds and flowers, and to cook. She introduced salads into our kitchen, as well as delicious dishes from Apulia, where her father was raised. Several of her recipes are included in our first book. Betty was at Paolo's side when he built and opened Tenuta Gangivecchio, his small inn with its own restaurant. When people who have read our first book come here now, they sometimes ask, "Where is Betty?" Paolo

always responds to that question with the same words: "*Non c'e* [She's not here]." At first, it was very sad. No longer. Paolo has returned to his former self. The twinkle in his eyes has returned. He works vigorously and is the jolly hotel proprietor and talented chef, welcoming and kind. My crystal ball informs me that he will find a lasting romance.

In the end, life here did not bring Betty what she needed or wanted. Perhaps she finally came to learn that whoever falls in love with a Tornabene must also fall in love with Gangivecchio.

Panini di Pomodori e Mozzarella
(Tomato and Mozzarella Sandwiches)

The happy marriage of fresh tomatoes, mozzarella, and basil, dressed with olive oil, salt, and pepper, is one of the most popular salads in the Mediterranean. Here, we serve it presented like an accordion.

SERVES 4

Place 1 tomato on each of 4 individual salad plates, stem side down. Cut 4 slits, at equal distances apart, from the bottom of each tomato down through to about ½ inch from the stem end. Separate the openings gently with your fingers and insert a slice of mozzarella into each opening. Sprinkle the tomatoes generously with olive oil, salt, and pepper. Shower with equal portions of the basil.

4 large ripe tomatoes
12 thin slices (about 1 pound) fresh mozzarella
Extra virgin olive oil
Salt and freshly ground pepper
12 fresh basil leaves, cut into very thin strips

Insalata di Melone e Prosciutto

(Melon and Ham Salad)

Serves 4

1 cantaloupe, seeded, peeled, and cubed

One ½-pound piece of boiled ham, cut into ½-inch cubes

2 tablespoons freshly chopped mint leaves

¼ cup extra virgin olive oil

3 tablespoons good-quality balsamic vinegar

Salt and freshly ground pepper

In a large bowl, combine the cantaloupe, ham, and mint.

In a small bowl, whisk together the olive oil and balsamic vinegar, and season to taste with salt and pepper. Sprinkle the dressing over the cantaloupe mixture. Gently toss, and serve at once.

Note This cooling salad is wonderful with fried fish.

Insalata di Polipetti (Baby Octopus Salad)

Serves 4

1½ pounds baby octopuses

Extra virgin olive oil

Salt and freshly ground pepper

1 garlic clove, minced

2 tablespoons freshly squeezed lemon juice

Pinch hot pepper flakes (optional)

⅓ cup freshly chopped Italian parsley

Heat the broiler.

Put the octopuses in a bowl and sprinkle lightly with oil, salt, and pepper. Toss. Arrange the octopuses in a single layer on a rack in a broiler pan. Broil 5 inches from the heat source until the octopuses begin to brown, about 5 minutes. Turn and cook 4 to 5 minutes on the other side.

Transfer the octopuses to a bowl.

In a small bowl, mix together ½ cup of olive oil, the garlic, lemon juice, and hot pepper flakes, if desired, and season to taste with salt and pepper. Pour the mixture over the octopuses and toss. Let rest at room temperature for 30 minutes.

Just before serving, sprinkle with the parsley, toss well, and serve immediately.

Insalata di Riso con Pesto e Gamberi

(Rice Salad with Pesto and Shrimp)

SERVES 4

In a small saucepan, cook the asparagus in lightly salted water over medium heat until al dente, about 5 minutes. Drain in a strainer under cold running water. Pat it dry on paper towels.

Transfer the cooked rice to a large bowl. Fluff it with a fork. Add the shrimp and asparagus. Toss gently.

To make the pesto, put the basil, pine nuts, Parmesan cheese, half the olive oil, and water into the bowl of a food processor. Begin to process. Immediately add the remaining oil, in a slow steady stream, through the feed tube. Process until smooth and creamy, less than a minute. Taste for seasoning, adding salt if necessary.

Add the pesto to the rice mixture and combine well. Garnish each of the 4 servings with 2 cherry tomatoes and a sprig of fresh basil.

12 fresh asparagus stalks, ends cut off, stems peeled with vegetable peeler, cut into 1-inch pieces

3 cups cooked Vialone Nano, Carnaroli, or Arborio rice, cooled

1 pound boiled medium shrimp, shelled, deveined, and chilled

8 cherry tomatoes

4 basil sprigs

PESTO

½ cup packed fresh basil leaves

¼ cup pine nuts

2 tablespoons freshly grated Parmesan cheese

¾ cup olive oil

2 tablespoons hot water

Salt

Dolci

(Desserts)

Dolci Tentazioni Siciliane

(Sicilian Sweet Temptations)

*L'Inferno, per me,
è Palermo senza
pasticcerie.*

(Hell, for me, would
be Palermo without
pastry.)

It has been my bittersweet tragedy in life to be constantly waging a war between my desire for desserts and the centimeters of my waistline. I was a fat child, and as an adult am on "*la dieta eterna* [the eternal diet]." I am both blessed and cursed to live in a country whose talented artisans make spectacular confections, famous all over the world, and also to have a mother whose first concern of any meal is its ending, the dessert.

Mamma adores making cakes, tarts, cookies, puddings, and candies—anything sweet—as much as she loves eating them. And naturally she never gains a gram. Wherever we travel, she must visit the *pasticcerie* and buy cakes, fritters, whatever catches her fancy. Driving from Gangivecchio to Palermo, a two-hour journey, we must always stop midway for a brioche filled with gelato or a delectable pastry.

Before we opened the restaurant in 1978, desserts at home were reserved mostly for holidays and special occasions, as is customary even today in most Sicilian homes. Seasonal fruits satisfy our craving for sweets, except in the case of my father, who, his entire life (spoiled by his mother and wife), went to bed with a cannoli or other delicacy placed on his nightstand, for sweet dreams. Mamma and I always smile when we stay at a hotel in America and discover a chocolate on our nightstands before bed: "*Come Papa, come Papa* [Like Papa, like Papa]." Mamma never eats the chocolate right away. Instead she leaves it on the table in front of the small framed photograph of Papa that accompanies her everywhere she travels. Mamma has her chocolate—and mine—for breakfast with her espresso.

Since the restaurant opened, my mother has prepared desserts practically every day. For me, they are sumptuous, torturous temptations, to which I often surrender.

Parfait di Mandorle (Almond Parfait)

This luscious, frozen almond parfait cake must be prepared one day in advance.

SERVES 12

1 tablespoon olive oil
1 cup blanched almond slivers
6 large egg yolks
1 cup sugar
6 tablespoons whole milk
Peel of 1 lemon, cut in 1 long piece
3 cups plus 3 tablespoons heavy cream
1 tablespoon pure vanilla extract

In a large frying pan, heat the oil, add the almonds, and toast over low heat, stirring often, until well browned (but don't allow to burn), about 15 minutes. Cool on paper towels.

In a medium saucepan, combine the egg yolks, ¾ cup of sugar, the milk, and the lemon peel. Cook over very low heat, stirring constantly, for about 25 minutes. Don't let the mixture boil. Transfer to a large bowl and cool. Discard the lemon peel.

Coarsely chop the almonds in the food processor. Evenly sprinkle half of the almonds over the bottom of a 10-by-4-inch, preferably nonstick, loaf pan.

Whip the cream until it begins to thicken. Whisk in the remaining ¼ cup of sugar and vanilla and beat until stiff.

Gradually fold the whipped cream into the egg mixture.

Pour the mixture over the almonds in the pan. Sprinkle the remaining almonds over the top. Cover with plastic wrap and freeze overnight.

To unmold the frozen cake, dip pan briefly in hot water. Place a rectangular-shaped serving dish, several inches larger than the size of the pan, over the cake. Invert and, holding both securely together, give 1 good shake. The parfait should release easily. Cut into slices and serve immediately.

Torta di Mele ed Amaretti (Apple and Amaretti Tart)

SERVES 8

1 cup sugar
1 large egg plus 1 large yolk
1 cup all-purpose flour
2 teaspoons baking powder

In a large bowl, combine the sugar and eggs with a wooden spoon until light and fluffy. In another bowl combine the flour, baking powder, and salt. Add dry ingredients to the egg mixture and combine well. Stir in the milk thoroughly.

Butter and flour a 9-inch round baking pan with 3- to 4-inch sides.

Preheat the oven to 350 degrees.

Cut the apples into quarters, core, and peel them. Cut the apple quarters into thin slices.

Spoon ⅓ of the cake batter over the bottom of the pan. Top with ⅓ of the apple slices arranged in circles in a single layer over the batter. Sprinkle the top with ⅓ of the amaretti crumbs. Make 2 more layers in the same manner.

Sprinkle the melted butter and Amaretto liqueur over the top. Bake in the oven for 1 hour. Cool for 30 minutes. Sprinkle with confectioners' sugar just before serving.

Pinch salt
1 cup milk
3 pounds Golden Delicious apples
8 amaretti cookies, crushed into coarse crumbs
½ cup melted unsalted butter
¼ cup Amaretto liqueur
Confectioners' sugar

Crostata di Amaretti e Cioccolato

(Amaretti and Chocolate Tart)

SERVES 6

In a large bowl, combine the flour and sugar with a pinch of salt and a pinch of baking soda. Make a well in the center of the dry ingredients, and combine the egg yolks and the melted butter in the well. Combine wet and dry ingredients and knead into a dough, working it as little as possible. Shape into a ball, cover, and refrigerate for 1 hour.

Butter and flour an 8-inch round springform baking pan.

In a medium bowl mix together the chocolate, almonds, and amaretti crumbs.

Preheat the oven to 350 degrees.

On a lightly floured work surface, roll out the dough into an 11-inch circle. Fit the circle into the prepared pan.

Whip the egg whites until stiff and fold them into the chocolate mixture. Pour the filling into the pastry shell. Bake for 40 minutes. Remove the wall of the pan and let cool. Dust with confectioners' sugar before serving.

PASTRY

1 cup all-purpose flour
½ cup sugar
Salt
Baking soda
2 large egg yolks
6 tablespoons melted butter
⅓ cup chopped bitter chocolate
⅓ cup chopped blanched almonds
⅓ cup crushed amaretti cookies
4 large egg whites
⅓ cup confectioners' sugar

Un Natale con Mia Nonna
(A Christmas with My Grandmother)

About thirty years ago, during the Christmas holidays, our family and a few friends were gathered at Gangivecchio. We had been invited by our old friends Ciccio and Anna to a party in their cottage high in the Madonie Mountains, about thirty miles away. When Anna called to invite us, she asked Mamma to bring some of her famous desserts.

So in addition to making all our Christmas desserts, my mother worked long hours for two days cooking desserts for Anna and Ciccio's event—incredible cannoli, *buccellati* (a classic cake stuffed with figs, raisins, and walnuts), a big chocolate cake, hazelnut and pear tarts, biscotti, and a stupendous pudding. They were wrapped in pretty packages and boxes and tied with red ribbons the night before the party.

At dawn the day of the party, an unexpected silence enveloped Gangivecchio—no birds chirping, no rooster crowing. Still in our beds, we all knew immediately what had happened. Snow had come during the night. From the windows, we watched it falling in gigantic, cottony flakes. Snow meant, of course, that we were not going anywhere; the roads would be impassable.

Although the nine of us were all adults, we were as disappointed as children. We thought of our stranded friends, high up in the mountains. "*Senza dolci* [without desserts]!" Mamma cried. We were complaining to each other about our terrible misfortune when my granny Giovanna, then eighty, appeared. In frail health, she was forbidden to travel, so she wasn't joining us for the trip to the party. She stood in the doorway and quietly said, "It always pleases me when it snows. Isn't it beautiful? And it pleases me that you cannot go anywhere. This was my last Christmas." (She'd been predicting that for the past ten years.) "You would have regretted leaving me here all alone the day after Christmas. We'll have a party here and eat all Wanda's lovely cakes ourselves. Wanda and I will make a delicious lunch. Enzo, go to the wine cellar and bring up five bottles of the best reds. Wanda, don't worry about your friends in the mountains. They can make *gelato fior di latte* [milk ice cream] from the snow."

And, of course, we did have a splendid time. The men kept the fire going to keep us warm. Mamma played the piano and we sang and danced, told stories and gossiped, and ate a huge meal, including the desserts, with abandon. Granny was so happy and so radiant. And it was, in fact, her last Christmas.

Crostata di Crema con Marmellata di Arance

(Orange Cream and Marmalade Tart)

SERVES 6

In a large bowl, combine the flour, baking powder, and sugar. Make a well in the center and add the eggs. Mix them well with a wooden spoon and stir in the melted butter. Combine ingredients into a dough, knead on a work surface for a few minutes, then cover and let rest for 30 minutes.

Preheat the oven to 350 degrees.

Butter and flour an 8-inch round baking pan.

On a lightly floured work surface, roll out the dough to an 11-inch circle. Fit the circle into the prepared baking pan. Trim the top of the dough evenly.

Spoon the marmalade onto the shell and smooth evenly. Top with the pastry cream. Arrange overlapping layers of the apple slices across the cream in 2 circles. Sprinkle with pine nuts. Cook for 45 minutes or until golden brown. Let rest 10 minutes before serving.

1½ cups all-purpose flour

1 tablespoon baking powder

¾ cup sugar

2 large eggs

5 tablespoons melted butter

¾ cup orange marmalade

2 cups pastry cream, made with orange peel instead of lemon (Crema Pasticciera, page 208)

3 large Red Delicious apples, cored, peeled, and thinly sliced

2 tablespoons pine nuts

Crema Pasticciera (Basic Pastry Cream)

This simple pastry cream is delicious on its own as a pudding, but it's also extremely useful as a filling for pastries or as a tasty base for tarts. We use it often at Gangivecchio. Giovanna likes to spread it over the bottom of a cooked tart shell (Pasta Frolla) and cover the top with a single kind of fruit, such as raspberries or strawberries. But she also makes a beautiful mixed fruit tart using fresh fruits and berries of the season. The recipe for Pasta Frolla follows.

MAKES ABOUT 2½ CUPS OF PASTRY CREAM.
THE RECIPE IS EASILY DOUBLED.

2¼ cups whole milk
½ teaspoon pure vanilla extract
Peel of 1 or 2 small lemons, cut in 1 long piece
4 large egg yolks, at room temperature
1 cup plus 2 tablespoons sugar
⅓ cup cornstarch

Over low heat, slowly bring the milk, vanilla, and lemon peel to a boil in a medium, heavy-bottomed saucepan, stirring often.

Beat the egg yolks with the sugar in a medium bowl until light and fluffy. Whisk in the cornstarch and blend well.

Remove the pan from the heat and discard the lemon peel. In a slow, steady stream, whisk ¾ cup of the hot milk into the eggs.

Slowly whisk the egg mixture into the remaining milk in the saucepan, stirring constantly. When it is thoroughly incorporated, return the pan to high heat and let the *crema* boil for 2 minutes, stirring constantly, until thick and creamy.

The pastry cream will keep, covered, in the refrigerator, for 2 days.

Variation   For orange pastry cream, substitute orange peel for the lemon peel in the recipe.

Pasta Frolla (Pastry Dough)

MAKES ONE 8- TO 9-INCH TART SHELL

Put the flour, sugar, and baking powder into a large bowl. Combine. Add the lemon zest, eggs, and vanilla, and mix together with a pastry blender or the blades of 2 ordinary kitchen knives. Little by little, incorporate all the butter. Coat your hands with a little flour and knead the dough only enough so that it sticks together; take care not to overwork it or it will toughen. Shape the dough into a ball.

Pasta Frolla can also be made in a food processor: Put the flour, sugar, baking powder, lemon zest, and butter into the bowl of the processor and blend until coarse-crumb consistency. With the machine running, add the eggs and vanilla through the feed tube. Process just a few seconds, until the dough is combined.

With a little flour on your hands, form the dough into a ball, then cover with plastic wrap and refrigerate overnight, if possible, but at least for 1 hour. The dough also freezes well for future use.

2 cups all-purpose flour
1 cup sugar
1 tablespoon baking powder
Finely grated zest of ½ lemon
3 large eggs, at room temperature
½ teaspoon vanilla extract
½ cup plus 3 tablespoons unsalted butter, melted then cooled to room temperature

La Vecchia Torta di Cioccolato

(The Old Chocolate Tart)

SERVES 6

Melt the butter over simmering water in a double boiler. Whisk in the sugar and egg yolks and cook for 5 minutes, stirring constantly. Whisk in the coffee, cocoa powder, rum, and almonds and cook until mixture is smooth and creamy, stirring constantly.

Preheat the oven to 350 degrees.

Transfer the mixture to a large bowl.

Butter and flour a 9-inch round baking pan.

Beat the egg whites until they just begin to stiffen. Fold into the chocolate mixture. Pour batter into the pan and bake for 30 minutes. Let cool for 30 minutes. Dust with confectioners' sugar.

6 tablespoons unsalted butter
1¼ cups sugar
6 large eggs, separated
5 tablespoons instant espresso or coffee powder
6 tablespoons bitter cocoa powder
3 tablespoons white rum
1¼ cups ground toasted blanched almonds
All-purpose flour
Confectioners' sugar

Torta di Ricotta con Frutta Secca

(Ricotta Tart with Nuts)

SERVES 6

One 8-ounce sheet frozen puff pastry, thawed

2 cups ricotta cheese

1 cup sugar

3 large egg yolks

⅓ cup diced candied fruit

¼ cup grappa

¼ cup chopped pistachios

1½ tablespoons chopped peanuts

Preheat the oven to 400 degrees.

Roll out the puff pastry, lightly dusted with flour, to about 8 by 12 inches. Place on a baking sheet. Prick the surface of the pastry with a fork in about a dozen places. Bake in the oven for 10 minutes.

Meanwhile, in a large bowl, combine the ricotta cheese, sugar, egg yolks, candied fruit, and grappa.

Remove the pastry from the oven. Lower the heat to 350 degrees.

Turn out the ricotta mixture over the pastry and spread it evenly to 1 inch from the edges. Bake for 30 minutes or until the filling is set and the crust golden brown. Bring to room temperature. Sprinkle with the pistachios and peanuts before serving.

Huge blond babas, Mont Blancs snowy with whipped cream, cakes speckled with white almonds and green pistachio nuts, hillocks of chocolate-covered pastry, brown and rich as the topsoil of the Catanian plain from which, in fact, through many a twist and turn they had come, pink ices, champagne ices, coffee ices, all parfaits, which fell apart with a squelch as the knife cleft them, melody in major of crystallized cherries, acid notes of yellow pineapple, and those cakes called "triumphs of gluttony" filled with green pistachio paste, and shameless "Virgins' cakes" shaped like breasts.

—From *The Leopard,* by Giuseppe Tomasi di Lampedusa

Sfoglio (Chocolate and Cheese Tart with Cinnamon)

SERVES 10

To make the pastry, combine the flour and 1 cup of the sugar in a large bowl. Make a well in the center and combine the melted lard or butter and 5 egg yolks in the well. Mix the ingredients into a dough with a wooden spoon. Add a little water if dough is too stiff. Knead the dough on a work surface for 1 minute. Set aside. In a small bowl, combine remaining sugar, the cinnamon, and the cocoa. Set aside.

Preheat the oven to 350 degrees.

Butter the bottom and sides of a 10-inch round baking pan.

Divide the dough in half. Roll each half of the dough out to a 12-inch circle. Fit 1 circle of dough into the bottom of the pan, letting it come up the sides about 2 inches. Let rest.

Beat the egg whites in a bowl until they just begin to stiffen. Add the sugar mixture a scoop at a time, and continue beating the whites until they are stiff. Fold in the candied citron and cheese.

Pour the filling into the pastry-lined pan and smooth the top evenly. Cover the mixture with the remaining circle of pastry. Crimp the edges of the dough together. Make a ¾-inch hole in the center of the top of the tart. Brush the top with the remaining egg yolk.

Bake the tart on a baking sheet on the center shelf of the oven for 1 hour or until golden brown.

Remove the tart from the oven and let cool on a rack for at least 30 minutes. Dust the tart with confectioners' sugar just before serving.

3¾ cups all-purpose flour
2⅓ cup sugar
¾ cup melted lard or unsalted butter
5 large eggs, separated, plus 1 egg yolk for brushing top of tart
1 teaspoon ground cinnamon
1 tablespoon cocoa powder
¼ cup diced candied citron
1 pound diced goat cheese
Confectioners' sugar

Una Strana Torta di Ricotta con Anisette

(A Strange Ricotta Tart with Anisette)

We had an old family friend who was the queen of gossip. She knew everything about everyone. Talking to her was better than the news on TV. She always found something strange in other people's lives or habits to comment on. "This recipe," she told my mother, "is the pharmacist's wife's secret."

Dried bread crumbs
3¾ cups ricotta
10 large eggs
3 cups sugar
½ teaspoon pure vanilla extract
3 tablespoons anisette

SERVES 8

Preheat the oven to 350 degrees.

Butter a 9-inch round springform pan and dust it with bread crumbs.

Pass the ricotta through a sieve, into a large bowl. Beat in the eggs, 1 at a time, thoroughly incorporating each into the ricotta before adding the next. Beat in the sugar, vanilla, and anisette and combine well.

Transfer the mixture to the prepared pan. Bake for 1 hour. If you see little bubbles appear on the surface during cooking, break them with a toothpick.

Remove the tart from the oven and cool to room temperature. This cake keeps, covered, in the refrigerator for 5 days.

La Festa dei Morti (The Feast of the Dead)

In Sicily, we are so used to suffering that we even invented "The Feast of the Dead," a day dedicated to remembering parents and other relatives who are no longer with us.

Like all Italians, the people of Palermo, following ancient and dark tradition, go to the cemetery on the second day of November, to bring flowers and to pray. *Palermitani* get organized early in the morning, dressing in their finest. The roads leading to the cemetery are caravans of cars—full of children, friends, and baskets of food. After the battle to find a parking space, there's the journey by foot to the family plot. After a few words of remembrance to the dearly departed—who were always the most wonderful people on earth—everyone happily begins to eat. I once heard a mother ask her daughter, "Did you offer a portion of your *timballo* to Granny?" Of course, Granny was unable to respond, because she was dead.

After the food, and some tears mixed with laughter and chatter, it's time to go to town, to the "Fair of the Dead," where stalls are full of sweets—cakes, cookies, biscuits, dried fruit, marzipan—and piles of toys. One of the main highlights of the day are the presents from the dead to the children of the family. In the past, the toys were hidden during the night in secret places all over the house. In the morning, the children went searching for dolls, balls, little trains, trucks, stuffed animals, and oh so many other things. My mother told me that when she was a child, she used to surround her bed with chairs to avoid close contact with any ghostly benefactor.

Anyway, at the stalls of the fair, marzipan is most beloved: wonderful fruit-shaped confections made of almond dough. Strawberries, figs, apples, clusters of grapes, apricots, cherries—every fruit imaginable, absolutely identical to the real ones. Treats so delicious you can forget, at least for a day, that they are caloric bombs.

Another important part of the fair is the fantastic *pupaccena* (sugar doll), a gaily colored sculpture of sugar, usually representing a paladin on a horse, with real feathers stuck into his sugary, helmeted head. Mamma's mother always bought the biggest and most beautiful sugar doll, but she wouldn't allow any of her three children to eat it. It stood proud and magnificent on the sideboard in the dining room. Every day, when no one was looking, my mother would eat little pieces from its back side. One day the sugar doll came tumbling down, missing most of its posterior. You can imagine the consequences.

I have always regarded "The Feast of the Dead" as a pleasant fantasy, a good way to exorcise death—a glass of wine, a piece of marzipan, and a brave sugar doll.

Iris (Fried Stuffed Pastries)

When Mamma was a little girl, her mother gave her lire every day for the school bus, but she preferred to walk and save the money to buy *iris* at a *pasticceria*.

1 envelope active dry yeast
½ cup warm water
1¾ cups all-purpose flour
2 tablespoons sugar
5 tablespoons melted lard or
    olive oil

STUFFING

2 cups ricotta cheese
1¼ cups sugar
¼ cup semisweet chocolate
    pieces
⅓ cup diced candied citron
2 large egg whites
2 cups fresh bread crumbs
Lard or sunflower oil, for
    deep-frying

MAKES ABOUT 10

Put the yeast in a small bowl with water and set aside for 10 minutes, until it foams. Stir it with a fork.

Put the flour and sugar into a large bowl. Make a well in the center and combine the yeast mixture and lard in the well. Mix ingredients together with a wooden spoon to form a dough. Add a little warm water if needed.

Knead the dough on a lightly floured work surface. Transfer to a clean bowl, cover, and let rise for 1 hour.

Meanwhile, in a medium bowl, mix the ricotta with the sugar. Stir in the chocolate pieces and candied citron. Let this mixture rest in the refrigerator.

When the dough has risen, roll it out into a ⅛-inch-thick circle. Cut out as many 4-inch circles as you can. Put a rounded tablespoon of the ricotta mixture in the center of a circle. Cover with another circle of dough. Press the edges of the 2 circles together securely and put on a tray. Prepare the remaining circles of dough in the same manner. Re-roll out the leftover dough and cut out as many more circles as you can, then fill them as directed. Let the *iris* rise for 30 minutes.

Brush each *iris* with egg white on both sides and lightly coat with bread crumbs.

Bring 3 inches of lard or sunflower oil to 360 degrees in a deep fryer. Cook the *iris* in batches by gently lowering 3 or 4 at a time into the hot oil with a flat metal skimmer. Cook until golden brown on each side. Drain on paper towels. Eat them while warm.

Cartocci (Fried Pastry Coils with Ricotta Cream)

MAKES 12

Put the yeast into a bowl with the water, and set aside for 10 minutes, until it foams. Stir with a fork.

Meanwhile, lightly rub vegetable oil on 12 cannoli tube forms and set aside.

To make the pastry, put the flour into a large bowl and mix with the sugar. Make a well in the center and add the lard or olive oil and the yeast mixture, plus ½ cup of tepid water. Blend well, mixing it into a dough. Turn out onto a lightly floured board and knead until soft.

Roll the dough into a rope about 12 inches long, and cut into 12 equal-sized pieces. Roll each piece into ropes about 8 inches long and ½ inch in diameter. Wrap 1 dough rope around an oiled cannoli tube about 3 times, tucking the end of the dough under the coil at the end. Place on lightly floured baking sheet. Make the 11 remaining *cartocci* in the same manner and let rise for 1 hour.

Heat 4 inches of oil in a large deep fryer until hot but not smoking. Fry the *cartocci*, a few at a time, until golden brown all over. As they are cooked, drain on paper towels. Using a pot holder, remove the tubes. Let the shells cool completely.

Pipe or spoon the ricotta cream in equal amounts into the center of each *cartocci* and sprinkle with confectioners' or granulated sugar.

2 envelopes active dry yeast
1¼ cups warm water
Vegetable oil
4 cups all-purpose flour
¼ cup sugar
¼ cup melted lard or olive oil
2 cups Crema di Ricotta, at room temperature; recipe follows (must be made 1 day in advance)
Confectioners' or granulated sugar

Crema di Ricotta (Ricotta Cream)

MAKES ABOUT 3 CUPS

Mix the ricotta and sugar together thoroughly and let rest at room temperature for 8 hours.

Pass the ricotta through a fine sieve into a large bowl. We use the bottom of a small, heavy glass jar to press the ricotta through the fine mesh.

Stir the vanilla into the mixture and combine well. Cover the bowl and refrigerate overnight.

1½ pounds ricotta cheese, fresh if possible
¾ cup sugar
1 teaspoon pure vanilla extract

Tatù (Chocolate Biscuit Balls)

MAKES 30

4½ cups all-purpose flour

1 tablespoon baking powder

3¾ cups sugar

1 teaspoon pure vanilla extract

⅔ cup melted lard or vegetable oil

2 cups milk

4 cups water

Zest of 1 lemon

3 tablespoons bitter cocoa powder

In a large bowl, combine the flour, baking powder, and 1¼ cups sugar. Add the vanilla and lard or vegetable oil and combine. Slowly stir in the milk. The mixture will be firm.

Preheat the oven to 350 degrees.

Cover a baking sheet with a piece of parchment paper.

Form the dough into balls the size of walnuts. Arrange the balls on the baking sheet a few inches apart. Bake for about 10 minutes. Remove and cool on a rack. Arrange and bake the next batch.

Prepare 2 separate mixtures. For the lemon sauce, put 2 cups of water, 1¼ cups of sugar, and the lemon zest in a saucepan. Bring to a boil. When the sugar has melted, remove from heat and let cool. For the chocolate sauce, put 2 cups of water, 1¼ cups of sugar, and the bitter cocoa powder in a saucepan and bring to a boil. Whisk until sugar has melted. Remove from heat and let cool.

When both mixtures are cool, dip half the *tatù* into the lemon sauce and let them dry on a cooling rack. Dip the remaining *tatù* into the chocolate sauce and let them dry on a cooling rack.

Serve with tea or sweet wine.

Cucchie (Raisin Cookies)

MAKES ABOUT 40 COOKIES

3 cups sugar

½ cup water

1½ cups coarsely chopped almonds

Zest of 1 lemon

4 cups raisins

2 tablespoons chopped pistachios

1 teaspoon ground cinnamon

In a saucepan over medium heat, heat 1½ cups of sugar in water. Stir in the almonds and lemon zest. Cook for 5 minutes, stirring often. Stir in the raisins, pistachios, cinnamon, almonds, and chopped candied pumpkin, if using. Mix well, and set aside.

In a large bowl, combine the flour with the remaining 1½ cups of sugar. Add the egg yolks and lard or olive oil and combine well.

Preheat the oven to 350 degrees.

Divide the dough in half and, on a lightly floured work surface,

roll each half out into a large rectangle. Spoon rounded tablespoons of the raisin mixture at 3-inch intervals over 1 of the rectangles, then cover with the second rectangle. Press around each mound of filling with your fingers, then cut around the mounds with heart-shaped cookie cutters. Place on baking sheets and bake for 30 minutes, in batches if necessary. Cool on racks.

2 tablespoons chopped blanched almonds
2 tablespoons candied pumpkin (optional)
4½ cups all-purpose flour
5 large egg yolks
2 cups melted lard or olive oil

Capelli d'Angeli (Angel's Hair)

MAKES 12

In a small bowl, beat the eggs with a pinch of salt. Heat a teaspoon of sunflower oil in a nonstick 7-inch omelette pan. Add ⅓ of the eggs and swirl in the pan, making a very thin, flat omelette. When set, flip and cook for a few seconds on the other side. Add another teaspoon of oil to the pan and make another omelette, then make a third omelette. Cool the omelettes completely, and then cut into very thin strips.

In a saucepan, heat the sugar in water until the sugar has dissolved and the mixture is thick and syrupy. Immediately remove from the heat.

Divide the egg strips into 12 portions on a work surface. Pour equal portions of the melted sugar over each. Immediately shape each portion into a ball.

Combine the hazelnuts and almonds. Roll each ball in the chopped nuts and sprinkle lightly with cinnamon.

4 large eggs
Salt
Sunflower oil
1 cup sugar
4 tablespoons water
½ cup finely chopped hazelnuts
½ cup finely chopped almonds
Ground cinnamon powder

Gelo di Caffè di Claire (Claire's Coffee Gelatine)

At the end of a meal in Sicily, especially at lunch, guests expect to have an espresso. But in the summer, when the sun is beating down and the temperature soars, a wonderfully refreshing way of serving coffee is in the form of a cooling gelatin. Even inveterate coffee drinkers are enthusiastic about our *gelo di caffè*. The recipe was a gift from an English woman, Claire Williams, who lives near us in a large estate called Casagiordano. She is an endless source of inspiring little tips and suggestions about food and recipes.

SERVES 4

3⅓ cups espresso
3 tablespoons cornstarch
1 tablespoon unsweetened
  cocoa powder
1 cup water
¾ cup sugar
Zest of 1 medium lemon
Lemon or other leaves as
  garnish

In a saucepan, combine the coffee, cornstarch, and cocoa powder. Stir in water, sugar, and lemon zest. Bring mixture to a boil, stirring constantly, until it thickens. Remove from the heat and let cool.

Pour the mixture into 4 individual dessert bowls and chill in the refrigerator for at least 3 hours. Garnish with lemon or other leaves.

Biancomangiare (Blancmange)

SERVES 6

4 cups whole milk
½ cup cornstarch
¾–1 cup sugar
½ teaspoon almond extract
Ground cinnamon
Chopped pistachio nuts

Pour the milk into a nonreactive medium saucepan. Whisk in the cornstarch until it is completely dissolved. Whisk in the sugar and almond extract and bring to a boil, whisking constantly. Boil for 1 to 2 minutes, still whisking constantly until mixture thickens. Remove from heat and cool to room temperature.

Pour the mixture into a 1-quart ring or mold or into 6 individ-

ual 1-cup molds. Cover with plastic wrap and refrigerate for at least 4 hours.

To serve, unmold and sprinkle with cinnamon and chopped pistachio nuts. Or you can serve the *biancomangiare* plain, surrounded by raspberries or other fruit or berries.

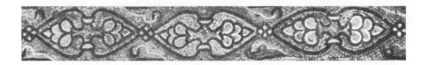

Vino e Liquori

(Wines and Liqueurs)

Laurino *(Bay Laurel Leaf Liqueur)*

La Vendemmia *(The Grape Harvest)*

Limoncello *(Lemon Liqueur)*

Arancello *(Orange Liqueur)*

Liquore di Mandarino *(Mandarin Liqueur)*

Liquore di Fragole *(Strawberry Liqueur)*

Liquore di Ciliege *(Cherry Liqueur)*

Rossi e Bianchi, Fatti in Casa o Comprati

(Red and White, Homemade or Bought)

In Sicily, we have always produced an enormous quantity of wine. In the past, most of the wines, with their high alcoholic content, were shipped in bulk to northern Italy, to be used for blending. For centuries, we have also produced fine wines, such as Regaleali, Corvo, and Rapitalà, which are now available in America. And Marsala—invented in 1773 by an Englishman, John Woodhouse—is Sicily's most famous fortified wine. Florio is the favored brand.

Happily, the roster of good Sicilian wines is slowly increasing, and we serve mostly Sicilian wines at Gangivecchio: Regaleali's wonderful reds and whites, Donnafugata's refreshing whites and full-bodied reds, and Corvo's *rosso* and *bianco* wines, especially Corvo Colomba Platino, from the Duca di Salaparuta vineyards.

Our amber-colored dessert wines are superb: Moscato di Pantelleria and Passito di Pantelleria (natural and sweet versions), with their delicate blends of *zibibbo* (fat Moscato) grapes, come from the island of Pantelleria, southwest of Sicily and off the coast of Tunisia. Carlo Hauner's Malvasia delle Lipari, from the Aeolian Islands, is another extraordinary amber-pink ambrosia, produced in limited quantities on the island of Salina. These wines are not easy to find in America, but if you come to Sicily, consider taking home a bottle or two. They are worthwhile souvenirs.

When you visit a Sicilian house, you will first be invited to sit down in the best armchair in the living room. Then, more than likely, you'll be offered a delicious homemade liqueur, a rare libation from their granny or an old aunt's secret recipe.

At Gangivecchio, we follow this tradition. I've done a lot of experimenting with my homemade liqueurs, transforming my family and friends into dizzy alcoholics. Now that the recipes are correct, I hope you get as much pleasure out of them as we have.

Laurino (Bay Laurel Leaf Liqueur)

MAKES 1 QUART

2 cups water

2 cups sugar

50 fresh bay laurel leaves

1 large cinnamon stick

2 cups vodka

Peeled zest of 1 large lemon,
with as much white pith
removed as possible

In a medium saucepan, heat the water and sugar and bring almost to a boil, stirring occasionally. Remove from the heat and stir until the sugar has dissolved. Let cool completely.

Put the bay leaves, cinnamon sticks, vodka, lemon zest, and sugar water into a wide-mouthed jar with a tight-fitting led. Close the jar tightly and shake the ingredients.

Store in a dark, cool place, shaking the mixture twice a day—in the morning and at the end of the day.

After 10 days, strain the liquid through a double piece of cheesecloth into a clean bowl. Using a funnel, transfer the liquid to a pretty bottle. Close the top with a cork or lid and store in the refrigerator. Serve well chilled.

La Vendemmia (The Grape Harvest)

Sometimes, when I gaze over the wild land, stretching out for miles beyond the abbey, I am greeted with a vision of the past. The tangled grass and weeds, the wild fennel, the impossibly dense thicket—it all disappears, and I see again the beautiful vineyards that were once at Gangivecchio and which made my father so proud: twelve thousand plants of *zibibbo, inzolia,* and *nero d'Avola,* among the best grapes Sicily has.

The soil was a rich, dark brown under the gold and green of the vines. In the summer, when we walked among the rows, a concert of bees was the only sound as *i grappoli* (the bunches of grapes) slowly grew more and more pregnant with sweet liquid, until they were ready for the harvest.

At the beginning of September, all the barrels were brought out from the cave to be

washed with hot water and a big dangling iron chain rolling around inside to clean them well. Then, in the middle of September, the big day came. Everyone arrived at dawn. All our farmers, and their wives and children, were ready to work, led by my father, my brother, and me. We each had a basket and a pair of scissors, except for Papa, who was in charge. A couple of mules, huge baskets straddled across their backs, completed our caravan.

I always started the harvest by cutting the first bunch of grapes. Then someone would immediately yell out, "*A signorina tagghiau!* [The miss has cut it!]" And everyone joined in the joyful competition of hard labor: to fill their own small basket first, empty it into a big one hanging on the sides of the mules, then repeat this task again and again.

My brother and I usually gave up after half an hour. Observing our father, we decided it was more comfortable to do nothing.

When all the grapes for the day were collected, another ceremony began. My father made all the male workers (women were excluded) scrub their feet with almost boiling-hot water. Then they wore clean slippers to walk to *il torchio*, the huge tub where they would press the grapes with their feet. The pressing was a sensual, rhythmic dance, like they were stepping up an invisible, endless staircase but always remaining in place. In later years, when my father converted to automated presses, I dearly missed those dancing feet.

When the day's work was over, everyone sat down at a long table for a well-deserved meal: pasta with fresh tomato sauce, followed by salt cod and potatoes. And wine, of course.

After the grape harvest, my father always spent a few sleepless nights worrying about controlling the must's fermentation. Stirring it with a wooden stick, he talked to it softly. After three days and three nights, the must was ready to be transferred to the barrels to age.

We usually waited until the first day of December to drink it. I was very young when my father gave me my first glass of wine, the wine that he made and that was his pride. Friends came from all over Sicily to drink my father's famous, delicious red wine.

My brother and I never asked Papa to explain to us his secret of the fermentation. Children never think that their father might suddenly die, but in August 1984, ours did, and he took his secret with him.

All the vines died a few months after we lost him, which we found mysteriously significant at the time. But we eventually learned that a disease had killed our vines, along with many others in the region.

Limoncello (Lemon Liqueur)

2 cups sugar

2 cups water

Peeled zest of 6 lemons, with as much white pith removed as possible

1 quart vodka

Heat the sugar and water in a medium saucepan, and bring almost to a boil, stirring constantly. Remove from the heat and stir until the sugar has dissolved. Let cool completely.

Put the lemon peels, cooled sugar syrup, and vodka in a wide-mouthed jar with a tight-fitting lid. Close the top tightly and shake well.

Store in a dark, cool place for 5 days, shaking the jar twice a day—in the morning and at the end of the day.

Strain the liquid through a double thickness of cheesecloth into a clean bowl. Using a funnel, transfer the liquid into a pretty bottle. Close the top with a cork or lid and store in the refrigerator. Serve well chilled.

Arancello (Orange Liqueur) Follow the directions for Limoncello, but substitute the peeled zest of 4 large oranges for the lemon zest.

Liquore di Mandarino (Mandarin Liqueur) Follow the directions for Limoncello, but substitute the peeled zest of 6 mandarins or tangerines for the lemon zest.

Liquore di Fragole (Strawberry Liqueur)

Prepare this liqueur at the end of spring and break it out in December.

MAKES ABOUT 2 QUARTS

Put the strawberries and vodka in a large wide-mouthed jar. Store in a dark, cool place for 2 weeks.

Prepare sugar syrup by heating the sugar and water together until almost boiling. Stir until the sugar dissolves and the water is clear. Cool completely.

Pour the vodka and strawberry mixture into a very large bowl. Stir in the sugar syrup. Ladle the mixture into 2 or 3 wide-mouthed jars with tight-fitting lids. Store in the refrigerator for 5 months. Strain through a double layer of cheesecloth before serving.

1 quart fresh strawberries, washed, hulled, and allowed to dry
1 quart vodka
6 cups sugar
1½ quarts water

Liquore di Ciliege (Cherry Liqueur) Follow the instructions for Liquore di Fragole, substituting 1 quart of pitted cherries for the strawberries.

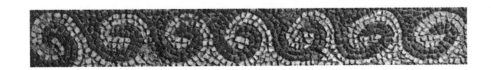

Quattro Menu di Gangivecchio
(Four Menus from Gangivecchio)

Un Pranzo Estivo Siciliano
(A Sicilian Summer Lunch)

Antipasto: La Caponata di Peperoni di Wanda
                (Wanda's Pepper Caponata)

Primo: I Veri Rigatoni all'Amatriciana
           (The True Rigatoni in the Style of Amatrice)

Secondo: Salmone Capriccioso
            (Capricious Salmon)
            Insalata di Cetrioli e Capperi
            (Cucumber and Caper Salad)

Dolce: Sfoglio
           (Chocolate and Cheese Tart with Cinnamon)

Una Cena d'Autunno
(A Fall Dinner)

Antipasto: Torta di Gorgonzola e Pere
                (Gorgonzola and Pear Tart)

Primo: Risotto Affumicato con Pistacchi di Paolo
           (Paolo's Risotto with Smoked Provolone and Pistachios)

Secondo: Stemperata di Pollo
            (Chicken with Vegetables, Green Olives, Capers, and Mint)

Dolce: Biancomangiare
           (Blancmange)

Una Cena d'Inverno con Amici
(A Winter Supper with Friends)

Antipasto: Pecorino Fresco con Miele e Pistacchi
(Fresh Pecorino with Honey and Pistachios)

Primo: Minestra di Funghi e Patate
(Mushroom and Potato Soup)

Secondo: Petto di Tacchino Farcito alla Siciliana
(Sicilian Stuffed Turkey Breast)
La Caponata di Peperoni di Wanda
(Wanda's Pepper Caponata)

Dolce: Parfait di Mandorle
(Almond Parfait)

Picnic di Primaverile in Campagna
(A Spring Picnic in the Country)

Antipasto: Uova Sode Ripiene al Gratin
(Au Gratin of Eggs Stuffed with Cheese)

Primo: Melanzane Ripiene di Anelletti
(Eggplant Stuffed with Anelletti)

Secondo: Le Cotolette dei Ragazzi
(My Boy's Cutlets)
Insalata di Finocchi e Carciofi
(Fennel and Artichoke Salad)

Dolce: Crostata di Amaretti e Cioccolato
(Amaretti and Chocolate Tart)

Poesia di Wanda
(Wanda's Poem)

Mamma wrote this poem a few years after her arrival at Gangivecchio. Enzo, her husband, was away in Palermo, so she composed a verse for him.

Momenti 1965 (Moments 1965)

Cielo pieno di stelle, tremule gocce di purissimo pianto,
sorriso di luna tra scuri cipressi,
solitarie acque scorrenti,
profumi leggeri rimossi dal vento.
Sussuri di voci tra canne fruscianti,
cuore natante in un lago di sogni,
folli desii di un'anima inquieta,
amato viso serrato al mio petto,
dolce, infinito, sublime momenti.

Lonely flowing waters, the sky scattered with stars,
Twinkling drops of purest tears.
The moon smiles on the dark cypresses
While the wind moves the sweetest scents.
Is that rustle of reeds whispering voices,
My heart floats in a lake of dreams,
With the foolish desires of a wondering heart,
And those beloved lips close to my face:
Sweet, endless, touching moments.

(Translation by Renata Pucci)

Indici (Indexes)

herb(s):
    -breaded fried turkey breast cutlets, 156
    pappardelle with ricotta and, 99
    Sicilian, pork stew with potatoes and,
        148
    summer couscous with, 128
    see also specific herbs
homemade pasta, 96–97
home-style bruschetta, 22–23
honey, fresh pecorino with pistachios and,
    34–35

imaginary fiancé's lobster, 168–69

jam omelette, wallet-shaped, 68–69

Kery's spaghetti with onions and fennel,
    97
Kery's spinach focaccia, 87–88
king's bread, the, 44–45

lamb, roasted "my idea," 149
lasagne, vegetable, 100
lemon:
    -flavored artichokes, Lina's, 175
    Giovanna's spaghetti, 103
    liqueur, 226
    Paolo's pappardelle with shrimp and, 116
lettuce:
    and ditali soup, 57
    tart, 37–38
Lina's lemon-flavored artichokes, 175
liqueurs, 221–27
    bay laurel leaf, 224
    lemon, 226
    strawberry, 227

lobster, imaginary fiancé's, 168–69
Lucia's fritters, 19

Mamma's veal casserole, 146
mandarins with caciocavallo, 35–36
Maria's fish soup, 58–59
marinated red winter pumpkin, 185
marmalade and orange cream tart,
    207
meat, Wanda's winter soup, 59
meatballs, Gangivecchio's sweet-and-sour,
    19
meat main-course dishes, 139–56
    chicken:
        soufflé, 150
        with vegetables, green olives, capers,
            and mint, 154
    lamb, roasted "my idea," 149
    pork:
        roasted rolled loin, 149
        roast shanks, 147–48
        stew with potatoes and Sicilian herbs,
            148
        and veal baked in dough, 146–47
    turkey breast:
        fried herb-breaded cutlets, 156
        Sicilian stuffed, 155
    veal:
        couscous with vegetables and,
            126–27
        delicious rib roast with mushrooms,
            144–45
        Mamma's casserole, 146
        my boy's cutlets, 147
        and pork baked in dough, 146–47
        Sicilian oven-braised shanks, 143
        stuffed packets of, 145
        Wanda's cutlets, 143–44
Mediterranean strudel, 41–42
melon:
    with balsamic vinegar and mint, 40
    and ham salad, 198

menus, 229–30
    fall dinner, 229
    Sicilian summer lunch, 229
    spring picnic in the country, 230
    winter supper with friends, 230
mint:
    beans with, 32
    bruschetta with swordfish and, 22
    chicken with vegetables, green olives,
        capers and, 154
    melon with balsamic vinegar and, 40
    omelette stuffed with zucchini and,
        66
mozzarella and tomato sandwiches, 197
mushroom(s):
    asparagus, and potato cake, 174
    delicious veal rib roast with, 144–45
    and potatoes, 182
    and potato soup, 52
    salad, 192
mussels, cherry tomatoes, and capers,
        tagliatelle with, 115
my boy's cutlets, 147

Nina's little sandwiches, Modica style,
        43–44
nun's eggs, 72

octopus, baby, salad, 198
olive(s):
    the actor's, 34
    Aunt Elvira's, 32–33
    black, spaghetti omelette with capers
        and, 20
    dressed, salad, 194–95
    green, chicken with vegetables, capers,
        mint and, 154
omelettes:
    potato, for Paolo, 68
    spaghetti, with capers and black olives,
        20

omelettes (*continued*)
    square, stuffed with spinach and cheese,
        67
    stuffed with zucchini and mint, 66
    wallet-shaped jam, 68–69
onion(s):
    focaccia with tomatoes and, 88–89
    Kery's spaghetti with fennel and, 97
    and pepper soufflé, 39–40
    red, tomato sauce, and caciocavallo
        pizza, 82
orange cream and marmalade tart, 207
oregano, crisp focaccia topped with olive oil
        and, 90

pancetta:
    Paolo's pennette with fresh figs and, 110–11
    pennette with vodka and, 119–20
    Paolo's pappardelle with shrimp and lemon,
        116
    Paolo's pennette with fresh figs and
        pancetta, 110–11
    Paolo's risotto with smoked provolone and
        pistachios, 134–35
pappardelle:
    with herbs and ricotta, 99
    Paolo's, with shrimp and lemon, 116
parfait, almond, 204
Parmesan cheese, prosciutto packets with
        arugula and, 195
pasta, 91–120
    with asparagus and ham, 104
    and bean soup, Granny Elena's, 51
    with *bottarga,* 113
    carbonara with vegetables, 98–99
    with cherry tomatoes, mussels, and
        capers, 115
    with eggplant, 105
    eggplant stuffed with, 101
    with fresh figs and pancetta, Paolo's,
        110–11
    with garlic, oil, and hot pepper, 102
    Giovanna's lemon, 103

A Note About the Authors

WANDA and GIOVANNA TORNABENE have run their restaurant out of the thirteenth-century abbey Gangivecchio, in Sicily's Madonie Mountains, since 1978. Their first book was *La Cucina Siliciana di Gangivecchio*, which won the 1997 James Beard Award for Best Italian Cookbook. Wanda and Giovanna spend most of their time at Gangivecchio and also have a home in Palermo.

MICHELE EVANS is the author of thirteen previous cookbooks and she is also a travel writer. Her *Caribbean Connoisseur: An Insider's Guide to the Islands' Best Hotels, Resorts, and Inns* is in its third edition. She is currently writing another cookbook, *Groceries*, and her first novel. She and her husband, Tully Plesser, are residents of St. Thomas, Virgin Islands.

A Note on the Type

This book was set in Adobe Garamond. Designed for the Adobe Corporation by Robert Slimbach, the fonts are based on types first cut by Claude Garamond (c. 1480–1561). Garamond was a pupil of Geoffroy Tory and is believed to have followed the Venetian models, although he introduced a number of important differences, and it is to him that we owe the letter we now know as "old style." He gave to his letters a certain elegance and feeling of movement that won their creator an immediate reputation and the patronage of Francis I of France.

Composed by North Market Street Graphics,
Lancaster, Pennsylvania
Printed and bound by Quebecor World,
Fairfield, Pennsylvania
Designed by Anthea Lingeman